Upside Down

Upside Down

A PRIMER FOR THE LOOKING-GLASS WORLD

Eduardo Galeano

With engravings by José Guadalupe Posada
Translated by Mark Fried

METROPOLITAN BOOKS
Henry Holt and Company   New York

Metropolitan Books
Henry Holt and Company, LLC
Publishers since 1866
115 West 18th Street
New York, New York 10011

Metropolitan Books™ is an imprint of
Henry Holt and Company, LLC.

Copyright © 1998 by Eduardo Galeano
Translation © 2000 by Mark Fried

Originally published in the Spanish language in 1998 by
Siglo Veintiuno Editores (Spain and Mexico), Catálogos (Argentina),
Ediciones del Chanchito (Uruguay), Tercer Mundo Editores (Colombia).

All rights reserved.

Library of Congress Cataloging-in-Publication Data
Galeano, Eduardo H., 1940–
[Patas arriba. English]
Upside down : a primer for the looking-glass world /
Eduardo Galeano ; with engravings by José Guadalupe Posada ;
translated by Mark Fried—1st American ed.
p.   cm.
Includes bibliographical references and index
ISBN 0-8050-6375-7 (hb)
1. Social problems. 2. Social history—20th century. 3. Economic
history—20th century. 4. World politics—20th century.
5. Developing countries—Social conditions. I. Title.
HN18.G25   1998
361.1—dc21   00-026787

Henry Holt books are available for special promotions and
premiums. For details contact: Director, Special Markets.

First American Edition 2000

Designed by Kelly S. Too

Printed in the United States of America

1 3 5 7 9 10 8 6 4 2

For Helena, this book that I owed her

Upside Down has many accomplices. It is a pleasure to finger them. José Guadalupe Posada, the great Mexican artist who died in 1913, is the only one who is innocent. The engravings that accompany this book, this chronicle, were published without the artist's knowledge. Others, in contrast, knew full well what they were doing and collaborated with an enthusiasm worthy of a better cause.

The author must begin by confessing that he would have been unable to commit the act of these pages without the assistance of Helena Villagra, Karl Hübener, Jorge Marchini, and his little electronic mouse.

By reading and commenting on the first criminal attempt, a number of others also took part in this mischief: Walter Achugar, Carlos Álvarez Insúa, Nilo Batista, Roberto Bergalli, David Cámpora, Antonio Doñate, Gonzlo Fernández, Mark Fried, Juan Gelman, Susana Iglesias, Carlos Machado, Mariana Mactas, Luis Niño, Raquel Villagra, and Daniel Weinberg.

A portion of the guilt—some more, some less—is borne by Rafael Balbi, José Barrientos, Mauricio Beltrán, Rosa del Olmo, Milton de Ritis, Claudio Durán, Juan Gasparini, Claudio Hughes, Pier Paolo Marchetti, Stella Maris Martínez, Dora Mirón Campos, Norberto Pérez, Ruben Prieto, Pilar Royo, Ángel Ruocco, Hilary Sandison, Pedro Scaron, Horacio Tubio, Pinio Ungerfeld, Alejandro Valle Baeza, Jorge Ventocilla, Guillermo Waksman, Gaby Weber, Winfried Wolf, and Jean Ziegler.

Also responsible to a large degree is Saint Rita, the patron of impossible deeds.

Montevideo, partway through 1998

This book now constitutes a threat to the English-speaking world. That would not have been possible without the fervent complicity of Mark Fried, Tom Engelhardt, Susan Bergholz, Bert Snyder, and the Metropolitan editorial team. One day, they will have to answer for their deeds.

Montevideo, partway through 2000

Ladies and Gentlemen, Come On In!

Come on in!
Step into the school of the upside-down world!
Rub the magic lantern!
Lights! Sound! The illusion of life!
Offered free to one and all!
Let it enlighten each of you and set a good example for future
    generations!
Come see the river that burns!
Lord Sun illuminating the night!
Dame Moon in the middle of the day!
Mam'selle Star tossed from the sky!
The jester on the king's throne!
Lucifer's breath clouding the universe!
The dead walking about with mirrors in their hands!
Witches! Acrobats!
Dragons and vampires!
The magic wand that turns a child into a coin!
The world lost in a throw of the dice!
Don't fall for cheap imitations!
God bless those who see it!
God forgive those who don't!
Rated R: Sensitive persons and minors not admitted.

—Based on eighteenth-century criers' pitch for magic lanterns

Program of Study

A Message to Parents

People respect nothing nowadays. Once we put virtue, honor, truth, and the law on a pedestal. . . . Graft is a byword in American life today. It is law where no other law is obeyed. It is undermining the country. Virtue, honor, truth and the law have all vanished from our life.

> —Al Capone, speaking to Cornelius Vanderbilt Jr.
> The interview was published in *Liberty* magazine on
> October 17, 1931, a few days before Capone went to jail.

If Alice Were to Return

One hundred and thirty years ago, after visiting Wonderland, Alice stepped into a mirror and discovered the world of the looking glass. If Alice were born today, she'd only have to peek out the window.

If you decide to train your dog, congratulations on your decision. You will soon discover that the roles of master and dog are perfectly clear.

—RALSTON PURINA INTERNATIONAL

THE LOOKING-GLASS SCHOOL

- Educating by Example
- The Students
- Injustice 101
- Racism and Sexism 101

Educating by Example

The looking-glass school is the most democratic of educational institutions. There are no admissions exams, no registration fees, and courses are offered free to everyone everywhere on earth as well as in heaven. It's not for nothing that this school is the child of the first system in history to rule the world.

 In the looking-glass school, lead learns to float and cork to sink. Snakes learn to fly and clouds drag themselves along the ground.

MODELS OF SUCCESS

The upside-down world rewards in reverse: it scorns honesty, punishes work, prizes lack of scruples, and feeds cannibalism. Its professors slander nature: injustice, they say, is a law of nature. Milton Friedman teaches us about the "natural rate of unemployment." Studying Richard Herrnstein and Charles Murray, we learn that blacks remain on the lowest rungs of the social ladder by "natural" law. From John D. Rockefeller's lectures, we know his success was due to the fact that "nature" rewards the fittest and punishes the useless: more than a century later, the owners of the world continue to believe Charles Darwin wrote his books in their honor.

Survival of the fittest? The "killer instinct" is an essential ingredient for getting ahead, a human virtue when it helps large companies digest small and strong countries devour weak but proof of bestiality when some jobless guy goes around with a knife in his fist. Those stricken with "antisocial pathology," the dangerous insanity afflicting all poor people, find inspiration in the models of good health exhibited by those who succeed. Lowlifes learn their skills by setting their sights on the summits. They study the examples of the winners and, for better or worse, do their best to live up to them. But "the damned will always be damned," as Don Emilio Azcárraga, once lord and master of Mexican television, liked to say. The chances that a banker who loots a bank can enjoy the fruits of his labor in peace are directly proportional to the chances that a crook who robs a bank will land in jail or the cemetery.

When a criminal kills someone for an unpaid debt, the execution is called a "settling of accounts." When the international technocracy settles accounts with an indebted country, the execution is called an "adjustment plan." Financial capos kidnap countries and suck them dry even when they pay the ransom: in comparison, most thugs are about as dangerous as Dracula in broad daylight. The world economy is the most efficient expression of organized crime. The international bodies that control currency, trade, and credit practice international terrorism against poor countries, and against the poor of all countries, with a cold-blooded professionalism that would make the best of the bomb throwers blush.

The arts of trickery, which con men practice by stalking the

gullible on the street, become sublime when certain politicians put their talents to work. In the shantytown nations of the world, heads of state sell off the remnants of their countries at fire-sale prices, just as in the shantytowns of cities criminals unload their booty for peanuts.

Hired guns do much the same work, albeit at retail, as the generals whose wholesale crimes get billed as acts of glory. Pickpockets lurking on street corners practice a low-tech version of the art of speculators who fleece the multitudes by computer. The worst violators of nature and human rights never go to jail. They hold the keys. In the world as it is, the looking-glass world, the countries that guard the peace also make and sell the most weapons. The most prestigious banks launder the most drug money and harbor the most stolen cash. The most successful industries are the most poisonous for the planet. And saving the environment is the brilliant endeavor of the very companies that profit from annihilating it. Those who kill the most people in the shortest time win immunity and praise, as do those who destroy the most nature at the lowest cost.

Walking is risky and breathing a challenge in the great cities of the looking-glass world. Whoever is not a prisoner of necessity is a prisoner of fear, deprived of sleep by anxiety over the things he lacks or by terror of losing the things he has. The looking-glass world trains us to view our neighbor as a threat, not a promise. It condemns us to solitude and consoles us with chemical drugs and cybernetic friends. We are sentenced to die of hunger, fear, or boredom—that is, if a stray bullet doesn't do the job first.

Is the freedom to choose among these unfortunate ends the only freedom left to us? The looking-glass school teaches us to suffer reality, not change it; to forget the past, not learn from it; to accept the future, not invent it. In its halls of criminal learning, impotence, amnesia, and resignation are required courses. Yet perhaps—who can say—there can be no disgrace without grace, no sign without a countersign, and no school that does not beget its counterschool.

THE STUDENTS

Day after day, children are denied the right to be children. The world treats rich kids as if they were money, teaching them to act the way money acts. The world treats poor kids as if they were garbage, to turn them into garbage. And those in the middle, neither rich nor poor, are chained to televisions and trained to live the life of prisoners.

The few children who manage to be children must have a lot of magic and a lot of luck.

TOP, BOTTOM, AND MIDDLE

In the ocean of desperation, there are islands of privilege, luxurious concentration camps where the powerful meet only the powerful and never, for even a moment, forget how powerful they are. In some Latin American cities where kidnappings have become commonplace, rich kids grow up sealed inside bubbles of fear. They live in fortresslike mansions or groups of homes ringed by electrified fences and guardhouses, watched day and night by bodyguards and closed-circuit security cameras. They travel like money in armored cars. They don't know their own city except by sight. They discover the subway in Paris or New York, but never use it in São Paulo or Mexico City.

They don't live in the city where they live. They're not allowed to set foot in the vast hell that threatens their tiny private heaven. Beyond the walls lie regions of terror filled with ugly, dirty, envious people. They grow up rootless, stripped of cultural identity, aware of society only as a threat. Their homeland lies in the designer names on their clothes, and their language is a modern Morse code. In cities around the globe, children of privilege are alike in their habits and beliefs, like shopping malls and airports, which lie outside the realms of time and space. Educated in virtual reality, they know nothing of real reality, which exists only to be feared or bought.

Fast food, fast cars, fast life: from birth, rich kids are trained for consumption and speed, and their voyage through childhood

A Child's World

You have to be very careful when you cross the street, Colombian teacher Gustavo Wilches explained to a group of children. "Even though the light is green, never cross without looking first one way, then the other."

Wilches told the children that once he was knocked down by a car in the middle of the street. His face darkened as he recalled the disaster that nearly cost him his life. The children asked: "What kind of car was it?" "Did it have air-conditioning?" "A sunroof?" "Did it have fog lights?" "How big was the motor?"

Store Windows

Toys for boys: Rambos, Robocops, Ninjas, Batmen, monsters,
machine guns, pistols, tanks, cars, motorcycles, trucks, planes,
spaceships.

Toys for girls: Barbies, Heidis, ironing boards, kitchens,
blenders, washing machines, televisions, babies, cribs, baby bottles, lipsticks, curlers, makeup kits, mirrors.

---

confirms that machines are more trustworthy than people. When
the day arrives for their rite of passage, they will be handed the
keys to their first four-wheel-drive all-terrain corsair. In the mean-
time, they construct their identities by driving full speed down
cybernetic highways, devouring images and merchandise, zapping
and shopping. They feel at home navigating cyberspace the way
homeless children do wandering city streets.

Long before rich kids stop being kids and discover expensive
drugs to fool their solitude and shroud their fear, poor kids are
sniffing gasoline and glue. While rich kids play war with laser-
beam guns, street kids are dodging real bullets.

In Latin America children and adolescents make up nearly half
the population. Half of that half lives in misery. Survivors: in Latin
America a hundred children die of hunger or curable disease every
hour, but that doesn't stem their numbers in the streets and fields of
a region that manufactures poor people and outlaws poverty. The
poor are mostly children and children are mostly poor. Among the
system's hostages, they have it the worst. Society squeezes them dry,

watches them constantly, punishes them, sometimes kills them; almost never are they listened to, never are they understood.

Everywhere on earth, these kids, the children of people who work hard or who have neither work nor home, must from an early age spend their waking hours at whatever breadwinning activity they can find, breaking their backs in return for food and little else. Once they can walk, they learn the rewards of behaving themselves—boys and girls who are free labor in workshops, stores, and makeshift bars or cheap labor in export industries, stitching sports clothes for multinational corporations. They are manual labor on farms and in cities or domestic labor at home, serving whoever gives the orders. They are little slaves in the family economy or in the informal sector of the global economy, where they occupy the lowest rung of the world labor market:

- in the garbage dumps of Mexico City, Manila, or Lagos they hunt glass, cans, and paper and fight the vultures for scraps
- in the Java Sea they dive for pearls
- they hunt diamonds in the mines of Congo
- they work as moles in the mine shafts of Peru, where their size makes them indispensable, and when their lungs give out they end up in unmarked graves
- in Colombia and Tanzania they harvest coffee and get poisoned by pesticides
- in Guatemala they harvest cotton and get poisoned by pesticides
- in Honduras they harvest bananas and get poisoned by pesticides
- they collect sap from rubber trees in Malaysia, working days that last from dark to dark
- they work the railroads in Burma

- in India they melt in glass ovens in the north and brick ovens in the south
- in Bangladesh they work at over three hundred occupations, earning salaries that range from nothing to nearly nothing for each endless day
- they ride in camel races for Arab sheiks and round up sheep and cattle on the ranches of the Rio de la Plata
- they serve the master's table in Port-au-Prince, Colombo, Jakarta, or Recife in return for the right to eat whatever falls from it
- they sell fruit in the markets of Bogotá and gum on the buses of São Paulo
- they wash windshields on corners in Lima, Quito, or San Salvador
- they shine shoes on the streets of Caracas or Guanajuato

Flight/1

Chatting with a swarm of street kids, the ones who cling to the bumpers of buses in Mexico City, reporter Karina Avilés asked about drugs.

"I feel great, I get rid of all my problems," said one. "When I come down and I'm just me," he added, "I feel trapped like a bird in a cage."

These children are regularly harassed by the police and their dogs in the Northern Bus Terminal. The company manager assured the reporter, "We don't let these children die, because in some way they are human."

- they stitch clothes in Thailand and soccer shoes in Vietnam
- they stitch soccer balls in Pakistan and baseballs in Honduras and Haiti
- to pay their parents' debts they pick tea or tobacco on the plantations of Sri Lanka and harvest jasmine in Egypt for French perfume
- rented out by their parents in Iran, Nepal, and India they weave rugs from before dawn until past midnight, and when someone tries to rescue them they ask, "Are you my new master?"
- sold by their parents for a hundred dollars in Sudan, they are put to work in the sex trade or at any other labor.

Armies in certain places in Africa, the Middle East, and Latin America recruit children by force. In war, these little soldiers work by killing and above all by dying. They make up half the victims of recent African wars.

In nearly all these tasks, except war, which tradition decrees and reality teaches is a male affair, girls' hands are just as useful as boys'. But the labor market treats girls the same way it treats women. They always earn less than the meager bit paid to boys, when they earn anything at all.

Prostitution is the fate of many girls and fewer boys around the world. Astonishing as it seems, there are at least a hundred thousand child prostitutes in the United States, according to a 1997 UNICEF report. But the vast majority of child victims of the sex trade work in the brothels and on the streets of the southern part of the globe. This multimillion-dollar industry, with its networks of traffickers, intermediaries, travel agents, and procurers, operates with scandalous ease. In Latin America, it is nothing new: child prostitution began in 1536, when the first "tolerance home"

Flight/2

In the streets of Mexico City, a girl inhales toluene, solvents, glue, you name it. When she stops trembling, she says: "I hallucinated the Devil, I mean I went into the Devil and right then, whoa! I was at the edge, I was about to jump, the building was eight stories high, and I was about to jump, but just then my hallucination stopped, the Devil left me. The hallucination I liked best was when the Virgin of Guadalupe appeared before me. I saw her twice."

opened in Puerto Rico. Today half a million Brazilian girls sell their bodies for the benefit of adults—as many as in Thailand, but not as many as in India. On some Caribbean beaches, the prosperous sex tourism industry offers virgins to whoever can pay the price. The number of girls placed on the market is rising steadily: according to estimates by international organizations, at least a million girls swell the ranks of the global supply of bodies every year.

The number of poor children who work, in their homes or out, for their families or for whomever, is uncountable. They work outside the law and outside statistics. And the rest? Many are superfluous. The market doesn't need them, nor will it ever. They aren't profitable; they never will be. From the point of view of the established order, they begin by stealing the air they breathe and soon steal anything they can lay their hands on. Hunger or bullets tend to shorten their voyage from crib to grave. The system that scorns the old also fears the young. Old age is a failure, childhood a threat. Ever more poor children are "born with a tendency toward crime," according to specialists. They are the most dangerous category of the "surplus population." The child as public threat: "the antisocial conduct of youth in Latin America" has been a recurring theme at the Pan-American Children's Congress for years. Governments and some experts on the subject share this obsession with violence, vice, and perdition. Each child is a potential El Niño, and the disasters he or she may cause must be prevented. At the first South American Police Congress, held in Montevideo in 1979, the Colombian delegate explained that "the rising daily increase in the population under eighteen leads us to expect a higher POTENTIALLY DELINQUENT population" (uppercase in original).

In Latin American countries, the hegemony of the market severs ties of solidarity and tears the social fabric to shreds. What fate awaits the nobodies, the owners of nothing, in countries where the right to own property is becoming the only right? And the children of the nobodies? Hunger drives many, who are always becoming many more, to thievery, begging, and prostitution. Consumer society insults them by offering what it denies. And then they take vengeance, united by the certainty of the death that awaits them. According to UNICEF, in 1995 there were eight million abandoned children on the streets of Latin America. According to Human Rights Watch, in 1993 death squads linked to the police murdered six children a day in Colombia, four a day in Brazil.

Between the extremes lies the middle. Between the prisoners of opulence and the prisoners of destitution are the children who have quite a bit more than nothing but much less than everything. They, too, are less and less free. "To be allowed to be or not to be allowed to be, that is the question," Spanish comic Chumy Chúmez liked to say. The freedom of these children is confiscated by societies that venerate order as they generate disorder. Fear of fear: the floor creaks under their feet and there are no guarantees.

So the Deaf Will Hear

The number of malnourished children in the world is growing. Twelve million children under the age of five die every year from diarrhea, anemia, and other illnesses caused by hunger. A 1998 UNICEF report, full of such statistics, suggests that the struggle against child hunger and death "become the world's highest priority." To make it that, the report turns to the only argument that seems to work today: "The lack of vitamins and minerals in the diet costs some countries the equivalent of more than 5% of their gross national product in lives lost, disability, and lower productivity."

Stability is unstable, jobs evaporate, money vanishes. Just to make it to the end of the month is a feat. "Welcome, middle class," is the greeting on a billboard at the entrance to one of the worst barrios of Buenos Aires. Middle-class people still live as impostors, pretending to obey the law and believe in it, pretending to have more than they have. But never before has it been so difficult for them to keep up this exhausting charade. Suffocated by debts and paralyzed by fear, the middle class raises its children in a state of panic. Fear of living, fear of falling, fear of losing your job, your car, your home, your possessions, fear of never having what you ought to have in order to be. In the widespread clamor for public security, imperiled by lurking criminal monsters, the members of the middle class shout loudest. They defend order as if they owned it, even though they're only tenants overwhelmed by high rents and the threat of eviction.

Caught in the trap of terror, more and more of their children are condemned to suffer the humiliation of perpetual imprisonment. In the city of the future, which is becoming the city of the present, telechildren watched by electronic nannies will contemplate the street from a window of their telehomes: the street, off-limits thanks to violence or fear of it, the street where the dangerous and sometimes prodigious spectacle of life takes place.

Injustice 101

Advertising enjoins everyone to consume, while the economy prohibits the vast majority of humanity from doing so. The command that everybody do what so many cannot becomes an invitation to crime. In the papers, crime stories have more to say about the contradictions of our times than all the articles about politics and economics.

This world, which puts on a banquet for all, then slams the door in the noses of so many, is simultaneously equalizing and unequal: *equalizing* in the ideas and habits it imposes and *unequal* in the opportunities it offers.

EQUALIZATION AND INEQUALITY

Twin totalitarianisms plague the world: the dictatorships of consumer society and obligatory injustice.

The machinery of compulsory equalization works against the finest trait of the human species, the fact that we recognize ourselves in our differences and build links based on them. The best of the world lies in the many worlds the world contains, the different melodies of life, their pains and strains: the thousand and one ways of living and speaking, thinking and creating, eating, working, dancing, playing, loving, suffering, and celebrating that we have discovered over so many thousands of years.

Equalization, which makes us all goofy and all the same, can't be measured. No computer could count the crimes that the pop culture business commits each day against the human rainbow and the human right to identity. But its devastating progress is mind-boggling. Time is emptied of history, and space no longer acknowledges the astonishing diversity of its parts. Through the mass media the owners of the world inform us all of our obligation to look at ourselves in a single mirror.

Whoever doesn't have, isn't. He who has no car or doesn't wear designer shoes or imported perfume is only pretending to exist. Importer economy, impostor culture: we are all obliged to take the consumer's cruise across the swirling waters of the market. Most of the passengers are swept overboard, but thanks to foreign debt the fares of those who make it are billed to us all. Loans allow the consuming minority to load themselves up with useless new things, and before everyone's eyes the media transform into genuine needs the artificial demands the North of the world ceaselessly invents and successfully projects onto the South. ("North" and "South," by the way, are terms used in this book to designate the carving up of the global pie and do not always coincide with geography.)

What about the millions upon millions of Latin American children who will soon be condemned to unemployment or hunger wages? Does advertising stimulate demand or, as seems more likely, incite violence? Television gives us the full treatment: it teaches us to confuse the quality of life with the quantity of things and offers daily audiovisual courses on violence with video games for extra

The Exception

There is only one place in the world where North and South meet on an equal footing: a soccer field at the mouth of the Amazon in Brazil. The equator cuts right through the middle of Zerão stadium in Amapá, so each team plays one half in the South and the other half in the North.

credit. Crime is the biggest hit on the small screen. "Strike first before they strike you," caution the video game professors. "You're all alone. Don't count on anyone else." Cars fly, people explode: "You, too, can kill." Meanwhile, in Latin America's cities, among the largest in the world, crime grows at an alarming rate.

The world economy requires consumer markets in perpetual expansion to absorb rising production and keep profit rates from falling. It also requires ridiculously cheap labor and raw materials to keep production costs down. The same system that needs to sell more and more needs to pay less and less. This paradox gives birth to another: to increase the number of consumers, the North issues ever more imperious orders to consume to the South and the East, but the number of criminals multiplies even faster. Muggers seize the fetishes that make people real, in order to become what their victims are. Glove thy neighbor: in the madhouse of the streets, anyone can be dealt a punch or a bullet, those born to die of indigestion as well as those born to die of hunger.

Cultural equalization, the process of casting all in the single mold of consumer society, can't be reduced to statistics, but inequality can. The World Bank, which does so much to encourage inequality, freely admits—and several agencies of the United Nations confirm—that never has the world economy been less democratic, never has the world been so scandalously unjust. In 1960, the richest 20 percent of humanity had thirty times as much as the poorest 20 percent. By 1990, that figure had increased to seventy times. And the scissors continue to open: in the year 2000 the gap will be ninety times.

Between the richest of the rich, who appear on the pornofinancial pages of *Forbes* and *Fortune,* and the poorest of the poor, who appear on the streets and in the fields, the chasm is even greater. A pregnant woman in Africa is a hundred times more likely to die than a pregnant woman in Europe. The value of pet products sold annually in the United States is four times the GNP of Ethiopia. The sales of just the two giants General Motors and Ford easily surpass the value of all black Africa's economies. According to the United Nations Development Program, "Ten people, the ten richest men on the planet, own wealth equivalent to the value of the total production of fifty countries, and 447 multimillionaires own a greater fortune than the annual income of half of humanity." The head of this UN agency, James Gustave Speth, declared in 1997 that over the past half century the number of rich people doubled while the number of poor tripled and that 1.6 billion people were worse off than they had been only fifteen years earlier.

Not long before that, the president of the World Bank, James Wolfensohn, threw cold water on the annual meeting of the bank and the International Monetary Fund. He warned those celebrating the achievements of the world government run by those two bodies that if things continue as they are, in thirty years there will be five billion poor people in the world, and inequality will explode in the face of future generations. Meanwhile, an anony-

mous hand wrote on a Buenos Aires wall, "Fight hunger and poverty! Eat poor people!"

As if to confirm our optimism, as Mexican writer Carlos Monsiváis suggests, the world carries on: the injustice that rules between countries is reproduced within each country, and year after year the gap between those who have everything and those who have nothing widens. We know it well in the Americas. In the United States half a century ago, the rich earned 20 percent of national income; now they get 40 percent. And in the South? Latin America is the most unjust region in the world. Nowhere else are bread and fish distributed as unfairly; nowhere else does such an immense distance separate the few who have the right to rule from the many who have the duty to obey.

Latin America is a slave economy masquerading as postmodern: it pays African wages, it charges European prices, and the merchandise it produces most efficiently is injustice and violence. Official statistics for Mexico City from 1997: 80 percent poor,

3 percent rich, the rest in the middle. The same Mexico City is the capital of the country that in the 1990s spawned more instant multimillionaires than anywhere else on earth: according to UN figures, one Mexican has as much wealth as seventeen million of his poor countrymen.

There is no country in the world as unequal as Brazil. Some analysts even speak of the "Brazilianization" of the planet in sketching a portrait of the world to come. By "Brazilianization" they certainly don't mean the spread of irrepressible soccer, spectacular carnivals, or music that awakens the dead, marvels that make Brazil shine brightest; rather they're describing the imposition of a model of progress based on social injustice and racial discrimination, where economic growth only increases poverty and exclusion. "Belindia" is another name for Brazil, coined by economist Edmar Bacha: a country where a minority lives like the rich in Belgium while the majority lives like the poor of India.

In this era of privatization and free markets, money governs without intermediaries. A state that is judge and police and not much else keeps cheap labor in line and represses the dangerous legions of those without work. In many countries, social justice has been reduced to criminal justice. The state takes charge of public security; everything else is left to the market. And where the police can't handle it, poverty—poor people, poor regions—is left to God. Even when government tries to dress up like some kindly mother, it has only the strength to exercise vigilance and mete out punishment. In these neoliberal times, public rights are reduced to public charity and handed out only on the eve of elections.

Every year poverty kills more people than the entire Second World War, which killed quite a few. But from the vantage point of the powerful, extermination is not a bad idea if it helps regulate a population that is growing too fast. Experts decry "surplus popu-

Points of View/1

From the point of view of the owl, the bat, the bohemian, and
the thief, sunset is time for breakfast.

 Rain is bad news for tourists and good news for farmers.

 From the point of view of the natives, it's the tourists who are
picturesque.

 From the point of view of the Indians of the Caribbean
islands, Christopher Columbus, with his plumed cap and red
velvet cape, was the biggest parrot they had ever seen.

lation" in the South, where ignorant masses violate the Sixth
Commandment day and night: "surplus population" in Brazil,
where there are seventeen inhabitants per square kilometer, or in
Colombia, where there are twenty-nine. Holland has four hundred
inhabitants per square kilometer and no Dutchman dies of hunger,
but Brazil and Colombia belong to a handful of gluttons. Haiti and
El Salvador are the most overpopulated countries in the
Americas—just as overpopulated as Germany.

 Power, which practices and lives by injustice, sweats violence
through every pore. The damned of dark skin, guilty of their
poverty and their hereditary criminal traits, exist in shantytown
hells. Advertising makes their mouths water and the police chase
them from the table. The system denies what it offers: magic lamps
that make dreams come true, neon lights announcing paradise in
the city night, the splendors of virtual wealth. As the owners of real
wealth know, there is no Valium to calm so much anxiety, no

Prozac to snuff out so much torment. Jails and bullets are the proper therapy for the poor.

Twenty or thirty years ago, poverty was the fruit of injustice. The left decried it, the center admitted it, the right rarely denied it. How quickly times have changed: now poverty is fair reward for inefficiency. Poverty may arouse pity, but it no longer causes indignation. People are poor by the law of chance or the hand of fate. The dominant language—mass-produced images and words—nearly always serves a carrot-and-stick system that conceives of life as a pitiless race between a few winners and many losers, who were born to lose anyway. Violence is generally portrayed not as the child of injustice but as the fruit of bad behavior by poor sports, the numerous socially inept who fill poor neighborhoods and poor countries. Violence is their nature. It corresponds, like poverty, to the natural order of things, to the biological or perhaps zoological order. That's how things are, that's how they've been, and that's how they will be.

The moral code of the end of the millennium condemns not injustice but failure. Robert McNamara, one of those responsible for the war in Vietnam, wrote a book in which he admitted it was a mistake. That war, which killed more than three million Vietnamese and fifty-eight thousand Americans, was a mistake not because it was unjust but because the United States carried on in full knowledge that it could not win. By 1965, according to McNamara, there was already overwhelming evidence that the invading force could not prevail; nonetheless, the U.S. government continued as if victory were possible. The fact that the United States spent fifteen years visiting international terrorism on Vietnam in order to impose a government the Vietnamese did not want does not even enter into the discussion. That the world's premier military power dropped more bombs on a small country than all the bombs dropped during the Second World War is utterly irrelevant.

Points of View/2

From the point of view of the South, summer in the North is winter.

From the point of view of a worm, a plate of spaghetti is an orgy.

Where Hindus see a sacred cow, others see an enormous hamburger.

From the point of view of Hippocrates, Galen, Maimonides, and Paracelsus, there was a disease called indigestion but none called hunger.

From the point of view of his neighbors in the town of Cardona, Toto Zaugg, who wore the same clothes in summer and winter, was an admirable man. "Toto's never cold," they said.

He said nothing. He was cold, but he had no coat.

After all, during that long butchery the United States was exercising the right of big powers to invade whomever they wish and impose whatever they choose. Officers, businessmen, bankers, and makers of opinions and emotions in ruling countries have the right to create military dictatorships or docile governments. They can dictate economic or any other kind of policy, give the orders to accept ruinous trade deals and usurious loans, demand servitude to their lifestyles, and enforce consumer trends. This right is a "natural one," consecrated by the impunity with which it is exercised and the rapidity with which its exercise is forgotten.

Power recalls the past not to remember but to sanctify, to

justify the perpetuation of privilege by right of inheritance, absolving those who rule of their crimes and supplying their speeches with alibis. What schools and the media teach as the only possible way of remembering the past simply passes on the voices that repeat the boring litany of power's self-sacralization. Exoneration requires unremembering. There are successful countries and people and there are failed countries and people because the efficient deserve rewards and the useless deserve punishment. To turn infamies into feats, the memory of the North is divorced from the memory of the South, accumulation is detached from despoliation, opulence has nothing to do with plunder. Broken memory leads us to believe that wealth is innocent of poverty. Wealth and poverty emerge from eternity and toward eternity they march, and that's the way things are because God or custom prefers it that way.

The Eighth Wonder of the World, Beethoven's Tenth, the Eleventh Commandment of the Lord: on all sides one hears hymns of praise to the free market, source of prosperity and guarantor of democracy. Free trade is sold as something new, as if born from a cabbage or the ear of a goat, despite its long history reaching back to the origins of the unjust system that reigns today:

- three or four centuries ago, England, Holland, and France practiced piracy in the name of free trade, through the good offices of Sir Francis Drake, Henry Morgan, Piet Heyn, François Lolonois, and other neoliberals of the day
- free trade was the alibi all Europe used while enriching itself selling human flesh in the slave trade
- later on, the United States brandished free trade to oblige many Latin American countries to accept its exports, loans, and military dictatorships
- wrapped in the folds of that same flag, British soldiers

Points of View/3

From the point of view of statistics, if a person earns a thousand dollars and another earns nothing, each of them appears to earn five hundred dollars when one calculates per capita income.

From the point of view of the struggle against inflation, adjustment policies are a good remedy. From the point of view of those who suffer such policies, they spread cholera, typhus, tuberculosis, and other damnations.

imposed opium smoking on China, while by fire and in the name of freedom, the filibuster William Walker reestablished slavery in Central America

◀ paying homage to free trade, British industry reduced India to the worst penury and British banks helped finance the extermination of Paraguay, which until 1870 had been the only truly independent country in Latin America

◀ time passed, and in 1954 it occurred to Guatemala to practice free trade by buying oil from the Soviet Union, and the United States promptly organized a devastating invasion to set things straight

◀ shortly thereafter, Cuba, also failing to see that free trade consisted of accepting prices as imposed, purchased outlawed Russian oil; the terrible fuss that ensued led to the Bay of Pigs invasion and the interminable blockade.

These historical antecedents teach us that free trade and other such monetary freedoms are to free peoples what Jack the Ripper was to Saint Francis of Assisi. The free market has transformed the countries of the South into bazaars filled with imported trinkets that most people can see but not touch. Nothing has changed since the far-off days when merchants and landowners usurped the independence won by barefoot soldiers and put it up for sale. That's when the workshops that might have incubated national industries were annihilated, when ports and big cities razed the hinterlands, choosing the delights of consumption over the challenges of creation. Years have passed and in Venezuela's supermarkets I have seen little plastic bags of water from Scotland to drink with your whiskey. In Central America's cities, where even rocks sweat buckets, I have seen fur stoles on fancy ladies. In Peru, I've seen German electric floor waxers for homes with dirt floors and no electricity; in Brazil, plastic palm trees bought in Miami.

Another path, the inverse one, was taken by developed countries. They never had Herod to their childhood birthday parties. The free market is the only commodity they produce without any subsidies, but it's only for export. They sell it, the South buys it. Their governments generously aid national agricultural production so that they can flood the South with food at ridiculously low prices despite ridiculously high costs, and so condemn the farmers of the South to ruin. The average rural producer in the United States receives state subsidies a hundred times greater than the income of a farmer in the Philippines, according to UN figures. And don't forget the ferocious protectionism practiced by developed countries when it's a matter of what they want most: a monopoly on state-of-the-art technologies, biotechnology, and the knowledge and communications industries. These privileges are defended at all cost so that the North will continue to know and the South will continue to repeat, and thus may it be for centuries upon centuries.

Many economic barriers remain high, and human barriers

Language/1

Companies are called "multinationals" because they operate in many countries at once, but they belong to the few countries that monopolize wealth; political, military, and cultural power; scientific knowledge; and advanced technology. The ten biggest multinationals today earn more than a hundred countries put together do.

"Developing countries" is the name that experts use to designate countries trampled by someone else's development. According to the United Nations, developing countries send developed countries ten times as much money through unequal trade and financial relations as they receive through foreign aid.

In international relations, "foreign aid" is what they call the little tax that vice pays to virtue. Foreign aid is generally distributed in ways that confirm injustice, rarely in ways that counter it. In 1995, black Africa suffered 75 percent of the world's AIDS cases but received 3 percent of the funds spent by international organizations on AIDS prevention.

higher yet. No need to look further than Europe's new immigration laws or the steel wall being erected by the United States along its border with Mexico. This is no homage to the Berlin Wall but one more door slammed in the face of Mexican workers who refuse to acknowledge that the freedom to change countries is money's privilege. (To make the wall less unpleasant, the plan is to paint it a salmon color, display tiles of children's artwork on it, and leave little holes to peek through.)

Every time they get together, and they get together with pointless frequency, the presidents of the Americas issue resolutions insisting that "the free market will contribute to prosperity." Whose prosperity, they don't say. Reality—which exists even if sometimes barely noted and which is not mute even if sometimes it keeps its mouth shut—tells us that the free flow of capital only fattens drug traffickers and the bankers who offer refuge to their narco-dollars. The collapse of public financial and economic controls provides good cover, allowing for the more efficient organization of drug distribution and money-laundering networks. Reality also tells us that the green light of the free market helps the North express its generosity, by offering the South and East as gifts its most polluting industries, its nuclear waste, and other garbage.

Language/2

In 1995, the Argentine press discovered that certain directors of the state-owned Banco Nación had received $37 million from IBM in return for a service contract $120 million above the usual price.

Three years later, the directors acknowledged that they had taken the money and deposited it in Swiss bank accounts, but they had the good taste to avoid using the word "bribe" or the rude expression "payoff": one of them used the word "gratuity," another said it was a "douceur," and the most delicate among them explained that it was just "a sign of IBM's happiness."

Language/3

In the Victorian period, one did not speak of trousers in the presence of an unmarried woman. Today, there are certain things one can't say in the face of public opinion:

- capitalism wears the stage name "market economy"
- imperialism is called "globalization"
- the victims of imperialism are called "developing countries," much as a dwarf might be called a "child"
- opportunism is called "pragmatism"
- treason is called "realism"
- poor people are called "low-income people"
- the expulsion of poor children from the school system is measured by the "dropout rate"
- the right of bosses to lay off workers with neither severance nor explanation is called "a flexible labor market"
- official rhetoric acknowledges women's rights among those of "minorities," as if the masculine half of humanity were the majority
- instead of military dictatorship, people say "process"
- torture is called "illegal compulsion" or "physical and psychological pressure"
- when thieves belong to a good family they're "kleptomaniacs"

- the looting of the public treasury by corrupt politicians answers to the name of "illicit enrichment"
- "accidents" are what they call crimes committed by cars
- for the blind, they say "the unseeing"
- a black man is "a man of color"
- where it says "long and difficult illness," it means cancer or AIDS
- "sudden illness" means heart attack
- people annihilated in military operations aren't dead: those killed in battle are "casualties," and civilians who get it are "collateral damage"
- in 1995, when France set off nuclear tests in the South Pacific, the French ambassador to New Zealand declared, "I don't like that word 'bomb.' They aren't bombs. They're exploding artifacts"
- "Getting Along" is what they call some of the death squads that operate under military protection in Colombia
- "Dignity" was what the Chilean dictatorship called one of its concentration camps, while "Liberty" was the largest jail of the Uruguayan dictatorship
- "Peace and Justice" is the name of the paramilitary group that in 1997 shot forty-five peasants, nearly all of them women and children, in the back as they prayed in the town church in Acteal, Chiapas, Mexico.

RACISM AND SEXISM 101

Subordinates owe eternal obedience to superiors, just as women owe obedience to men. Some are born to rule, others to be ruled.

Racism, like sexism, is justified by genetic inheritance. The poor are damned not by history but by biology. Their fate is written in the blood, and worse yet, their inferiority chromosomes carry the evil seeds of crime. When a poor, dark-skinned man approaches, red lights flash and alarm bells ring.

FABLES, LABELS, AND SIMPLE UNABLES

In the Americas and Europe the police hunt stereotypes guilty of wearing an unconcealed face. Every nonwhite suspect confirms the rule written in invisible ink in the depths of our collective conscience: crime is black or brown, or at least yellow.

This demonization ignores history. Over the past five centuries, white crimes aren't hard to find. No more than one-fifth of the world's population in the Renaissance, whites already claimed to embody God's will. In his name they exterminated untold millions of Indians in the Americas and abducted untold millions of blacks from Africa. White of skin were the kings, vampires, and flesh traders who founded hereditary slavery in the Americas and Africa, so that the children of slaves would be born slaves in the mines and on the plantations. White were the authors of the countless acts of barbarism that civilization committed over the centuries, imposing white imperial power on the four corners of the earth by blood and fire. White were the heads of state and the warrior chiefs who, with a hand from the Japanese, organized and executed two world wars in the twentieth century, killing sixty-four million people, most of them civilians. And white were those who planned and carried out the Holocaust against the Jews, Reds, Gypsies, and gays in the Nazi death camps.

The certainty that some are born to be free and others to be slaves has guided all empires since the world began. But it was with the Renaissance and the conquest of the Americas that racism became a system of moral absolution at the service of European gluttony. Since then, racism has ruled, dismissing majorities among the colonized and excluding minorities among the colonizers. In the colonial era racism was as essential as gunpowder, and in Rome pope after pope slandered God by attributing to him the order to loot and plunder.

In America a new vocabulary was invented to locate people on the social scale according to their degree of degradation by miscegenation. "Mulatto" was, and is, a mixture of white and black, an evident allusion to the mule, the sterile offspring of a male donkey and a mare. Other terms classified the thousand colors engendered by the successive embraces of Europeans, Americans, and Africans in the New World: English names like half-caste, quadroon, octoroon, mustee, sambo, griffe, or the Spanish *castizo, cuarterón, quinterón, morisco, cholo, albino, lobo, zambaigo, cambujo, albarazado, barcino, coyote, chamiso, zambo, jíbaro, tresalbo, jarocho,*

Identity

Where are my ancestors? Whom shall I celebrate? Where shall I
find the raw material? My first American ancestor . . . was an
Indian, an early Indian; your ancestors skinned him alive, and I
am an orphan.

—Mark Twain, who was white, in the
New York Times, December 26, 1881

lunarejo, and *rayado.* And there were Spanish names meaning
"turn-back," "there-you-stay," "hang-in-the-air," and "I-don't-
understand-you," to baptize the fruits of these tropical salsas and to
define greater or lesser degrees of hereditary damnation.

Of all the names, "I-don't-understand-you" is the most revealing. In the five centuries since the so-called discovery of America,
we've had nothing but I-don't-understand-yous. Christopher
Columbus thought that the Indians were from India, that Cubans
lived in China and Haitians in Japan. His brother Bartholomew
burned six Indians alive when all they had done was bury Catholic
medallions so the new gods would make their crops fertile. When
the conquistadors arrived on the eastern coast of Mexico they
asked, "What is this place?" The natives answered, "We don't
understand a thing," which in the Mayan language sounded like
"Yucatan," and that is what the region has been called ever since.
When the conquistadors reached the heart of South America they
asked, "What is this lake?" The natives answered, "Water, sir?"
which in the Guaraní language sounded like "Ypacaraí," the name

promptly conferred on the lake near Asunción, Paraguay. Indians were always beardless, but in his *Dictionnaire universel* of 1694 Antoine Furetière described them as "furry and covered with hair," because the European iconographic tradition held that savages were always hairy like monkeys. In 1774, the priest charged with teaching catechism in the town of San Andrés Itzapa in Guatemala discovered that the Indians worshiped not the Virgin Mary but the serpent crushed under her foot, the serpent being a Mayan divinity. He also discovered that they venerated the cross because it was shaped like the sacred meeting of the rain and the earth. At the same time in the German city of Königsberg, Immanuel Kant, who had never been to America, declared that Indians were "incapable of civilization" and were destined to be exterminated. In fact, extermination was occurring, though it had little to do with their nature: not many Indians survived the harquebusades and cannonades, the attacks of virus and bacteria unknown in the Americas, and the endless days of forced labor in the fields and in the gold and silver mines. Many were condemned to the lash, the stake, or the gallows for the sin of idolatry. Those "incapable of civilization" lived in communion with nature and believed, like many of their descendants today, that the earth is sacred, as is all that walks on it or grows from it.

Century after century, the whites kept getting it wrong. At the end of the nineteenth century, the military campaigns to annihilate the Indians in southern Argentina were called "the conquest of the desert," even though Patagonia was less deserted then than it is today. A few years ago the Argentine civil registry refused to accept indigenous names "because they are foreign." Anthropologist Catalina Buliubasich discovered that the registry was giving undocumented Indians from highlands near Salta birth certificates on which their aboriginal names were exchanged for unforeign

---

For the Course on Penal Law

In 1986, a Mexican congressman visited the jail in Cerro Hueco, in Chiapas. There he found a Tzotzil Indian who had slit his father's throat and been sentenced to thirty years. But every day at noon, as the congressman discovered, the dead father brought tortillas and beans to his son in jail.

The Tzotzil prisoner had been interrogated and judged in Spanish, of which he understood little or nothing, and with the help of a good beating he confessed to something called parricide.

---

ones like Chevroleta, Ford, Twenty-Seven, Eight, and Thirteen. Some were even rebaptized Domingo Faustino Sarmiento, the whole shebang, in homage to the founding father who felt nothing but disgust for the native population.

Today, Indians are considered deadwood in the economies that live off their hard labor, and a millstone for the plastic culture to which these countries aspire. In Guatemala, one of the few countries where Indians managed to recover from their demographic catastrophe, they suffer mistreatment as an excluded minority even though they are the majority. Mestizos and whites (or those who call themselves white) dress and live (or wish they could dress and live) Miami-style so that they won't look like Indians, while thousands of foreigners make the pilgrimage to the market at Chichicastenango, a pillar of world beauty, to buy the marvels woven by indigenous artists. Colonel Carlos Castillo Armas, who took power in 1954, dreamed of turning Guatemala into

Disneyland. To save the Indians from ignorance and backward-ness, the colonel proposed "awakening their aesthetic sense," as an official pamphlet explained, "by teaching them weaving, embroi-dery, and other trades." Death surprised him in the midst of this task.

"You look like an Indian" or "You smell like a black," say some mothers in countries with a large Indian or black presence when their children don't want to take a bath. Yet the chroniclers of the Conquest noted the Spaniards' astonishment at the frequency with which Indians bathed. It was Indians, and later African slaves, who had the courtesy to pass their hygienic habits on to other Americans from Canada to Chile.

The Christian faith distrusted bathing, suspecting it of being a sin because it felt so good. In Spain during the Inquisition, fre-quent bathers, accused of Moslem heresy, could end up burned at the stake. In Spain today, someone is a real Arab if he vacations at Marbella on the Costa del Sol, but a poor Arab is just a Moor, per-haps "a stinking Moor." Anyone who has visited the Alhambra, that festival of water in Granada, knows Islam has been a culture of water since way back when Christians wouldn't touch it except to drink. In reality, showers became popular in Europe quite recently, more or less at the same time as television.

They say Indians are supposed to be cowards and blacks easily frightened, but they've always been good cannon fodder in wars of conquest, wars of independence, civil wars, and border wars in Latin America. The Spanish used Indian soldiers to massacre Indians during the Conquest. The nineteenth-century wars of independence were a hecatomb for Argentine blacks, who were always sent to the front lines. In the war against Paraguay, the bod-ies of black Brazilians littered the battlefields. Indians were the troops Peru and Bolivia used in the war against Chile. "That abject and degraded race," as Peruvian writer Ricardo Palma called them, were sent to the slaughterhouse as the officers fled shouting "Long live the fatherland!" More recently, it was Indians who died in the war between Ecuador and Peru and Indian soldiers who destroyed Indian villages in the Guatemalan highlands. For their mestizo officers each crime was a grisly rite meant to exorcise half their blood.

The Goddess

On the night celebrating Iemanyá, the entire coast is a feast. Bahía, Rio de Janeiro, Montevideo, and other shores celebrate the goddess of the sea. Crowds turn the beach into a sea of candles and the waters into a garden of flowers and perfumes, necklaces, cakes, candies, and other trifles and treats she may fancy.

Then the worshipers make a wish:

The map of buried treasure,
The key to forbidden love,
The return of the lost,
The resurrection of the dead.

The worshipers ask and their wishes come true. Perhaps the miracle lasts no longer than it takes to utter the words that name it, but in that fleeting moment when the impossible happens, the worshipers shine with their own light, luminous in the dark.

Once the waves have carried away their offerings, the worshipers retreat, their eyes on the horizon, so as not to turn their backs on the goddess. And very slowly they return to the city.

The same people who claim blacks are lazy also say admiringly, "He works like a black." They say, "Whites run, blacks flee." The white who runs was robbed; the black who flees is a thief. Even Martín Fierro, the character from the Argentine literary classic, who best embodies all poor and persecuted gauchos, thinks blacks are thieves created by the Devil to the disgrace of hell. Indians, too: "The Indian is Indian and will not try/To change his ways so forlorn/An Indian thief he was first born/And like an Indian thief he will die." Black thief, Indian thief: the I-don't-understand-you tradition insists that thieves be the ones who are robbed the most.

Since the days of conquest and slavery, Indians and blacks have been robbed of their hands and their lands, their labor and their wealth—their words and memory as well. In the Rio de la Plata, "*quilombo*" now means brothel, chaos, disorder, confusion, but this Bantu word really meant training camp. In Brazil, *quilombos* were the sanctuaries founded in the jungle by fugitive slaves, some of which lasted a long time. The free kingdom of Palmares in the hinterlands of Alagoas lasted an entire century, resisting more than thirty military expeditions by the armies of Holland and Portugal. The true history of the conquest and colonization of America is a

Hell

In colonial times, Palenque was a sanctuary of freedom deep in the jungle, a refuge for fugitive black slaves from Cartagena de Indias and the plantations of the Colombian coast. Years have gone by, centuries, and Palenque survives. The people of Palenque continue to believe that the earth, their earth, is a body made of fields, jungles, wind, people, that it breathes through trees and cries through streams. They continue to believe that those who have enjoyed life will be rewarded in paradise and those who haven't will burn in hell, in the eternal fire reserved for the cold women and men who disobeyed the sacred voices that command us to live life with pleasure and passion.

story of unceasing dignity. There was not a day without rebellion. Yet official history has erased every one of those uprisings with the disdain reserved for ill-mannered servants. After all, when blacks and Indians refused to accept slavery or forced labor as their fate, they were trying to subvert the organizing principles of the universe. Between the amoeba and God, universal order was founded on a long chain of successive subordinations: like the planets that orbit the sun, serfs revolved around their lords. Social inequality and racial discrimination are still an integral part of the harmony of the cosmos, and not only in the Americas. As Italian politician Pietro Ingrao noted in 1995: "I have a Philippine maid at home. It's so strange. It's hard for me to imagine a Philippine family that would have a white maid in their home."

Thinkers capable of elevating the prejudices of the ruling class to the category of science have never been lacking, but in nineteenth-century Europe they were particularly bountiful. The philosopher Auguste Comte, a founder of modern sociology, believed in the superiority of the white race and the perpetual childhood of women. Like nearly all his colleagues, Comte harbored no doubts about one essential principle: white men are the most fit to rule over those condemned to the lower rungs of the social ladder.

Cesare Lombroso turned racism into criminology. To demonstrate the innate dangerousness of "primitive savages," this Italian professor, who happened to be Jewish, developed a method quite similar to the one Hitler would use half a century later to justify anti-Semitism. According to Lombroso, criminals are born criminals and the animal features that give them away are the very same ones that black Africans and American Indians inherited from the Mongoloid race. Murderers have high cheekbones, frizzy black hair, sparse beards, large incisors. Robbers have flat noses; rapists, swollen lips and eyelids. Like savages, criminals do not blush, which allows them to lie shamelessly. Women do blush, though Lombroso discovered that "even women considered normal have some criminal features." Revolutionaries, too: "I have never seen an anarchist with a symmetrical face."

Herbert Spencer attributed to the empire of reason inequalities that today spring from the law of the market. Though a century has passed, some of his truths sound rather modern, well suited to our neoliberal days. According to Spencer the state ought to remain on the margins and not interfere with the processes of "natural selection" that give power to the strongest and best-endowed. Social welfare only adds to the herd of lazy bums, and public education sows discontent. The state ought to stick to

Heroes and Villains

Inside some athletes lives a crowd. In the forties, when blacks couldn't even share a cemetery with whites in the United States, Jackie Robinson was a baseball star. Millions of oppressed blacks found dignity through this athlete who shone like no one else in an exclusively white sport. Fans threw insults and peanuts at him; players spat on him; death threats welcomed him home.

In 1996, while the world was busy acclaiming Nelson Mandela and his long struggle against racism, the athlete Josia Thugwane became the first black South African to win an Olympic medal. Over the past few years, it has become normal for Olympic medals to end up in the hands of Kenyans, Ethiopians, Somalis, Burundis, or South Africans. Tiger Woods, the Mozart of golf, is a star in a rich white sport, and for years now basketball and boxing have been dominated by blacks. Blacks and mulattos are the players who give soccer most of its joy and beauty.

In racism's doublespeak, it is perfectly acceptable to applaud successful blacks and damn the rest. At the World Cup won by France in 1998, nearly all the players in blue who started each match to the tune of the "Marseillaise" were immigrants. A poll taken during the Cup confirmed that four of every ten people in France harbor racial prejudice, but every Frenchman celebrated that triumph as if those blacks and Arabs were the sons of Joan of Arc.

instructing "inferior races" in manual trades and keeping them away from alcohol.

As when the police conduct a search, racism finds whatever it has planted. Until the early years of the twentieth century, weighing brains was a common way of measuring intelligence. This scientific method, which gave rise to obscene exhibitions of encephalitic matter, demonstrated that Indians, blacks, and women had rather light brains. Gabriel René Moreno, the great intellectual of nineteenth-century Bolivia, proved, scale in hand, that Indian and mestizo brains weighed five to ten ounces less than white brains. The weight of the brain has about as much to do with intelligence as the size of the penis does with sexual ability—in other words, none. But scientists tracked down famous brains, undaunted by disconcerting results. The brain of Anatole France, for example, weighed half as much as Ivan Turgenev's, even though their literary merits were considered more or less the same.

A century ago in Paris, Alfred Binet invented the first IQ test, with the laudable objective of identifying children who needed more help from their teachers. The inventor was the first to say that this instrument was of no use in measuring intelligence, which cannot be measured, and should not be used to disqualify anyone from anything. But by 1913, U.S. officials were already using the Binet test at the very gates of New York, right near the Statue of Liberty, on recently arrived Jewish, Hungarian, Italian, and Russian immigrants. They found that eight out of every ten immigrants had the minds of children. Three years later, Bolivian authorities put the test to work in the public schools of Potosí: eight out of every ten children there were abnormal. And ever since, racial and social prejudice has relied on the scientific aura of intellectual coefficients, treating people as if they were numbers.

Names

The marathon runner Doroteo Guamuch, a Quiché Indian, was the greatest athlete in Guatemalan history. Since he was the pride and glory of his country, he had to change his Mayan name and call himself Mateo Flores.

In homage to his feats, the country's largest soccer stadium was named Mateo Flores while the man himself earned his living as a caddy, carrying clubs and collecting balls and tips at the Mayan Golf Club.

In 1994, *The Bell Curve* was a spectacular best-seller in the United States. Written by two university professors, it proclaimed unabashedly what many thought but didn't dare say above a whisper: that blacks and poor people have lower IQs than whites and the rich thanks to their genetic makeup. To waste money on education and social assistance for them would be like throwing water into the sea. The poor, especially those with black skin, are donkeys, and not because they're poor. Rather they're poor because they're donkeys.

Racism only acknowledges evidence that supports its own prejudices. African art has been a primordial source of inspiration for, and often the object of blatant plagiarism by, the most famous painters and sculptors of the twentieth century. And where would we be without the music that came out of Africa to spawn new magic in Brazil, the United States, and the Caribbean? African rhythms saved the world from dying of boredom or sorrow. Nevertheless, to Jorge Luis Borges, Arnold Toynbee, and many other worthy modern intellectuals, the cultural sterility of blacks was self-evident.

In the Americas, our culture is the daughter of several mothers. Our multiple identity gains its creative vitality from the fertile contradiction of its parts. But we have been trained not to see ourselves, not to see the full splendor of the human condition in all its glory. The Americas are sick with racism, blind in both eyes from North to South. Latin Americans of my generation were educated by Hollywood. Indians were guys with long faces wearing feathers and war paint, seasick from riding in circles. Of Africa all we knew was what we learned from Professor Tarzan, the invention of a novelist who never set foot on that continent.

Non-European cultures are not seen as cultures but as catch basins of ignorance, useful at best for proving the impotence of inferior races, or attracting tourists, or giving holiday parties a decorative touch. But in the real garden of mestizo culture, indigenous and African roots flower with as much potency as their European counterparts. Their bountiful fruits can be plainly seen not only in high art but in arts scorned as handicrafts and in religions dismissed as superstition. Those roots, ignored but not ignorant, feed the daily lives of people of flesh and blood even if some don't realize it or would rather not see it. They are alive in the languages that reveal who we are by what we say and what we keep silent, in our ways of eating and preparing what we eat, in the melodies that make us dance, the games that make us play, and the thousand and one secret or shared ceremonies that help us live.

For centuries the divinities that came from the American past and the coasts of Africa were outlawed and lived in hiding. Although they are still disdained today, many believing whites and mestizos pay them homage or acknowledge them and ask their favors. In the Andean countries, it's not only Indians who tilt their glasses and allow the first swallow to spill so that Pachamama, goddess of the earth, may drink. On the islands of the Caribbean and the Atlantic coasts of South America, it's no longer only blacks who offer flowers and treats to Iemanyá, goddess of the sea. The days are over when Indian and black gods had to dress up as Christian saints in order to exist. Still, they remain objects of scorn by official culture. In our alienated societies, trained for centuries to spit in the mirror, it isn't easy to accept that religions which originated in the Americas or came on slave ships from Africa are as worthy of respect as Christianity. Not more, but not a bit less. Religions? Those superstitions? Those pagan exaltations of nature, those dangerous celebrations of human passion? Picturesque, maybe even pleasant, but deep down what are they? Just expressions of ignorance and backwardness.

Justice

In 1997, an expensive new car with official plates traveled at a normal speed down a São Paulo avenue. Three men rode inside. At a corner they were stopped by a policeman who made them get out and stand against the car, hands in the air, for over an hour while he asked them again and again where they had stolen the car.

The three men were black. One of them, Edivaldo Brito, was the head of the São Paulo Justice Department. For Brito this was nothing new. In less than a year it had already happened five times.

The policeman who stopped them was also black.

Viewing blacks and their symbols of identity that way is a long-standing tradition. In 1937, to open the road to progress in the Dominican Republic, Generalissimo Rafael Leónidas Trujillo ordered twenty-five thousand black Haitians cut to pieces with machetes. The generalissimo, a mulatto whose grandmother was Haitian, used to whiten his face with rice powder and he wanted to whiten the country, too. As an indemnity, the Dominican government paid $29 per body to Haiti. After lengthy negotiations, Trujillo admitted to eighteen thousands deaths, for a total of $522,000.

Meanwhile, far from there, Adolf Hitler was sterilizing Gypsies and the mulatto children of Senegalese soldiers who had come to Germany in French uniforms. The Nazi plan to achieve Aryan purity began with the sterilization of criminals and people with hereditary diseases and then moved on to the Jews.

The world's first euthanasia law was approved in 1901 by the state of Indiana. By 1930, thirty U.S. states had legalized the sterilization of the retarded, dangerous murderers, rapists, and those who belonged to categories as fuzzy as "social perverts," "alcoholics and other drug addicts," and "sick and degenerate people." Most of those sterilized were, of course, black. In Europe, Germany wasn't alone in enacting laws inspired by dreams of social hygiene and racial purity. Sweden, for example, has recently admitted to sterilizing more than sixty thousand people under a 1930s law not repealed until 1976.

In the twenties and thirties the most prestigious educators in the Americas spoke of the need to "regenerate the race," "improve the species," or "change the biological quality of children." When Peruvian dictator Augusto Leguía opened the Pan-American Children's Congress in 1930, he emphasized "ethnic improvement," echoing Peru's recent National Conference on Children,

Points of View/4

In the East of the world, Western day is night.

In India, those in mourning wear white.

In ancient Europe, black, the color of the fertile earth, was the color of life, and white, the color of bones, was the color of death.

According to the wise old men of Colombia's Chocó region, Adam and Eve were black, and so were their sons, Cain and Abel. When Cain killed his brother with one blow, God's fury thundered across the heavens. Cringing before the Lord's rage, the murderer turned so pale from guilt and fear that he stayed white until the end of his days. We whites are all children of Cain.

which had raised the alarm about "child retards, degenerates, and criminals." Six years earlier, when the congress was held in Chile, many speakers insisted on the necessity of "selecting the seeds to be sown, to avoid impure children," while the Argentine daily *La Nación* editorialized about the need "to look out for the future of the race" and in Chile *El Mercurio* warned that Indian "habits and ignorance impede the adoption of certain modern customs and concepts."

A leading participant in the congress in Chile, a socialist medical doctor named José Ingenieros, wrote in 1905 that blacks, "opprobrious scoriae," merited enslavement for reasons "of purely biological reality." The rights of man could not be extended to "these simian beings, who seem closer to anthropoid monkeys than to civilized whites." According to Ingenieros—a guiding light of Argentine youth—neither should "these scraps of human flesh" aspire to be citizens, "because they shouldn't be considered people in the juridical sense." A few years earlier, another doctor, Raymundo Nina Rodrigues, had spoken in no less outrageous terms. This pioneer of anthropology in Brazil declared that "the study of inferior races has offered science well-observed examples of their organic cerebral incapacity."

Most of the intellectuals of the Americas were convinced that "inferior races" blocked the road to progress. Nearly all governments held the same opinion. In the south of the United States mixed marriages were outlawed and blacks couldn't get into schools, washrooms, or cemeteries reserved for whites. The blacks of Costa Rica couldn't enter the city of San José without a permit. No black was allowed to cross the border into El Salvador. Indians weren't allowed on the sidewalks of the Mexican city of San Cristóbal de las Casas.

But Latin America never had euthanasia laws, maybe because hunger and the police were already on the job. Today, indigenous children in Guatemala, Bolivia, and Peru are still dying like flies from hunger and curable diseases, and in Brazil eight out of every ten street kids murdered by death squads are black. The last U.S. euthanasia law was repealed in 1972 in Virginia, but in the United States the mortality rate of black infants is twice that of whites, and four out of every ten adults executed in the electric chair, by lethal injection, pills, firing squad, or hanging are black.

During the Second World War, while many black Americans lay dying on European battlefields, the U.S. Red Cross refused blood donations from blacks, lest the mixing outlawed in bedrooms occur by transfusion. Fear of contamination, as seen in some of William Faulkner's literary marvels and in the many hor-

Thus It Is Proven That Indians Are Inferior
(According to the Conquistadors of the Sixteenth and Seventeenth Centuries)

The Indians of the Caribbean islands commit suicide? *Because they are lazy and refuse to work.*

They go about naked, as if their entire bodies were faces? *Because savages have no shame.*

They know nothing of the right of property, share everything, and have no desire for riches? *Because they are closer to the apes than to man.*

They bathe with suspicious frequency? *Because they are like the heretics of the sect of Mohammed, who burn well in the fires of the Inquisition.*

They believe in dreams and obey their voices? *The influence of Satan or plain stupidity.*

Homosexuality is practiced freely? Virginity has no importance? *Because they are promiscuous and live at hell's door.*

They never hit their children and they let them run free? *Because they are incapable of punishment or discipline.*

They eat when they are hungry and not at mealtimes? *Because they are incapable of dominating their instincts.*

They adore nature, which they consider their mother, and believe she is sacred? *Because they are incapable of religion and can profess only idolatry.*

Thus It Is Proven That Blacks Are Inferior
(According to the Thinkers of the Eighteenth and Nineteenth Centuries)

Voltaire, anticlerical writer, advocate of tolerance and reason:
Blacks are inferior to Europeans but superior to apes.

Carolus Linnaeus, classifier of plants and animals: The black
is a vagabond, lazy, negligent, indolent, and of dissolute morals.

David Hume, master of human understanding: The black
might develop certain attributes of human beings, the way the
parrot manages to speak a few words.

Etienne Serres, sage of anatomy: Blacks are condemned to be
primitive because of the short distance between their belly buttons and their penises.

*Francis Galton, father of eugenics, the scientific method for
impeding the propagation of the unfit:* A crocodile will never
become a gazelle, nor will a black ever become a member of the
middle class.

Louis Agassiz, prominent zoologist: The brain of the adult
black is equivalent to that of a seven-month-old white fetus; the
development of the brain is blocked because the black cranium
closes much earlier than the white cranium.

rors of the hooded Ku Klux Klan, is a ghost that has not disappeared from the nightmares of North Americans. No one can deny
the spectacular achievements of the civil rights movement over the
past few decades. Yet blacks still face an unemployment rate twice
that of whites, and more of them end up in jail than in college. One

out of every four has been or is currently imprisoned. Three out of every four black residents of Washington, D.C., have been arrested at least once. In Los Angeles, blacks driving expensive cars are systematically stopped by police offering the usual humiliations and the occasional beating as well, like the one given to Rodney King in 1991, setting off an explosion of collective anger that made the city tremble. In 1995 Ambassador James Cheek of the United States flippantly dismissed Argentina's patent law, a timid effort at independence, as "worthy of Burundi," and he didn't offend a soul, not in Argentina, the United States, or Burundi. By the way, Burundi was at war at the time, as was Yugoslavia. According to the news agencies, Burundi suffered tribal conflict, but in Yugoslavia the conflict was—take your pick—ethnic, national, or religious.

Two hundred years ago, the German scientist Alexander von Humboldt, who truly understood Spanish America, wrote that "lighter or darker skin determines the class a man occupies in society." Those words continue to paint a fairly accurate picture not only of Spanish America but of all the Americas, from North to South, even though Bolivia recently had an Indian vice president and the United States can show off a well-known black general brimming with medals, some prominent black politicians, and successful black businessmen.

At the end of the eighteenth century, the few Latin American mulattos who had become wealthy could buy *certificados de blancura* from the Spanish crown or *cartas de branquidão* from the Portuguese crown, testaments to a sudden change of skin color that bestowed a corresponding change in rights. Over the centuries, money continued to be capable of such alchemy. In exceptional cases, so could talent: the Brazilian Machado de Assis, the greatest Latin American writer of the nineteenth century, was mulatto but, as his compatriot Joaquim Nabuco liked to say, his literary talent turned him white. "Racial democracy" remains a social pyramid with a summit that is white or pretends to be.

The situation of Indians in Canada is reasonably similar to that of blacks in the United States: they make up less than 5 percent of the population, but three out of every ten prisoners are Indian and their infant mortality rate is twice that of whites. In Mexico, the average wage for Indians is barely half the national average and the rate of malnutrition is double. Rarely are black-skinned Brazilians found in universities, on soap operas, or in advertisements. Official Brazilian statistics show many fewer blacks than there really are, and the followers of African religions are listed as Catholics. In the Dominican Republic, where for better or worse everyone has some black ancestor, identity documents register skin color but the word "black" is never used: "I don't put down 'black' so they won't be disgraced their whole lives," an official explained to me.

The Dominican border with Haiti, a black country, is called "the Bad Pass." Throughout Latin America, classified ads that ask for "well-groomed employees" are really asking for light-skinned ones. A black lawyer in Lima told me judges are always confusing him with the defendant. In 1996, the mayor of São Paulo had to issue a decree to open elevators in private buildings to everyone. They had usually been off-limits to the poor, which is to say, to blacks and dark-skinned mulattos. At the end of that year, just before Christmas, the Nativity scene in the cathedral of Salta in northern Argentina caused a scandal. The shepherds and the three kings, the Virgin and Saint Joseph, even the baby Jesus were all Indians, with Indian clothes and features. Such a sacrilege could not last. After expressions of indignation from local high society and threats of arson, the Nativity scene was removed.

At the time of the Conquest it was already clear that Indians would be condemned to servitude in this life and hell in the next. There was plenty of evidence of Satan's reign in the Americas. Among the more irrefutable proofs: homosexuality was practiced freely in the Caribbean and elsewhere. In 1446, King Alfonso V ordered Portuguese homosexuals burned at the stake: "We order and dispose by general law that any man who commits such a sin under any guise shall be burned and reduced to dust by fire, so that memory of neither his body nor his burial shall ever be heard." In 1497, Ferdinand and Isabella, the Catholic monarchs of Spain, ordered burned alive those guilty of the "nefarious sin of sodomy," who previously had been stoned to death or hanged. The conquistadors offered their own worthy contributions to the technology of punishing homosexuals. In 1513, two days before what is called the discovery of the Pacific Ocean, Captain Vasco Núñez de Balboa "dogged" fifty Indians who offended God by committing "the abominable sin against nature." Instead of burning them alive, he threw them to dogs trained to devour human flesh. The spectacle took place in Panama by the light of bonfires. Balboa's dog, Leoncico, earned the salary of a second lieutenant.

Nearly five centuries later, in May 1997, in the small Brazilian city of São Gonçalo de Amarante, a man killed fifteen people, then committed suicide by shooting himself in the chest because people in town were saying he was gay. Ever since the Conquest, the established order has worked feverishly to uphold the biblical tradition not by socializing worldly goods—God forbid—but by perpetuating its most horrendous phobias.

Today, the gay and lesbian movement has won broad freedoms and respect, above all in the North, but cobwebs still cloud our vision. Too many people see homosexuality as a sin that cannot be expiated, an indelible and contagious stigma or an invitation to ruin that tempts the innocent. The sinners, whether viewed as diseased or delinquent, constitute a public threat. Many homosexuals fall victim to "social cleansing groups" in Colombia, death squads in Brazil, or any number of fanatics in uniform or civilian clothes around the world who exorcise their own demons by beating or stabbing or shooting. According to anthropologist Luiz Mott of the Gay Group of Bahía, no less than eighteen hundred homosexuals have been murdered in the past fifteen years in Brazil. "They kill one another," say the police. "That's how fags are." One hears exactly the same explanation for wars in Africa ("That's how blacks are") and for massacres of Indians in the Americas ("That's how Indians are").

"That's how women are" is also said. Racism and sexism drink from the same wells and spit out similar words. According to Argentine criminologist Eugenio Raúl Zaffaroni, the founding text of all penal law is *The Witches' Hammer,* a manual from the Inquisition directed against half of humanity and published in 1546. The inquisitors spend the entire book, first page to last, justifying the punishment of women by their biological inferiority. Women had long been mistreated in the Bible and in Greek mythology, from the days when foolish Eve made God throw us out of paradise and when that idiot Pandora opened the box and filled the world with misfortune. "The head of woman is that of man," explained Saint Paul to the Corinthians, and nineteen centuries later Gustave Le Bon, one of the founders of social psychology, was able to prove that an intelligent woman is as rare as a two-headed gorilla. Charles Darwin acknowledged some feminine virtues, like intuition, but these were "virtues characteristic of inferior races."

Since the earliest days of the Conquest of America, homosexuals have been accused of treason to masculinity. Then, the most unpardonable of affronts to the Lord, who was obviously male, was the femininity of those Indians who to be women needed only to have tits and to give birth, as Balboa is said to have put it. Today, treason against femininity is the accusation leveled at lesbians, those degenerates who don't reproduce. Born to make children, undress drunks, and dress up saints, women have traditionally been accused of congenital stupidity, like Indians, like blacks. And like them they have been condemned to the shanty-towns of history. Official history in the Americas concedes only a tiny role to those loyal shadows of male heroes, resigned mothers and suffering widows: the flag, embroidery, and mourning. Rarely is mention made of the European women who fought in the Conquest or the women born in the Americas who raised their swords in the wars of independence, although macho historians should at least applaud their virtues as warriors. Even less does

Points of View/5

Had the Holy Apostles who wrote the Gospels been women, how would they have portrayed the first night of the Christian era?

Saint Joseph, the Apostles would have written, was in a foul mood, the only one with a long face in that stable where the baby Jesus shone in his manger. Everybody else was smiling: the Virgin Mary, the little angels, the shepherds, the sheep, the oxen, the donkey, the kings who had come from the East, and the star that had led them to Bethlehem. Everybody smiled except for sullen Saint Joseph, who grumbled, "I wanted a girl."

Points of View/6

If Eve had written Genesis, what would she have said about the first night of human love?

Eve would have begun by making it clear that she was not born from anyone's rib, nor did she know any serpents, nor did she offer anyone apples, and God never told her that giving birth would hurt or that your husband would tell you what to do. All those stories were just lies Adam told the press.

one hear of the Indian and black women who led several of the many rebellions in the colonial period. Invisible, they appear only miraculously, when you dig deep enough. Not long ago, reading a book about Surinam, I learned of Kaála, leader of free people, who roused fugitive slaves with her sacred staff and abandoned her husband because he was feeble at love.

Like Indians and blacks, women, though inferior, are a threat. "Better a man's spite than a woman's kindness," warns Ecclesiasticus. And Odysseus knew enough to avoid the songs of mermaids meant to entice men from their course. There is no cultural tradition that does not justify the masculine monopoly on weapons and words, nor is there a popular tradition that fails to perpetuate disdain for women or to denounce them as a danger. Proverbs transmitted from generation to generation teach that women and lies were born the same day and that a woman's word isn't worth a pin. The peasant mythology of Latin America is filled with ghosts of women seeking vengeance as fearsome spirits, "evil lights" that lie in wait for travelers at night. In vigil and in sleep,

men betray their terror that females may invade the forbidden territories of pleasure and power, and thus it has been from time immemorial.

It's not for nothing that witch-hunts went after women, and not only during the Inquisition. Spasms and moans, maybe orgasms—even worse, multiple orgasms—these were the evidence of a woman bewitched. Only possession by the Devil could explain so much forbidden fire, which by fire was punished: God commanded that female sinners burning with passion be burned alive. Envy and terror of female pleasure are nothing new. A myth common to many cultures over the ages and across the world is that of the vagina dentata, the woman's sex like a mouth filled with teeth, the insatiable piranha that feeds on male flesh. And in the world today there are twenty million women whose clitorises have been mutilated.

No woman is free from suspicion. In boleros they're all ungrateful; in tangos, they're all whores (except for mama). In the countries of the South, one woman out of every three married women is routinely beaten for what she has done or could do. "We are asleep," says a woman worker in Montevideo's barrio Casavalle. "Some prince gives you a kiss and puts you to sleep. When you awake, the prince is beating you up." Another: "I've got my mother's fear, and my mother had my grandmother's." Men confirm their right of ownership over women with their fists, just as men and women do over children.

And rapes, aren't they also rites to enforce that right? Rapists don't seek pleasure, nor do they find it. Rape brands a mark of ownership on the victim's buttocks, the most brutal expression of the phallic power of the arrow, the spade, the rifle, the cannon, the missile, or any other erection. In the United States a woman is raped every six minutes, in Mexico every nine minutes. A Mexican woman says: "There is no difference between being raped and being hit by a truck, except that after rape men ask if you liked it."

Statistics track only those rapes that get reported, which in Latin America are always many fewer than occur. Most rape victims remain silent out of fear. Many girls, raped in their homes, end up on the streets, which they work as cheap bodies. Some of them, like all street kids, make their homes on the pavement. Fourteen-year-old Lélia, raised by the grace of God on the streets of Rio de Janeiro, says, "Everybody steals. I steal and people steal from me." When Lélia sells her body, they pay her little or they pay her with blows. And when she steals, the police steal what she stole and her body as well. Angélica, thrown onto the streets of Mexico City at sixteen, says: "I told my mother that my brother had abused me, and she kicked me out of the house. Now I live with a guy and I'm pregnant. He says he'll support me if I have a boy. If I have a girl, he doesn't say."

"In today's world, being born female is a risk," says the director of UNICEF. In 1995 in Beijing, the international women's conference noted that women today earn one-third what men earn for equal work. Of every ten poor people, seven are women, and barely one woman in a hundred owns property. Minus a wing, humanity flies crooked. For every ten legislators, there is, on average, one woman, and in some parliaments there are none. Women are acknowledged as useful at home, in factories, or in offices and even as necessary in bed or in the kitchen, but public spaces are virtually monopolized by men born with the urge to have power and make war. That a woman, Carol Bellamy, heads UNICEF is unusual. The United Nations preaches equality but doesn't practice it: at the highest levels of this, the highest international organization, men occupy eight out of every ten positions.

The Despised Mother

Black Africa's works of art, the fruits of collective creation by nobody and everybody, are rarely exhibited on an equal footing with those of artists considered worthy of the name. The booty of colonial pillage can sometimes be found in a few museums and art galleries or in private collections in Europe and the United States, but its "natural" place is in the anthropology museum. Reduced to handicrafts or folklore, African art is dealt with only as one of several customs of exotic peoples.

The centers of so-called civilization, accustomed as they are to acting as creditors for the rest of the world, have no great interest in acknowledging their debts. Yet anyone who has eyes to see and admire might wonder what would have happened to twentieth-century art without the black contribution? Without the African mother from whom they nursed, would the most famous paintings and sculptures of our times have been possible? On page after page in a revealing book published by New York's Museum of Modern Art, William Rubin and other experts document the debt that the art we call art owes to the art of peoples we call "primitive."

The principal figures of contemporary painting and sculpture were nourished by African art, and some of them copied it without even a thank-you. The greatest artistic genius of the twentieth century, Pablo Picasso, always worked surrounded by African masks and weavings, and their influence is evident in the many marvels he left. The painting that gave rise to Cubism, *Les Demoiselles d'Avignon* (the ladies of the red-light district of Barcelona), offers one of many examples. The most famous face in it, the one that breaks most strikingly with traditional symmetry, is an exact reproduction of a mask from the Congo, representing a face deformed by syphilis, that hangs in the Royal Central African Museum in Belgium.

Certain carved heads by Amedeo Modigliani are twin sisters of masks from Mali and Nigeria. The hieroglyphic borders on traditional Mali weavings were the model for Paul Klee's graphs. Some stylized carvings from the Congo or Kenya made before Alberto Giacometti was born could pass for Giacomettis in any museum. You could try to guess which is a Max Ernst oil of a man's head and which is the Ivory Coast sculpture *Head of a Knight* in a private New York collection, but it wouldn't be easy. *Moonlight on a Breeze* by Alexander Calder contains a face that is a clone of a Luba mask from Congo displayed in the Seattle Art Museum.

Justice is like a snake: it only bites the barefooted.

—MONSIGNOR OSCAR ARNULFO ROMERO,
ARCHBISHOP OF SAN SALVADOR,
ASSASSINATED IN 1980

LECTURES ON FEAR

- The Teaching of Fear
- The Industry of Fear
- Sewing: How to Make Enemies to Measure

THE TEACHING OF FEAR

I n a world that prefers security to justice, there is loud applause whenever justice is sacrificed on the altar of security. The rite takes place in the streets. Every time a criminal falls in a hail of bullets, society feels some relief from the disease that makes it tremble. The death of each lowlife has a pharmaceutical effect on those living the high life. The word "pharmacy" comes from *pharmakos,* the Greek name for humans sacrificed to the gods in times of crisis.

THE GREAT THREAT OF THE FIN DE SIÈCLE

At the end of 1982 a routine event occurred in Rio de Janeiro. The police killed a man suspected of robbery. The bullet entered the man's back, as tends to happen when officers of the law kill in self-defense, and the case was filed away. In his report, the chief explained that the suspect was "a true social microbe," who had been "absolved on this planet by his death." The papers, radio, and TV in Brazil often use a vocabulary drawn from medicine and zoology to describe criminals: "virus," "cancer," "social infection," "animals," "predators," "insects," "wild beasts," even "small beasts" when referring to children. These terms always allude to poor people. When criminals aren't poor, the story leaps to the front page: "Young Mugger Killed Was Middle-Class," went a *Folha de São Paulo* headline of October 25, 1995.

Not counting the many victims of gangs linked to the police, *officially* the São Paulo state police killed four people a day in 1992; by year's end the total was four times the number killed by the military dictatorship that ruled Brazil for fifteen years. At the end of 1995, the Rio police were given a raise for "bravery and fearlessness." That pay hike brought another sort of raise in its wake: the number of "alleged criminals" shot dead. "They aren't citizens, they're bandits," explained General Nilton Cerqueira, once a star of the military dictatorship and now responsible for public security in Rio. He has always believed that, like good soldiers, good policemen shoot first and ask questions later.

After the earthquake of the Cuban Revolution of 1959, Latin America's armed forces turned their attention from the traditional role of defending borders to "internal enemies": guerrilla subversion and its many incubators. With the free world and democratic rule at stake, these militaries were inspired to do away with freedom and democracy. In just four years, between 1962 and 1966, there were nine coups d'état in Latin America. Following the doctrine of national security to a tee, the brass continued to overthrow civilian governments and massacre people for years thereafter. Time has passed, civilian rule has been reestablished. The enemy remains "internal" but isn't what it used to be. Now the armed forces are taking up the fight against so-called common crime. Instead of the doctrine of national security, we have the hysteria of public security. Generally speaking, the officers don't like it one bit that they've been demoted to mere policemen—but reality insists.

Global Fear

Those who work are afraid they'll lose their jobs.

Those who don't are afraid they'll never find one.

Whoever doesn't fear hunger is afraid of eating.

Drivers are afraid of walking and pedestrians are afraid of getting run over.

Democracy is afraid of remembering and language is afraid of speaking.

Civilians fear the military, the military fears a shortage of weapons, weapons fear a shortage of wars.

It is the time of fear.

Women's fear of violent men and men's fear of fearless women.

Fear of thieves, fear of the police.

Fear of doors without locks, of time without watches, of children without television; fear of night without sleeping pills and day without pills to wake up.

Fear of crowds, fear of solitude, fear of what was and what could be, fear of dying, fear of living.

About thirty years ago the establishment had enemies of all colors, from pale pink to fire-engine red. The work of chicken thieves and knife-carrying slum dwellers was of interest only to crime-page readers, devotees of cruelty, and experts in criminology. Today, "common crime" is a universal obsession, democratized and within the reach of all: many practice it, everyone suffers from it. Crime is the most potent source of inspiration for politicians and journalists who scream for an iron hand and the death penalty, and it gives certain military officers a golden opportunity to pursue civilian careers. Maybe the collective terror that identifies democracy with chaos and insecurity helps explain why some Latin American generals who only a few years ago were running bloody dictatorships have been so successful as politicians. General Ríos Montt, the exterminating angel of Guatemalan Indians, led the polls until his presidential candidacy was ruled illegal, and the same happened with General Oviedo in Paraguay. General Bussi, who killed suspects with one hand while with the other depositing the sweat of his brow in Swiss banks, was elected and reelected governor of the Argentine province of Tucumán. Another uniformed assassin, General Banzer, was rewarded with the presidency of Bolivia.

The experts at the Inter-American Development Bank, who can translate life and death into dollars and cents, calculate that Latin America loses $168 billion a year to crime. We are winning the World Cup of crime. Latin America's murder rate is six times the world average. If the economy only grew like crime, the region would be the most prosperous on the planet. Peace in El Salvador? What peace? At the rate of a murder an hour, El Salvador is keeping pace with the worst years of the war. Kidnapping is the most lucrative industry in Colombia, Brazil, and Mexico. In our large cities, no one would be considered normal if he hadn't been mugged at least once. There are five times as many murders in Rio as in New York. Bogotá is the capital of violence, Medellín the city of widows. Elite cops, members of "special groups," have begun to patrol the streets of some Latin American cities outfitted from head to toe for World War III. They have infrared night visors, headphones, microphones, and bulletproof vests; on their belts

---

Typical Scenes from Latin America

States stop running businesses and concentrate on running jails.
  Presidents become local managers of foreign companies.
  Finance ministers make good translators.
  The captains of industry become importers.
  The many more depend more and more on the leftovers of
the ever-fewer few.
  Workers lose their jobs.
  Peasants lose their plots.
  Children lose their right to be children.
  Youth lose the capacity to believe.
  Old folks lose their pensions.
  "Life is a lottery," say the winners.

---

they carry pepper spray and bullets; an automatic rifle is in their hands and a pistol on their thighs.

Of every hundred crimes committed in Colombia, ninety-seven are never solved. The proportion is similar in the barrios of Buenos Aires, where the police spend most of their time committing crimes and killing young people. From 1983, when democracy was restored, to the middle of 1997, the police blew away 314 suspicious-looking boys. In the course of a police shake-up at the end of 1997, the press discovered that nobody knew what five thousand officers on the payroll did or where they were. Polls showed that few Argentines or Uruguayans would turn to the police if they had a serious problem. Six out of ten Uruguayans

favored taking justice into their own hands, and some had signed up for shooting lessons.

In the United States four out of every ten people admit to having changed their routines because of crime, and south of the Rio Grande people talk about muggings and robberies as much as about soccer or the weather. The public opinion industry throws oil on the fire, doing its best to turn public security into public obsession, but the fact is, reality does more. Reality assures us that violence is rising even faster than the statistics confess. In many countries people don't report crimes, because they don't trust the police or they fear them. The Uruguayan papers call gangs that pull off spectacular robberies "supergangs," and those who have police officers among their members are called "poligangs." Of every ten Venezuelans, nine believe the police commit crimes. In 1996, the majority of Rio de Janeiro's finest admitted that they had been offered bribes, while their chief said that "the police were created to be corrupt" and that a society "that wants corrupt and violent police" is to blame.

An internal police report leaked to Amnesty International shows that six out of every ten crimes in Mexico City are committed by the police. To catch a hundred criminals in a year, it takes 14 police in Washington, 15 in Paris, 18 in London, and 1,295 in Mexico City. "We have allowed the police to become excessively corrupt," the mayor of that city admitted in 1997. "Excessively?" asked the ever-curious Carlos Monsiváis. "What's wrong with them? Are they corrupt or are they getting away with honesty? Put them to work."

At century's end, everything is becoming globalized and everything is becoming alike: clothes, food, the lack of food, ideas, the lack of ideas, and crime, too, not to speak of the fear of crime. Throughout the world, crime is rising faster than the numbers can sing, even though they sing with gusto. Since 1970, reported crimes have grown three times faster than the world's population. In Eastern Europe, while consumerism buried Communism in the 1990s, daily violence multiplied at the same rate that wages fell: by three in Bulgaria, the Czech Republic, Hungary, Latvia, Lithuania, and Estonia. Organized and disorganized crime have taken over Russia, where juvenile crime is flowering as nowhere else. The kids who wander the streets of Russian cities are called "the forgotten"; "We have hundreds of thousands of homeless children," admitted President Boris Yeltsin.

At the end of 1997, terror of assaults was written into law in most eloquent fashion in Louisiana, where drivers were authorized to kill anyone who tried to rob them, even if the crook was unarmed. This no-holds-barred approach was then promoted on TV thanks to the toothy smile of the reigning Miss Louisiana. Meanwhile the popularity of New York mayor Rudolph Giuliani rose spectacularly when he hit criminals hard with a "zero tolerance" policy. The crime rate dropped in the same measure as charges of police brutality rose. Beastly repression, a magic potion adored by the media, fell savagely on blacks and the other "minorities" that make up the majority of New York's residents. "Zero tolerance" quickly became a beacon for Latin America's cities.

Presidential elections in Honduras, 1997: crime is the key issue in the speeches of all the candidates, every one of whom promises security to a people cowering in fear. Legislative elections in Argentina, the same year: candidate Norma Miralles comes out for the death penalty, but not if it's painless: "It's no big deal to kill a condemned man, because he doesn't suffer." Not long before, Rio de Janeiro mayor Luiz Paulo Conde said he preferred life sentences or forced labor, because the death penalty has the drawback of being "a very quick thing."

But no law can stop the invasion of those who live outside the law. The frightened only multiply in number, and they can be more dangerous than the danger that frightens them. Not only do the hustlers and spongers who live in prosperity feel threatened, so do many who survive in scarcity, poor people who suffer the attacks of people poorer or more desperate than themselves. "Frenzied Mob Burns Child Alive for Stealing an Orange," reads the headline. The blind fury of poor against poor: between 1979 and 1988 the Brazilian press reported 272 lynchings by people who had no money to pay the police to do the job for them. Poor, too, were those responsible for the 52 lynchings that occurred in Guatemala in 1997 and the 166 lynchings between 1986 and 1991 in Jamaica. During those same five years, quick-triggered Jamaican police killed over a thousand suspects. A poll found that a third of the population believed delinquents should be hanged, since neither street vengeance nor police violence did the trick. Polls in 1997 in

Rio de Janeiro and São Paulo revealed that more than half the people considered lynching criminals to be "normal."

A good part of the population also openly or discreetly applauds the death squads that mete out capital punishment even when it's against the law and do so with the participation or complicity of the police and the military. In Brazil they started by killing guerrillas. Then they moved on to adult criminals, later to homosexuals and panhandlers, and finally to teenagers and children. Silvio Cunha, the president of a merchants' association in Rio, said in 1991, "Killing a young slum dweller is a service to society." The owner of a shop in the barrio of Botafogo was robbed four times in two months. A policeman explained why: there's no point arresting children today, since the judge will set them free to rob tomorrow. "It's up to you," the policeman said. And for a reasonable price he offered to take care of things when he was off-duty, "to get rid of them," he said.

"Get rid of them?"

"That's right."

Under contract to store owners, the death squads in Brazil, which like to call themselves "self-defense groups," clean up the cities while in the countryside their colleagues under contract to big landowners gun down landless peasants and other bothersome people. According to the May 20, 1998, issue of *Isto é* magazine, in the state of Maranhão the life of a judge is worth five hundred dol-

Public Enemy/1

In April 1997, Brazilian television viewers were invited to vote on the fate of a young perpetrator of a violent assault. Execution won by a landslide, two to one over prison.

According to researcher Vera Malaguti, the image of public enemy number one is modeled on a great-grandchild of slaves who lives in the favelas, can't read, adores "funk" music, uses or sells drugs, is arrogant and pushy, and fails to show the least remorse.

lars, that of a priest four hundred. It's only three hundred to knock off a lawyer. Murderers for hire offer their services by Internet, with discounts for subscribers.

Death squads in Colombia—known officially as "self-defense groups," they call themselves "social cleansing groups"—also began by killing guerrillas and now, under contract to store owners, landowners, or whoever will pay, they'll kill anyone. Many of their members are policemen or soldiers without uniform, but they also train young executioners. In Medellín, several schools for hit men attract teenagers with offers of easy money and cheap thrills. These fifteen-year-olds trained in the arts of crime are sometimes hired to kill other children as dead of hunger as they are. Poor against poor, as usual: poverty is a blanket that's too narrow, and everyone pulls it to his own side. But the victims might also be prominent politicians or famous journalists. The chosen target is called a "dog" or a "package." The young assassins get paid

Public Enemy/2

At the beginning of 1998, journalist Samuel Blixen made an eloquent comparison. The take from fifty muggings carried out by the best-known criminal gangs in Uruguay added up to $5 million. The take from two muggings carried out without a shot by a bank and a financier totaled $70 million.

according to the importance of the dog and the risks of the operation. Often the executioners are protected by the legal mask of security companies. At the end of 1997, the Colombian government acknowledged that it had only thirty inspectors for three thousand private security firms. Last year in an exemplary operation that lasted a week, one agent inspected four hundred "self-defense groups." He found nothing out of the ordinary.

Death squads leave no fingerprints. Rarely is the silence broken. An exception occurred in Colombia in mid-1991: sixty beggars were shot dead in the city of Pereira. The murderers weren't arrested, but fifteen police officers, two of high rank, were "disciplined" and forced to retire. Another exception occurred in Rio de Janeiro in mid-1993: fifty homeless children sleeping at the gates of Candelaria Church were shot; eight of them died. The massacre was news around the world and, in the end, two of the military police who carried out the operation went to jail. A miracle.

Afanásio Jazadji was elected to the legislature with the largest vote in the history of the state of São Paulo. He earned his popularity preaching on the radio, day after day, microphone in hand.

Enough talk of problems, he said, it's time for solutions. Overcrowded jails? "We should take all those incorrigible prisoners, put them up against the wall, and incinerate them with a flamethrower. Or set off a bomb. Boom. Problem solved. Those bums are costing us millions." Interviewed in 1987 by Bell Chevigny, Jazadji explained that torture is okay because the police torture only the guilty. Sometimes, he said, the police don't know what crimes the crook has committed and can find out only by beating him, just like a husband when he beats his wife. Torture, he concluded, is the only way to discover the truth.

Back in the year 1252 Pope Innocent IV authorized the torture of those suspected of heresy. The Inquisition invented new techniques for the production of pain, which twentieth-century technology has elevated to industrial perfection. Amnesty International has documented the systematic practice of electric-shock torture in fifty countries. In the thirteenth century the powerful called a spade a spade; now torture is committed but not discussed. Power avoids bad words. At the end of 1996, when the Israeli Supreme Court authorized the torture of Palestinian prisoners, the justices called it "moderate physical pressure." In Latin America torture is called "legal compulsion." Common criminals, or those

who look like them, have always suffered "compulsion" in the police stations here. It's a custom, considered normal, for the police to extract confessions by the same means of torment that military dictatorships recently used on political prisoners. The difference is that many of those political prisoners were middle-class, some upper-class, and social class is the only boundary impunity occasionally acknowledges. During the military horror, campaigns by human rights groups didn't always ring like a wooden bell; sometimes they struck a chord in the closed environment of life under dictatorship and even in the world beyond. Who, in contrast, will listen to common criminals, socially despised and legally invisible? When one of them commits insanity by announcing that he's been tortured, the police send him back for more intensive care.

Filthy jails, prisoners like sardines in a can—most of them have not been convicted, many haven't even been tried. They're just there and nobody knows why. Compared with these seething prisons, Dante's Inferno looks like Disneyland. Riots break out continually, and the forces of order spray the disorderly with bullets, in the process killing as many as they can to ease the overcrowding. In 1992, there were over fifty uprisings in Latin America's most overcrowded prisons. Nine hundred were killed, most of them in cold blood.

Thanks to torture, which makes the mute sing, many are imprisoned for crimes they did not commit, since it's better to have an innocent behind bars than a criminal walking free. Others confess to murders that are child's play compared with the feats of certain generals or to robberies that are jokes compared with the frauds run by businessmen and bankers or the commissions charged by politicians every time they sell off another piece of the country. The military dictatorships are gone, but the jails of Latin America's democracies are filled to bursting. The prisoners are

poor, as you'd expect, because only the poor go to jail in countries where nobody goes to jail for the collapse of a brand-new bridge, the bankruptcy of a looted bank, or the crumbling of a building with no foundation.

The system of power that creates poverty is the same one that wages war without quarter on the desperate people it begets. A century ago, Georges Vacher de Lapouge demanded more guillotines to purify the race. This French thinker, who believed that all geniuses were German, was convinced that only the guillotine could correct the errors of "natural selection" and end the alarming proliferation of incompetents and criminals. "A good crook is a dead crook," say those who today demand ironhanded social therapy. Society has the right to kill in legitimate defense of public health, given the danger posed by slums infected with ne'er-do-wells and drug addicts. With social problems reduced to police problems, there is a growing clamor for the death penalty, a fair punishment that will reduce the cost of prisons, have a healthy, intimidating effect, and solve the problem of recidivism by eliminating potential repeat offenders. You learn by dying. In most Latin American countries the law does not allow capital punishment, but it gets carried out every time a police warning shot enters the back of a suspect's neck or death squads kill with impunity. With or without the law, the state practices premeditated homicide, treachery, and discrimination. Yet no matter how many people the state kills, it can't seem to do a thing about the no-man's-land the street has become.

Power keeps hacking away at the weeds, but it can't pull out the roots without threatening itself. Criminals get sentenced but not the machine that keeps churning them out, just as drug addicts get sentenced but not the lifestyle that cries out for chemical consolation and an illusion of escape. Society is thus exonerated from responsibility. The law is like a spider's web, says author Daniel Drew, spun to trap flies and other small insects, not to block the way of larger species. Over a century ago, the poet José Hernández compared the law to a knife that never turns on those who wield it. Official speeches invoke the law as if it applied to everyone, not just to the unfortunates who can't evade it. Poor criminals are the bad guys in this movie; rich criminals write the script and direct the action.

In other times, the police served an economic system that needed abundant docile labor. The justice system punished vagrants by forcing them into factories at bayonet point. That's how European society industrialized the peasantry and managed to impose the work ethic in its cities. But today the question is how to impose the unemployment ethic. What mandatory obedience techniques are there to manage the growing multitudes who have no work or hope of ever getting any? What can be done to keep all those who have fallen overboard from trying to climb back in and capsizing the ship?

The raison d'être of the state today is the same as that of the financial markets that rule the world and produce nothing but speculation. Subcommandante Marcos, the spokesman for the Indians of Chiapas, described the process aptly: we are witnessing, he said, a striptease. The state takes off everything down to its underwear, that indispensable intimate garment which is repression. The moment of truth: the state exists only to pay the foreign debt and guarantee social peace.

The state murders by omission as well as commission. At the end of 1995, there were these items of news from Brazil and Argentina:

Crime by commission: the Rio de Janeiro military police killed civilians at eight times the rate of the previous year, and the police in Buenos Aires barrios hunted young people as if they were wild beasts.

Crime by omission: forty kidney patients lay dying in the town of Caruarú in northeast Brazil after a public hospital used polluted water for dialysis, while in Argentina's northeast province of Misiones, pesticide-laced drinking water was producing babies with leprous lips and deformations of the spinal medulla.

In the favelas of Rio, women carry cans of water on their heads like crowns, while children fly kites in the wind as warnings that the police are coming. At carnival time, black-skinned queens and kings come down from the hills in wigs of white curls, collars of lights, silken coats. On Ash Wednesday, when carnival ends and the tourists depart, anyone still in costume gets thrown in jail. And every other day of the year, the state makes sure the plebeians who were monarchs for a moment toe the line.

At the beginning of the century there was only one favela in Rio. In the forties, by which time there were a few, writer Stefan Zweig paid them a visit and found neither violence nor sadness.

Today, there are over five hundred favelas in Rio. Many working people live there, cheap hands who serve tables or wash cars and clothes and bathrooms in wealthy neighborhoods. There, too, live many who are shut out of any market, a number of whom find in drugs some income or relief. From the point of view of the society that created them, favelas are no more than a refuge for organized crime and the cocaine trade. The military police invade them frequently in Vietnam War–lookalike operations, and dozens of death squads work them as well. The dead—illiterate children of illiterates—are mostly black adolescents.

A century ago, the head of a reform school in Illinois concluded that one-third of his internees could not be redeemed. They were future criminals who loved the world, the flesh, and the Devil. It was not clear what could be done with them, but back then a few scientists like the Englishman Cyril Burt proposed fighting crime at the source by eliminating the poorest of the poor, "impeding the propagation of their species." A hundred years later, the countries of the South treat the poorest poor as if they were toxic waste. The countries of the North export their dangerous industrial waste to the South, but the South can't return the favor. What then can be done with its dangerous human waste that cannot be redeemed? Bullets do their best to impede "the

Let's Tell It Like It Is

The first South American Police Congress met in Uruguay in 1979 under the military dictatorship. The congress decided to continue its work in Chile under the military dictatorship, "to benefit the high interests that sparkle along the path of the peoples of America," as the final resolution put it.

The delegation from Argentina, also under military dictatorship, highlighted the role of the forces of order in the struggle against child and youth crime. Its report was eloquent, as only the police can be: "Although it may seem simplistic, to get to the root of the problem, to its essence in the animating substratum of its dynamism and evolution, we will state and reiterate that the minimal common base is family reality, which has little to do with the socioeconomic-cultural side. . . . Needy adolescents try to find models of identity in other subcultures (hippie, criminal, etc.), thereby causing an interruption in the socialization process. . . . The maintenance of public order transcends the interindividual level and, reaching the intraindividual level, takes up that unique and indivisible reality of the individual being and the social being. . . . If some minors have demonstrated conduct that could degenerate into inadequate behavior presenting an individual-social threat, they have been easily detected and reoriented, and the problem resolved.

propagation of their species," and indeed the Pentagon, military vanguard of the world, says that the wars of the twenty-first century will require ever more specialized weapons for street riots and looting. In some cities of the Americas, like Washington and Santiago de Chile, as in many British cities, video cameras keep a watchful eye on the streets.

Consumer society consumes people and things like so many shooting stars. Things made not to last die soon after birth, and more and more people are condemned from the moment they peek out of the womb. Abandoned children on the streets of Bogotá used to be called "gamines"; now they're called "disposable kids" and they're marked to die. In the technocratic language of the moment, the many nobodies are "economically inviable." What fate awaits these human leftovers? The world invites them to disappear, saying, "You don't exist because you don't deserve to exist." Official reality tries to ignore them: the fastest-growing slum in Buenos Aires is called Hidden City, while in Mexico City the barrios of tin and cardboard sprouting in gullies and garbage dumps are called "lost cities."

Covenant House interviewed more than 140 orphans and abandoned children living on the streets of Guatemala City: all of them sold their bodies for coins, all had venereal disease, all sniffed glue or solvents. One morning in the middle of 1990, some of those children were talking in a park when several armed men took them away in a truck. One girl escaped by hiding in a garbage can. Four of their bodies turned up a few days later without ears, without eyes, without tongues. The police had taught them a lesson.

In April 1997, Galdino Jesús dos Santos, an indigenous leader visiting Brasilia, was burned alive as he slept at a bus stop. Five teenagers from good families, out on the town, had sprayed him with alcohol and set him alight. They justified what they did by saying, "We thought he was a beggar." A year later they received light prison sentences; after all, it wasn't a case of premeditated homicide. As the spokesman for the federal district court explained, the boys used only half the fuel they were carrying, which proved they acted "with the intention of having a good time, not of killing." The burning of beggars is a sport practiced by the youth of Brazil's upper class with some regularity, but the news doesn't usually reach the papers.

Leftovers: street kids, vagrants, beggars, prostitutes, transvestites, homosexuals, pickpockets, small-time thieves, drug addicts, drunks, squeegee kids. In 1993, Colombia's "disposable kids" crawled out from under their rocks to protest. The demonstration erupted when it hit the news that "social cleansing groups" were killing beggars and selling the bodies to anatomy students at the Free University of Barranquilla. At the demonstration, storyteller Nicolás Buenaventura told those vomited up by the system the real story of the Creation: every time God created something, he had a little bit left over. While the sun and the moon, time and the world, the seas and the jungles were being born from his hand, God kept tossing the leftovers into the abyss. But God, being rather scatterbrained, forgot to make the first woman and man, and they had no choice but to make themselves. Way down there in God's garbage dump, at the bottom of that abyss, the first woman and the first man made themselves out of God's leftovers. We human beings were born from garbage, and that's why we all have a bit of day and a bit of night, and we're all time and earth and water and wind.

The Industry of Fear

Fear is the raw material that sustains the flourishing industries of private security and social control, and it's in steady supply. Demand in these industries is growing as fast as or faster than the crime rate that drives it, and experts predict that it's going to keep on climbing. The market for private police and private jails is booming, while all of us—some more, some less—are turning into guards and prisoners: guards keeping an eye on whoever's nearby and prisoners of fear.

TIME OF CAPTIVE JAILERS

"The TV news is our best ad," say security salesmen, and they ought to know. In Guatemala there are 180 security firms, in Mexico 600, and in Peru 1,500. There are 3,000 in Colombia. In Canada and the United States twice as much is spent on private security as on public security. At the turn of the century there will be two million private police in the United States. In Argentina security is a billion-dollar-a-year business. Every day in Uruguay there are more homeowners who lock four locks instead of three, making some doors look like knights from the Crusades.

A Chico Buarque song starts out with the wail of a police siren: "Call the thief! Call the thief!" pleads the Brazilian singer. In Latin America the crime-control industry feeds on an incessant torrent of news about assaults, kidnappings, rapes, and other crimes. But it also relies on the poor reputation of the public police, who commit crimes with enthusiasm and pursue criminals with suspicious inefficiency. The homes of everyone who has anything to lose, however little, are already behind bars or barbed wire. And even we atheists call on God before we call the police.

In countries where the public police are more effective, alarm at the specter of crime also leads to the privatization of panic. Not only is the number of private policemen in the United States skyrocketing, but so is the number of guns on night tables and in glove compartments. The National Rifle Association, presided over by actor Charlton Heston, has nearly three million members and cites Scripture to justify bearing arms. You can't blame its leaders for swelling with pride when they proclaim that there are 230 million firearms in the hands of U.S. citizens, an average of one weapon per soul, leaving aside babies and toddlers. In reality, this arsenal is held by a third of the population. For that third, a gun is like a lover or a credit card: without it you can't sleep or leave home.

All over the world, fewer and fewer dogs enjoy the luxury of just being pets; ever more of them earn their bone by frightening strangers. Car alarms sell like hotcakes, and so do the little personal alarms that shriek in a woman's handbag or a gentleman's pocket. Same story with portable electric cattle prods, the "shockers" that knock out suspects, and with sprays that paralyze from a distance. A security company recently began marketing an elegant coat that attracts glances and repels bullets. Protect yourself and your family, counsels the Internet ad for these sporty leather

---

Let the Children Come unto Me

The sale of guns to minors is against the law in the United States, but advertising targets that clientele anyway. National Rifle Association literature sees the future of shooting sports in the hands of our grandchildren, and a pamphlet from the National Shooting Sports Foundation explains that every ten-year-old alone at home or traveling alone to the store ought to have a gun. In the New England Firearms catalog, too, children are the future of the sport.

According to statistics from the Violence Policy Center, *every day* in the United States, through crime, suicide, or accident, bullets kill fourteen children under the age of nineteen. The country grunts in disgust and shakes its head at the frequency with which schools are turned into battlefields. The killers are usually not black boys from the slums but white, freckled suburbanites.

cuirasses. (In Colombia, the flourishing bulletproof-vest industry sells more and more in children's sizes.)

Electronic monitoring via closed-circuit TV and other devices keeps an eye on things in many places. It's undertaken by individuals and businesses, not to mention the state. In Argentina the ten thousand employees of state intelligence agencies spend two million dollars a day spying on people: they tap phones, they film, they record.

No country fails to use public security as an alibi or a pretext. Hidden cameras and microphones are placed in banks and supermarkets, offices and stadiums, and sometimes they follow people right into their bedrooms. Is there an eye hidden in the TV remote control? Ears listening from the ashtray? Billy Graham, who makes millions preaching the poverty of Jesus on TV, has acknowledged that he is careful when he talks on the phone and even when he talks to his wife in bed. "Our business isn't to promote Big Brother," a spokesman for the U.S. Security Industry Association insists defensively. In his prophetic novel written half a century ago, George Orwell imagined a city where Big Brother used TV to keep tabs on everyone. He called it *1984,* but perhaps he didn't get the date quite right.

Who are the jailers and who the jailed? In one way or another we're all imprisoned, those in jail and those of us outside. How can the prisoners of need be free, since they live to work and can't afford the luxury of working to live? And the prisoners of desperation, who have no work and never will and who survive only by robbery or by miracle? What about the prisoners of fear, are we free? Aren't we all prisoners of fear, those on top, on the bottom, and in the middle, too? In societies obliged to live by everyone-for-himself, we're all prisoners, the guarded and the guards, the chosen and the pariahs. The Argentine cartoonist Nik drew a reporter interviewing a man gripping the bars of a window in his house:

"We've all installed bars, TV cameras, floodlights, double locks, and tinted glass. . . ."

"Don't your relatives come over?"

"Yes, I have visiting hours."

"And what do the police say?"

"If I keep up my good behavior, Sunday morning I can go out to the bakery."

I've seen bars on shantytown hovels made of scrap wood and

tin, poor people defending themselves from other poor people. Urban development metastasizes inequality: in the suburbs, hovels and gardens spring up side by side. Rich suburbs tend to be not too far from the shantytowns that supply them with maids, gardeners, and watchmen. In places of despair, those who eat only now and then lie in wait. In places of privilege, the rich live under house arrest. On a private block in San Isidro in Buenos Aires, the man delivering newspapers jokes, "Live here? No thanks. If I have nothing to hide, why would I?"

Helicopters cross the skies above the city of São Paulo, coming and going between luxury prison homes and downtown rooftops. The streets, kidnapped by thugs and poisoned by pollution, are a trap to be avoided. Fugitives from violence and smog, the rich are obliged to live in hiding. Paradoxes of exhibitionism: opulence is concealed behind ever-higher walls in houses without faces, invisible to the envy and covetousness of everyone else. Microcities rise

Family Chronicle

Nicolás Escobar's aunt died in her sleep, peacefully, at home in
Asunción, Paraguay. Nicolás was six and had already logged
thousands of hours of television when he learned that he had
lost his beloved elderly relative. He asked, "Who killed her?"

up on the edges of the great cities. There mansions huddle, protected by complex electronic security systems and armed guards
who patrol their borders. Just as malls are like the cathedrals of
other times, these castles of our days have watchtowers, cressets,
and embrasures to spy the enemy and keep him at bay. On the
other hand, they have neither the magnificence nor the beauty of
those old stone fortresses.

The captives of fear don't realize they are prisoners. But the
prisoners of the penal system, who wear numbers on their chests,
have lost both their freedom and the right to delude themselves.
The most modern jails, the latest thing in fashion, tend to be
maximum-security prisons. No one suggests returning criminals to
society, saving those who have lost their way, as it was once so
quaintly put. Nowadays, the only desire is to shut them away forever, and no one bothers to preach lies. Justice blindfolds herself
to keep from seeing where a criminal comes from or why he committed a crime, which ought to be the first step toward his possible
rehabilitation. The model fin-de-siècle jail is not the least concerned with redemption or even with teaching a lesson. Society
locks up public menaces, then throws away the key.

In some new prisons in the United States, the cell walls are steel and windowless; the doors open and close electronically. The U.S. penitentiary system is generous only when it hands out televisions, for their narcotic effect, and a growing number of prisoners have little or no contact with other prisoners. A prisoner might see a guard once in a while, but even guards are growing scarce. Today's technology allows a single employee in a control room to keep watch over a hundred prisoners. Machines take care of everything.

Those under house arrest have also been controlled by electronic means, ever since a judge named Love, Jack Love, invented a lovely remote-control bracelet. Attached to the criminal's wrist or ankle, it keeps track of his movements and knows if he's trying to take it off, or if he drinks alcohol, or if he leaves the house. At this rate, predicts criminologist Nils Christie, trials will soon be held by video with the accused never seen in person by the prosecutor, the defense attorney, or the judge.

In 1997, there were 1.8 million prisoners in U.S. jails, more than double the number ten years earlier. But that figure would triple if it encompassed those under house arrest, out on bail, or on parole. That total would include five times as many black prisoners as all those imprisoned under apartheid at its height, a number equal to the entire population of Denmark. This gigantic clientele, tempting for any investor, has encouraged privatization. Private jails continue to sprout in the United States, even though they've shown themselves to be purveyors of horrible food and poor treatment—eloquent proof that for the taxpayer private jails are no cheaper than public ones, since their huge profits far outweigh their low costs.

Back in the seventeenth century, English jailers bribed judges to get more prisoners. When their sentences were up, prisoners were so deep in debt that they had to work for their jailers, often as beggars, for the rest of their lives. At the end of the twentieth century, a private U.S. prison company, Corrections Corporation of America, was one of the five highest-priced companies on the New York Stock Exchange. Founded in 1983 with capital from Kentucky Fried Chicken, the company made it clear from the start that it intended to sell jails like chicken dinners. By the end of 1997, the value of its stock had multiplied seventy times, and the company had set up prisons in England, Australia, and Puerto Rico. But the domestic market is the meat and potatoes of its business. In the United States, where prisoners are always plentiful, jails are hotels that never have a vacancy. In 1992, over a hundred companies were designing, building, or administering prisons.

In 1996, World Research Group sponsored a conference on how to maximize the profits of this dynamic industry. The invitation read: "While arrests and convictions are on the rise, profits are to be made—profits from crime." The fact is that the incidence of crime in the United States has been falling in recent years, but the market still serves up ever more prisoners. He who is not jailed for what he has done is jailed for what he might do. There's no reason why falling crime statistics should disturb the brilliant growth of this enterprise. Besides, as executive Diane McClure assured investors in October 1997, "Our market analysis shows that *juvenile* crime will continue growing."

In an interview at the beginning of 1998, novelist Toni Morrison pointed out that "the brutal treatment of prisoners in private jails has grown so scandalous that even Texans are concerned. Texas, a place not known for its big heart, is rescinding contracts." But the prisoners, the unfree, must serve the free market. They don't deserve better treatment than any other commodity. The National Criminal Justice Commission estimates that at

For Sale

Here are some of the ads published in the April 1998 issue of the U.S. magazine *Corrections Today:*

Bell Atlantic offers the "most secure phone systems" for monitoring and screening calls: "Full control over who, when and how inmates call."

The ad for US West's inmate telephone service shows a crouching prisoner with a cigarette butt hanging from his lips: "He could cut you up. Somewhere, there could be a hardened criminal concealing a sharpened weapon."

On another page a threatening shadow, another prisoner, lies in wait: "Don't give an inch," warns LCN's ad for high-security closers. "Any door, not fully latched, is an open invitation to trouble."

"Inmates are built tougher than ever before," warns Modu-Form. "Fortunately, so is our furniture."

Motor Coach Industries shows off its latest-model jail on wheels, something akin to a doghouse divided into steel cages. "Save time. Save dollars," suggests Mark Correctional Systems, a builder of prisons. "Economy! Quality! Speed! Durability! Security!"

the current rate of change in the prison population, by the year 2020 six out of every ten black men will be behind bars. Over the past twenty years, public spending on prisons has grown by 900 percent. That hasn't alleviated public fears one bit, but it has done lots for the health of the prison industry.

"After all, jail means money," concludes Nils Christie. And he tells the story of a British parliamentarian, Sir Edward Gardner, who in the 1980s crossed the Atlantic at the head of a European commission to study prison privatization in the United States. Sir Edward was an enemy of private prisons. When he returned to London, he had changed his mind and so became president of the company Contract Prisons, PLC.

Sewing: How to Make Enemies to Measure

Never have so many economic resources and so much scientific and technological knowledge been brought to bear on the production of death. The countries that sell the world the most weapons are the same ones in charge of world peace. Fortunately for them, the threat of world peace is receding. The war market is on the rebound and the outlook for profits from butchery is promising. The weapons factories are as busy as those producing enemies to fit their needs.

THE DEVIL'S AMPLE WARDROBE

Good news for the military economy, which is to say, good news for the economy: the weapons industry, selling death, exporting violence, is flourishing. Demand is steady, the market is growing, and good harvests continue to be reaped from the cultivation of injustice across the globe. Crime and drug addiction, social unrest, and national, regional, local, and personal hatred are all on the rise.

After a few years of decline at the end of the Cold War, arms sales have turned around. The world market in weaponry, with total sales of $40 billion, grew 8 percent in 1996. Leading the list of buyers was Saudi Arabia at $9 billion. For several years that country has also led the list of countries that violate human rights. In 1996, says Amnesty International, "reports of torture and ill-treatment of detainees continued, and the judicial punishment of flogging was frequently imposed. At least 27 individuals were sentenced to flogging, ranging from 120 to 200 lashes. They included 24 Philippine nationals who were reportedly sentenced for homosexual behavior. At least 69 people were executed." And also: "The government of King Fahd bin 'Abdul 'Aziz maintained its ban on political parties and trade unions. Press censorship continued to be strictly enforced."

For many years that oil-rich monarchy has been the top client for U.S. weapons and British war planes. Arms and oil, two key factors in national prosperity: the healthy trade of oil for weapons allows the Saudi dictatorship to drown domestic protest in blood,

Points of View/7

On a wall in San Francisco: "If voting changed anything, it would be illegal."

On a wall in Rio de Janeiro: "If men gave birth, abortion would be legal."

In the jungle, do they call the habit of devouring the weakest the "law of the city"?

From the point of view of a sick people, what's the meaning of a healthy currency?

Weapons sales are good news for the economy. Are they also good news for those who end up dead?

Points of View/8

Until not so many years ago, historians of Athenian democracy never mentioned slaves or women, except in passing. Slaves were a majority of the Greek population and women half of it. What would Athenian democracy have looked like from their point of view?

The U.S. Declaration of Independence declared in 1776 that "all men are created equal." What did that mean from the point of view of the half a million black slaves whose status remained unchanged after the declaration was made? And to women, who still had no rights? To whom were they created equal?

From the point of view of the United States, engraving the names of citizens who died in the Vietnam War on an immense marble wall in Washington was a just act. From the point of view of the Vietnamese killed in the U.S. invasion, there are sixty walls missing.

---

while feeding the U.S. and British war economies and protecting their sources of energy from threat. A skeptic might conclude that those billion-dollar purchase orders bought King Fahd impunity. For reasons that only Allah knows, we never see, hear, or read anything about Saudi Arabia's atrocities in the media, the same media that tend to get quite worked up about human rights abuses in other Arab countries. Best friends are those who buy the most weapons. The U.S. arms industry wages a struggle against terrorism by selling weapons to terrorist governments whose only relation to human rights is to do all they can to trample them.

In the Era of Peace, the name applied to the historical period that began in 1946, wars have slaughtered no less than twenty-two million people and have displaced from their lands, homes, or countries over forty million more. Consumers of TV news never lack a war or at least a brushfire to munch on. But never do the reporters report, or the commentators comment, on anything that might help explain what's going on. To do that they would have to start by answering some very basic questions: Who benefits from all that human pain? Who profits from this tragedy? "And the executioner's face is always well hidden," Bob Dylan once sang.

In 1968, two months before a bullet killed him, the Reverend Dr. Martin Luther King Jr. declared that his country was "the world's greatest purveyor of violence." Thirty years later the figures bear him out: of every ten dollars spent on arms in the world, four and a half end up in the United States. Statistics compiled by the International Institute of Strategic Studies show the largest weapons dealers to be the United States, the United Kingdom, France, and Russia. China figures on the list as well, a few places back. And these five countries, by some odd coincidence, are the very ones that can exercise vetoes in the UN Security Council. The right to a veto really means the power to decide. The General Assembly of the highest international institution, in which all countries take part, makes recommendations, but it's the Security Council that makes decisions. The Assembly speaks or remains silent; the Council does or undoes. In other words, world peace lies in the hands of the five powers that profit most from the big business of war.

So it's no surprise that the permanent members of the Security Council enjoy the right to do whatever they like. In recent years, for example, the United States freely bombed the poorest neighborhood in Panama City and later flattened Iraq. Russia punished

Enigmas

What are those skulls laughing at?

Who is the author of anonymous jokes? Who *is* that old guy making wisecracks and spreading them about the world? What cave does he hide out in?

Why did Noah let mosquitoes on the Ark?

Did Saint Francis of Assisi love mosquitoes too?

Are the statues we ought to have as numerous as the ones we have and don't need?

If communications technology is more and more advanced, why do people communicate less and less?

Why is it no one understands communications experts, not even God?

Why do sex education books make us want to give up sex for several years?

In wars, who sells the weapons?

Chechnya's cries for independence with blood and fire. France raped the South Pacific with its nuclear tests. And every year China legally executes ten times as many people by firing squad as died in Tienanmen Square. As in the Falklands war the previous decade, the invasion of Panama gave the air force an opportunity to test its new toys, and television turned the invasion of Iraq into a global display case for the latest weapons on the market: Come and see the new trinkets of death at the great fair of Baghdad.

Neither should anyone be surprised by the unhappy global imbalance between war and peace. For every dollar spent by the United Nations on peacekeeping, the world spends two thousand dollars on warkeeping. In the ensuing sacrificial rites, hunter and prey are of the same species and the winner is he who kills more of his brothers. Theodore Roosevelt put it well: "No triumph of peace is quite so great as the supreme triumphs of war." In 1906, he was awarded the Nobel Peace Prize.

There are thirty-five thousand nuclear weapons in the world. The United States has half of them; Russia and, to a lesser degree, other powers, the rest. The owners of the nuclear monopoly scream to the high heavens when India or Pakistan or anyone else achieves the dream of having its own bomb. That's when they decry the deadly threat of such weapons to the world: each weapon could kill several million people, and it would take only a few to end the human adventure on this planet and the planet itself. But the great powers never bother to say when God decided to award them a monopoly or why they continue building such weapons. During the Cold War, nuclear arms were an extremely dangerous instrument of reciprocal intimidation. But now that the United States and Russia walk arm in arm, what are those immense arsenals for? Whom are these countries trying to scare? All of humanity?

Every war has the drawback of requiring an enemy—if possible, more than one. Without threat or aggression—spontaneous or provoked, real or fabricated—the possibility of war is hardly convincing and the demand for weaponry might face a dramatic decline. In 1989, a new Barbie doll dressed in military fatigues and giving a smart salute was launched onto the world market. Barbie picked a bad time to start her military career. At the end of that year the Berlin Wall fell; everything else collapsed soon after. The Evil Empire came tumbling down and suddenly God was orphaned of the Devil. The Pentagon and the arms trade found themselves in a rather tight spot.

Enemy wanted. The Germans and the Japanese had gone from Bad to Good years earlier, and now, from one day to the next, the Russians lost their fangs and their sulfurous odor. Fortunately, lack-of-villain syndrome found a quick fix in Hollywood. Ronald Reagan, lucid prophet that he was, had already announced that the Cold War had to be won in outer space. Hollywood's vast talent and money were put to work to fabricate enemies in the galaxies. Extraterrestrial invasion had been the subject of films before, but

Points of View/9

From the point of view of the economy, the sale of weapons is indistinguishable from the sale of food.

When a building collapses or a plane crashes, it's rather inconvenient from the point of view of those inside, but it's altogether convenient for the growth of the gross national product, which sometimes ought to be called the "gross criminal product."

it was never depicted with much sorrow or glory. Now the studios rushed to portray ferocious Martians and other reptilian or cockroachlike foreigners with the knack of adopting human form to fool the gullible or reduce production costs. And they met with tremendous box-office success.

Meanwhile, here on earth, the panorama improved. True, the supply of evils had fallen off, but in the South there were longstanding villains who could still be called on. The Pentagon should put up a monument to Fidel Castro for his forty long years of generous service. Muammar al-Qaddafi, once a villain in great demand, barely works anymore, but Saddam Hussein, who was a good guy in the eighties, became in the nineties the worst of the worst. He remains so useful that, at the beginning of 1998, the United States threatened to invade Iraq a second time so people would stop talking about the sexual habits of President Bill Clinton.

At the beginning of 1991, another president, George Bush, saw there was no need to look to outer space for enemies. After invading Panama, and while he was in the process of invading Iraq, Bush declared: "The world is a dangerous place." This pearl of wisdom has remained over the years the most irrefutable justification for the highest war budget on the planet, mysteriously called

the "defense budget." The name constitutes an enigma. The United States hasn't been invaded by anybody since the English burned Washington in 1812. Except for Pancho Villa's fleeting excursion during the Mexican Revolution, no enemy has crossed its borders. The United States, in contrast, has always had the unpleasant habit of invading others.

A good part of the U.S. public, astonishingly ignorant about everything beyond its shores, fears and disdains all that it does not understand. The country that has done more than any other to

A Star Is Born?

In mid-1998, the White House put another villain up on the global marquee. He uses the stage name Osama bin Laden; he's an Islamic fundamentalist, sports a beard, wears a turban, and caresses the rifle in his lap. Will this new star's career take off? Will he be a box-office hit? Will he manage to undermine the foundations of Western civilization or will he only play a supporting role? In horror movies, you never know.

develop information technology produces television news that barely touches on world events except to confirm that foreigners tend to be terrorists and ingrates. Every act of rebellion or explosion of violence, wherever it occurs, becomes new proof that the international conspiracy continues its inexorable march, egged on by hatred and envy. Little does it matter that the Cold War is over, because the Devil has a large wardrobe and doesn't dress just in red. Polls indicate that Russia now sits at the bottom of any enemy list, but people fear a nuclear attack from some terrorist group or other. No one knows what terrorist group has nuclear weapons, but as the noted sociologist Woody Allen points out, "Nobody can bite into a hamburger anymore without being afraid it's going to explode." In reality, the worst terrorist attack in U.S. history took place in 1995 in Oklahoma City, and the attacker wasn't a foreigner bearing nuclear arms but a white U.S. citizen with a fertilizer bomb who had been decorated in the war against Iraq.

Among the ghosts of international terrorism, "narcoterrorism" is the one that's most frightening. To say "drugs" is like saying "the plague" in another epoch: it evokes the same terror, the same sense of impotence, of a mysterious curse from the Devil incarnate, who tempts his victims and carries them off. Like all misfortune, it comes from outside. Not much is said anymore about marijuana, once the "killer weed," and perhaps that has something to do with the way it has become a successful part of local agriculture in eleven states of the Union. In contrast, heroin and cocaine, produced in foreign countries, have been elevated to the category of enemies that erode the very foundations of the nation.

Official sources estimate that U.S. citizens spend $110 billion a year on drugs, the equivalent of one-tenth the value of the country's entire industrial production. Authorities have never caught a

Desire

A man found Aladdin's lamp lying around. Since he was a big
reader, the man recognized it and rubbed it right away. The
genie appeared, bowed deeply, and said: "At your service, master. Your wish is my command. But there will be only one wish."

Since he was a good boy, the man said, "I wish for my dead
mother to be brought back."

The genie made a face. "I'm sorry, master, but that wish is
impossible. Make another."

Since he was a nice guy, the man said, "I wish the world
would stop spending money to kill people."

The genie swallowed. "Uhh . . . What did you say your
mother's name was?"

single U.S. trafficker of any real importance, but the war against
drugs has certainly increased the number of consumers. As happened with alcohol during Prohibition, outlawing only stimulates
demand and boosts profits. According to Joe McNamara, former
chief of the San Jose police force in California, profits can be as
high as 17,000 percent.

Drugs are as "American" as apple pie—a U.S. tragedy, a U.S.
business, but they're the fault of Colombia, Bolivia, Peru, Mexico,
and other ingrate nations. In a scene straight out of the Vietnam
War, helicopters and planes bomb guilty-looking Latin American
fields with poisons made by Dow Chemical, Chevron, Monsanto,
and other chemical companies. Devastating to the earth and to
human health, the sprayings are next to useless because the drug

plantations simply relocate. The peasants who cultivate coca or poppies, the moving targets in these military campaigns, are the smallest fish in the drug ocean. The cost of the raw materials has little effect on the final price. From the fields where coca is harvested to the streets of New York where cocaine is sold, the price multiplies one hundred to five hundred times, depending on the ups and downs of the underground market for white powder.

Is there a better ally than drug trafficking for banks, weapons manufacturers, or the military hierarchy? Drugs make fortunes for the bankers and offer useful pretexts for the machinery of war. An illegal industry of death thus serves the legal industry of death: vocabulary and reality become militarized. According to a spokesman for the military dictatorship that razed Brazil from 1964 on, drugs and free love were "tactics of revolutionary war" against Christian civilization. In 1985, the U.S. delegate to a conference on narcotic and psychotropic drugs in Santiago, Chile, announced that the fight against drugs had become "a world war." In 1990, Los Angeles police chief Daryl Gates suggested that drug users be riddled with bullets "because we are at war." Shortly before that, President George Bush had exhorted the nation to "win the war" against drugs, explaining that it was "an international war" because the drugs came from overseas and constituted the gravest threat to the nation. This war is the one subject never absent from presidential speeches, whether it's the president of a neighborhood club inaugurating a swimming pool or the president of the United States, who never misses a chance to exercise his right to grant or deny other countries certification for their good conduct in it.

A problem of public health has been turned into a problem of public security that respects no borders. It's the Pentagon's duty to intervene on any battlefield where the war against "narco-

subversion" and "narco-terrorism" (two new words that put rebellion and crime in the same bag) is being waged. After all, the
National Anti-Drug Strategy is directed not by a doctor but by a
military officer.

Frank Hall, former head of the New York police narcotics
squad, once said, "If imported cocaine were to disappear, in two
months it would be replaced by synthetic drugs." Common-
sensical as that might seem, the fight against the Latin American
sources of evil continues because it offers the best cover for main-
taining military and, to a large degree, political control over the
region. The Pentagon wants to set up a Multilateral Anti-Drug
Center in Panama to run the drug war waged by the armies of the
Americas. For the entire twentieth century, Panama was a major
U.S. military base. The treaty that imposed that humiliation on the
country expired on the final day of the century, but the drug war
could well require that the country be rented out for another
eternity.

For some time now drugs have been the major justification for
military intervention in the countries south of the Rio Grande.
Panama was the first to fall victim. In 1989, twenty-six thousand
soldiers burst into Panama, guns blazing, and imposed as presi-

dent the unpresentable Guillermo Endara, who proceeded to step up drug trafficking under the pretext of fighting it. In the name of the war on drugs, the Pentagon is making itself at home in Colombia, Peru, and Bolivia. This sacred crusade—Get thee hence, Satan!—also gives Latin America's armies another reason for existing, hastens their return to the public stage, and provides them with the resources they need to deal with frequent explosions of social protest.

General Jesús Gutiérrez Rebollo, who headed up the war on drugs in Mexico, no longer sleeps at home. Since February 1997, he's been in jail for trafficking cocaine. But the helicopters and sophisticated weaponry the United States sent him to fight drugs with have proved quite useful against upstart peasants in Chiapas and elsewhere. A large portion of U.S. antidrug aid to Colombia is used to kill peasants in areas that have nothing to do with drugs. The armed forces that most systematically violate human rights, like Colombia's, are those that receive the most U.S. aid in weapons and technical assistance. For years, they have been making war on the poor, enemies of the established order, while defending the established order, enemy of the poor.

After all, that's what it's about: the war on drugs is a cover for social war. Just like the poor who steal, drug addicts, especially poor ones, are demonized in order to absolve the society that produces them. Against whom is the law enforced? In Argentina, a quarter of the people behind bars who have not been sentenced are there for possession of less than five grams of marijuana or cocaine. In the United States, the antidrug crusade is focused on crack, that devastating poor cousin of cocaine consumed by blacks, Latins, and other prison fodder. U.S. Public Health Service statistics show that eight out of ten drug users are white, but of those in jail for drugs only one in ten is white. Several uprisings in federal prisons labeled "racial riots" by the media have been protests against unjust sentencing policies. Crack addicts are punished a hundred times more severely than cocaine users. Literally one hundred times: according to federal law, a gram of crack is equivalent to one hundred grams of cocaine. Practically everyone imprisoned for crack is black.

In Latin America, where poor criminals are the new "internal enemy," the war on drugs takes aim at a target described by Nilo Batista in Brazil: "black teenagers from the slums who sell drugs to well-off white teenagers." Is this a question of drugs or of social and racial power? In Brazil and everywhere else, those who die in the war on drugs far outnumber those who die from an overdose.

I'm Curious

Why do people mix up coca and cocaine?

If coca is so perverse, why is one of the symbols of Western civilization called Coca-Cola?

If coca is outlawed because it is used for bad ends, why isn't television outlawed too?

If the drug industry is outlawed because it's a murderous business, why don't they outlaw the arms industry, which is the most murderous of all?

By what right does the United States act as the world's drug police, when it buys half of all the drugs the world produces?

How is it that small planes loaded with drugs enter and leave the United States with such astonishing ease? How come state-of-the-art technology that can photograph a flea on the horizon can't detect a plane flying by the window?

Why hasn't a single one of the snow kings who reign over the drug trade in the United States ever been caught?

Why do the mass media talk so much about drugs and so little about why people take them? Why do they condemn drug addicts instead of the lifestyle that ratchets up anxiety, anguish, loneliness, and fear or the consumer culture that leads people to seek chemical consolation?

If an illness is made into a crime and that crime is made into a business, is it fair to punish those who are sick?

Why doesn't the United States wage war on its own banks, the ones that launder all those drug dollars? Or against the Swiss bankers who wash them whiter yet?

Why are the drug dealers the most fervent supporters of antidrug laws?

Doesn't the free circulation of goods and capital favor illegal trafficking? Isn't the drug business the most perfect prototype of neoliberal thinking? Aren't the traffickers just following the golden rule of the market, that every demand will be met by a supply?

Why is it that the most popular drugs today are the drugs of productivity? The ones that hide exhaustion and fear, that fake omnipotence, that help you produce more and earn more? Couldn't we read in that a sign of the times? Could it just be happenstance that unproductive hallucinogens like LSD, the drugs of the sixties, have receded into prehistory? Were the desperate of those times different? What about their desperations?

A baby who doesn't cry gets no milk,
and a man who doesn't hustle is a fool.

—FROM THE TANGO "CAMBALACHE"
BY ENRIQUE SANTOS DISCÉPOLO

SEMINAR ON ETHICS

- Practicum: How to Make Friends and Succeed in Life
- Lessons for Resisting Useless Vices

Practicum: How to Make Friends and Succeed in Life

Crime is the mirror image of order. The criminals who fill jails are poor and nearly always use small arms and crude methods. If not for those defects of poverty and preindustrial technology, slum criminals could well be wearing the crowns of kings, the wide-brimmed hats of gentlemen, the miters of bishops, or the caps of generals, and they would be signing government decrees instead of placing their thumbprints on confessions.

IMPERIAL POWER

Queen Victoria of England gave her name to an epoch that was indeed victorious, a time of splendor for an empire that ruled the seas and a good part of the lands as well. As the *Encyclopaedia Britannica* tells us under the letter *V,* the queen led her subjects by the example of her austere life, always upholding strict morals and good habits, and it is to her in great measure that we owe the spread of concepts like dignity, authority, and respect for family, which were characteristic of Victorian society. In portraits she always wears a scowl, due perhaps to the difficulties she faced and the boredom she suffered in pursuit of the virtuous life.

Although the *Encyclopaedia Britannica* doesn't mention this detail, Queen Victoria was also the greatest drug trafficker of the nineteenth century. Under her long reign, opium became the most valuable commodity of imperial trade. Large-scale poppy cultivation and opium production were developed in India at British initiative and under British control. A large portion of that opium entered China as contraband, and the drug industry pried open a growing consumer market. The number of addicts was said to have grown to about 12 million by 1839, when, observing its devastating effects on the population, the Chinese emperor outlawed the trafficking and use of opium and ordered the cargoes of several British ships impounded. The queen, who never in her life uttered the word "drug," decried that unpardonable sacrilege against free trade and sent her fleet of warships to the coasts of China. During the two decades, with a few interruptions, that the opium war lasted, the word "war" was also never uttered.

On the tail of the warships came cargo ships loaded with opium. At the conclusion of each military action, commercial operations resumed. In one of the first battles, the taking of the port of Tin-hai in 1841, three Britons died and so did more than two thousand Chinese. The balance of losses continued more or less like that in the years that followed. The first truce ended in 1856, when the city of Canton was bombarded by order of Sir John Bowring, a devout Christian who liked to say, "Jesus is free trade, and free

trade is Jesus." The second truce ended in 1860, when Queen Victoria's patience ran out. It was time to put an end to the obstinacy of the Chinese. Peking fell under cannon fire and the invading troops assaulted and burned the imperial summer palace. After that, China accepted opium, the number of drug addicts skyrocketed, and British merchants lived happily ever after.

THE POWER OF SECRECY

The richest countries in the world are Switzerland and Luxembourg. Two small nations, two large financial markets. About minuscule Luxembourg, little or nothing is known. Switzerland, in contrast, is famous for the marksmanship of William Tell, the precision of its watches, and the discretion of its bankers.

The prestige of Swiss banks is long-standing; a seven-century tradition guarantees their seriousness and security. But it was during World War II that Switzerland became a great financial power. Loyal to its equally long tradition of neutrality, Switzerland did not take part in the war. It did, however, take part in the business of war, selling its services, and at a very good price, to Nazi Germany. The deal was brilliant: Swiss banks took the gold that Hitler stole from the countries he occupied and from the Jews he trapped, including gold teeth from the dead in gas chambers and concentration camps, and turned it into convertible currency. The gold crossed into Switzerland without any problem, while people persecuted by the Nazis were turned away at the border.

Bertolt Brecht used to say that robbing a bank is a crime but the greater crime is to found one. After the war, Switzerland became the cave of Ali Baba for the world's dictators, crooked politicians, tax-evading acrobats, and traffickers in drugs and arms. Under the resplendent sidewalks of the Banhofstrasse in Zurich and the Corraterie in Geneva lie the fruits of looting and fraud, transformed into stacks of gold bars and mountains of bills.

Besieged by scandals and lawsuits, numbered accounts are not what they used to be, but for better or worse the engine of national prosperity hums along. Money still has the right to wear a costume and a mask in this never-ending carnival, and referendums have proved that the majority of the population finds nothing wrong with that.

Though the money arrives as dirty as can be and the washings are incredibly complicated, this launderette leaves it spotless. In the eighties, when Ronald Reagan presided over the United States, Switzerland was the center of operations for the many-faceted manipulations of Oliver North. As Swiss journalist Jean Ziegler discovered, U.S. arms went to Iran, an enemy country, which paid for them in part with morphine and heroin. From Switzerland the drugs were sold and in Switzerland the money was deposited that later financed the mercenaries who bombed cooperatives and schools in Nicaragua. Back then, Reagan liked to compare those mercenaries to the U.S. Founding Fathers.

Whether temples with high marble columns or discreet chapels, Swiss sanctuaries dodge questions and proffer mystery. Ferdinand Marcos, despot of the Philippines, kept between $1 billion and $1.5 billion in forty Swiss banks. The Philippine consul in Zurich was a director of Crédit Suisse. At the beginning of 1998, twelve years after Marcos's fall and after many suits and counter-suits, the Federal Tribunal ordered $570 million returned to the Philippine government. It wasn't everything, but it was something and an exception to the rule: normally, stolen money disappears without a trace. Swiss surgeons give it a new face and name, fabricating a new legal life and a fake identity for it. Of the booty looted by the Somoza dynasty, vampires of Nicaragua, nothing at all turned up. Practically nothing was found, and nothing at all was returned, of what the Duvalier dynasty stole from Haiti. Mobutu Sese Seko, who squeezed the last drop out of Congo, always visited his bankers in Geneva in a fleet of armored Mercedes. Mobutu had between $4 billion and $5 billion: only $6 million could be found after his dictatorship fell. The dictator of Mali, Moussa Traoré, had a little over $1 billion; Swiss bankers returned $4 million.

The money of the Argentine officers who sacrificed themselves for the fatherland by waging terror from 1976 on ended up in Switzerland. Twenty-two years later, a lawsuit revealed the tip of that iceberg. How many millions vanished into the mist that shrouds their phantom accounts? In the nineties, the Salinas family stripped Mexico clean. Raúl Salinas, the president's brother, was called "Mr. Ten Percent" in recognition of the commissions he pocketed from privatizing public services and protecting the drug mafia. The press reported that his river of dollars ended up in Citibank, the Union des Banques Suisses, the Société de Banque Suisse, and other affiliates of money's Red Cross. How much will be recovered? Money plunges into the magic waters of Lake Geneva and becomes invisible.

There are those who praise Uruguay by calling it the "Switzerland of America." We Uruguayans aren't too sure about that tribute. Does it honor our democratic traditions or our own secret banking laws? Since numbered accounts came in a few years ago, Uruguay has become the Southern Cone's cashier, a huge bank with an ocean view.

DIVINE POWER

On the last night of 1970, three of God's bankers met in a hotel in Nassau. Caressed by tropical breezes, surrounded by postcard scenery, Roberto Calvi, Michele Sindona, and Paul Marcinkus celebrated the birth of the new year by raising their glasses in a prayer for the annihilation of Marxism. Twelve years later, they annihilated the Banco Ambrosiano.

The Banco Ambrosiano wasn't Marxist. Known as *"la banca dei preti,"* the priests' bank, Ambrosiano would not accept stockholders who had not been baptized. It wasn't the only banking institution linked to the Church. Back in 1605, Pope Paul V had founded the Bank of the Holy Ghost, which no longer performed financial miracles for divine benefit, as it had been taken over by the Italian state, but the Vatican had, and continues to have, its own official bank, piously called the Institute for Religious Works. In any case, Ambrosiano was very important, the second-largest private bank in Italy, and the *Financial Times* called its collapse the gravest crisis in the history of Western banking. In this colossal swindle, over a billion dollars went missing and the Vatican itself, one of the bank's primary stockholders and greatest beneficiaries of its loans, was directly implicated.

Many camels went through the eye of that needle. Ambrosiano wove a global spider's web for laundering money from drug traf-

For Religion Class

When I went to Rome for the first time I no longer believed in God, and for me earth was the only heaven and the only hell. But my memory of God the father from my childhood wasn't a bad one, and deep inside I kept a special place for God the son, the rebel of Galilee who defied the imperial city where my Alitalia flight was then landing. Of the Holy Ghost, I confess, not much stayed with me, just a vague recollection of a white dove that dives down with outspread wings and impregnates virgins.

As soon as I walked into the Rome airport a huge sign loomed before my eyes: BANK OF THE HOLY GHOST.

I was young and it made quite an impression on me that this was what the Holy Ghost was up to.

ficking and arms dealing, working hand in hand with the Sicilian and U.S. mafias and with drug networks in Turkey and Colombia. The Cosa Nostra used it to evade taxes on the profits of its smuggling and kidnapping operations, and it sent a shower of dollars to Polish unions fighting against the Communist regime. The bank also generously supplied the Contras in Nicaragua and the P-2 Lodge in Italy, Masons who allied with their traditional enemy the Church to fight the red threat. The capos of the P-2 received a hundred million dollars from Ambrosiano, which contributed to their family prosperity and helped them set up a parallel government for carrying out terrorist attacks meant to punish the Italian left and sow panic among the population.

The bank was cleaned out over a number of years, its assets flowing into a number of open financial mouths in Switzerland, the Bahamas, Panama, and other fiscal paradises. Heads of government, ministers, cardinals, bankers, captains of industry, and top bureaucrats were all accomplices in the looting organized by Calvi, Sindona, and Marcinkus. Calvi, who administered monies for the Holy See and presided over Ambrosiano, was famous for his icy smile and his accounting pirouettes. Sindona, king of the Italian stock exchange, trusted by the Vatican to handle its investments in real estate and finance, also served as a bag man for the U.S. embassy's donations to right-wing parties. He owned banks, factories, and hotels in several countries and was even the owner of the Watergate building in Washington, which earned a spot in the history books thanks to the curiosity of Richard Nixon. Archbishop Marcinkus, who presided over the Institute for Religious Works, was born in Chicago, in the same neighborhood as Al Capone. A muscular man always chomping on a cigar, he had been the pope's bodyguard before he became his business manager.

The three men worked for the greater glory of God and their own pocketbooks. It could be said that they had successful careers. But none of them escaped the persecution and martyrdom trumpeted in the Gospels for apostles of the faith. Shortly before Banco Ambrosiano went belly-up, Roberto Calvi was found hanged under a bridge in London. Four years later, Michele Sindona, then in a maximum-security prison, asked for coffee with sugar. They didn't quite catch the order and gave him coffee with cyanide. A few months after that, an arrest warrant was issued for Archbishop Marcinkus, for fraudulent bankruptcy.

POLITICAL POWER

Sixty years ago the Argentine writer Roberto Arlt had some advice for anyone wanting to pursue a career in politics: "Proclaim: 'I have robbed, and I aspire to robbing on a larger scale.' Promise to sell off every last inch of Argentine soil, to sell the Congress building and turn the Palace of Justice into a tenement. In your speeches, say: 'Stealing isn't easy, gentlemen. You have to be a cynic, and that's what I am. You have to be a traitor, and that's what I am.'"

Arlt thought this would be a sure-fire formula for success, since all the scoundrels speak of is honesty and people tire of lies. A Brazilian politician, Adhemar de Barros, won over the electorate of the state of São Paulo, the richest in the country, with the slogan *"Rouba mas faz"*—"He steals but he gets things done." In Argentina, in contrast, Arlt's advice never caught on and today it's still impossible to find a politician who has the courage to admit he will steal or to confess he has stolen. And none of these looters of the public purse is capable of acknowledging, "I stole for myself. I stole to give myself the good life." If any of them had a conscience that could torment him, he would at least say: "I did it for the party, for the people, for the country." Some politicians love their country so much they take it all home.

Roberto Arlt's formula won't work. No Brazilian politician has copied Adhemar de Barros's recipe. As a general rule, what garners the most votes are the arts of theater—good acting, well-chosen masks. As another Argentine writer, José Pablo Feinmann,

Prices

In 1993, the tiny Brazilian Social Democratic Party didn't have the minimum number of representatives in Congress to be eligible for the presidential elections. For a price that varied between $30,000 and $50,000, it bought a number of congressmen from other parties. One of them admitted it and, what's more, he offered an explanation: "That's what soccer players do when they change clubs."

Four years later, prices had gone up in Brasilia. Two congressmen received $200,000 apiece for voting in favor of a constitutional amendment to allow President Cardoso to run for reelection.

once put it, electoral politics tends to reward doublespeak and split personalities. Many professional politicians cultivate the schizophrenia that turns timid Clark Kent into Superman just by his removing his glasses and insipid Bruce Wayne into Batman when he puts on his bat cape.

You don't need to be a poli-sci major to realize that political speeches usually have to be read backwards for their real meaning. There are few exceptions to the rule: politicians promise change and once they're elected they change . . . their minds. Sometimes they turn around so fast they get dizzy and you get a stiff neck from watching them spin to the right. "Education and health first!" they proclaim like the captain of a ship crying, "Women and children first!" and sure enough, education and health are the first to drown. Their words praise hard work, and their deeds damn the workers. Politicians who swear, hand over heart, that national sovereignty has no price tend to be the ones who give it away for nothing. And those who proclaim they'll round up all the crooks tend to be the ones who steal even the shoes off horses galloping by.

In mid-1996, Abdalá Bucaram won the presidency of Ecuador by calling himself the lash of the corrupt. Bucaram, a boisterous politician who thought he sang like Julio Iglesias and was actually proud of that, provoked widespread outrage and was thrown out of office after only a few months. One of the straws that broke the back of people's patience was the party he threw for his eighteen-year-old son, Jacobito, to celebrate the first million he made performing miracles in the customs office.

In 1990, Fernando Collor became president of Brazil. In a

For International Relations Class

Terence Todman and James Cheek were U.S. ambassadors to Argentina in recent years. One after the other, they followed the same trajectory: for love of the tango, they came right back. As soon as their diplomatic stints ended, they returned to Buenos Aires as lobbyists.

Both of them used their influence with the Argentine government to assist private companies eager to pocket the country's airports. Shortly afterward, a picture of Cheek with a doll in his lap was all over television and the papers. With his victorious airport campaign behind him, Cheek went to work for Barbie, the little woman who tempts us to commit the sin of plastic.

Generous Souls

In the United States, the sale of political favors is legal and can be carried on openly—no need to pretend, no risk of scandal.

Over ten thousand bribery pros work in Washington, plying their trade with members of Congress and the tenants of the White House. In an account that was certainly not exhaustive, the Center for Responsive Politics recorded $1.2 billion legally paid out in 1997 by numerous business and professional organizations, an average of $100 million a month. Leading the long list of "donors" was the American Medical Association, which is linked to the private health care business, the Chamber of Commerce, and the companies Philip Morris, General Motors, and Edison Electric Institute.

The figure, which rises year after year, does not include payments made under the table. As Johnnie Chung, a businessman who acknowledged making illegal donations, explained in 1998, "The White House is like a subway: You have to put in coins to open the gates."

quick and dirty election campaign made possible by television, Collor gave speech after moralistic speech attacking the "maharajahs," or top bureaucrats, who were looting the state. Two and a half years later, up to his neck in scandal, Collor was impeached for his secret bank accounts and ostentatious displays of instant wealth. In 1993, the president of Venezuela, Carlos Andrés Pérez, was also thrown out of office and sentenced to house arrest for embezzling funds. Never in the history of Latin America has anyone been

Exemplary Lives/1

In September 1994, in the Brasilia studios of Globo television, Treasury Minister Rubens Ricupero was waiting to be interviewed. While the lights and microphones were adjusted, he chatted with the journalist. Relaxed and speaking off the record, the minister admitted he only gives out economic information favorable to the government and hides figures that aren't. "I have no scruples," he said.

And he told the journalist confidentially: "Once the elections are over, we'll sic the police on the strikers."

But there was a mix-up. This private chat was picked up by satellite and transmitted to every parabolic antenna in Brazil. The words of the minister were broadcast throughout the country. On that historic occasion, Brazilians heard the truth. For once, and by mistake, they heard the truth.

Afterward, the minister didn't crawl the path of Saint James on his knees or flagellate himself or throw ash on his head; nor did he seek refuge in the heights of the Himalayas. Rubens Ricupero became secretary-general of the United Nations Conference on Trade and Development (UNCTAD).

obliged to return the money he stole—neither overthrown presidents, nor the many ministers forced out by overwhelming evidence of corruption, nor the directors of public services, nor the legislators, nor the petty officials who take money under the table. No one has ever returned a cent. I'm not saying they didn't intend to, it's just that it never occurred to anyone to ask.

Money isn't all they steal. Sometimes they steal elections too, as occurred in Mexico in 1988, when the presidency was snatched away from the left-wing opposition candidate, Cuauhtémoc Cárdenas, who had won a majority at the polls. Years later, in 1997, several legislators from the governing party accused the leader of the right-wing opposition, Diego Fernández de Cevallos, of receiving fourteen million dollars in return for his complicity in that electoral fraud. The press had a field day because an exchange of blows turned the parliamentary session into a boxing match, and the accusation of bribery got a lot of publicity. But passed over as hardly worth mentioning was something much more serious: the accusation itself was an implicit confession of electoral fraud by congressmen from the party that had committed it.

The greatest crimes are on the order of bad habits considered normal. While democracy gets besmirched, the ethic of anything goes is embraced: no one succeeds by pissing holy water. How many North Americans believe their senators have "very high

morals"? All of 2 percent. At the end of 1996, the Buenos Aires daily *Página 12* published a Gallup poll: seven of every ten Argentine youth claimed that dishonesty is the only way to succeed. And of all those polled, young and old, nine out of ten acknowledged that evading taxes and bribing officials or the police are common practices.

What is rewarded above is punished below. Petty robbery is a crime against property; grand larceny is a property owner's right. Unscrupulous politicians do no more than act in accordance with a system where success justifies the means that make it possible, dirty as they may be: cheating the tax man and your neighbor, falsifying accounts, hiding assets, looting companies, inventing fictitious enterprises, underbilling, overbilling, fraudulent commissions . . .

THE POWER OF KIDNAPPERS

According to the dictionary, "kidnap" means to hold someone illegally in order to obtain a ransom. The crime draws a stiff sentence

Exemplary Lives/2

At the end of the eighties, all young men in Spain wanted to be like him. The polls agreed: this star from Spain's financial world, this King Midas of the banks, had eclipsed El Cid and Don Quixote as the model of choice for generations to come. An acrobat who did high jumps up the social ladder, this native of a little town in Galicia had reached the summits of power and success. The readers of romance magazines showered him with praise, calling him the most attractive man in Spain, the most marriageable. Always smiling, every hair in place, he looked fresh from the dry cleaners whether they photographed him reading spreadsheets, dancing *sevillanas,* or yachting in the Mediterranean. "I Want to Be Mario Conde" was the name of a hit song.

In 1997, the prosecutor demanded forty-four years for Mario Conde, not much for the man who masterminded the greatest financial swindle in the history of Spain.

in every penal code, but no one would dream of jailing the financial bigwigs who hold countries hostage and, delightfully immune to consequences, collect fabulous ransoms day after day.

In the olden days, the marines would take over the customs houses in Central America and the islands of the Caribbean to collect the debts those countries owed. The U.S. occupation of Haiti lasted nineteen years, from 1915 to 1934. The invaders did not leave until Citibank had collected on all its loans, multiplied several times over by usurious interest rates. In their place, the marines left a national army created to prop up the dictatorship and keep the payments flowing. Today, in these democratic times, international technocrats are more effective than military expeditions. The Haitian people did not elect, did not even cast a single vote for, the directors of the International Monetary Fund or the World Bank, but that's who decides the fate of every dollar that enters Haiti's public coffers. As in all other poor countries, more powerful than the vote is the veto: the democratic vote proposes and the financial veto disposes.

The Monetary Fund is called International, just as the Bank is called World, but these twin brothers live, collect, and decide in Washington, and their well-populated technocracy never spits in the plate from which they eat. Although the United States is by far the most indebted country in the world, no outsider orders it to put a FOR SALE sign on the White House; such an act of insolence would never occur to any international bureaucrat. In contrast, the countries of the South, which service their debts at the rate of $250,000 *per minute,* are captives, and creditors cut their sovereignty to ribbons just as Roman patricians in previous imperial times cut their plebeian debtors to ribbons in the public plaza. No matter how much these countries pay, there is no way to quench the thirst of that huge leaky jug called the foreign debt. The more they pay, the more they owe; and the more they owe, the more they are obliged to obey orders to dismantle the state, mortgage their political independence, and alienate the national economy. "He lived paying and he died owing" could be written on their gravestones.

Saint Hedwig, patron saint of the indebted, is the saint who garners the most prayers in Brazil. Thousands upon thousands of desperate debtors make their pilgrimage to her, pleading for her to keep creditors from taking away their televisions, cars, or

homes. Sometimes Saint Hedwig performs a miracle. But how can the saint help countries when creditors have already carted off the government, countries free to do whatever they're told by faceless, far-off men who practice financial blackmail by remote control? Creditors open and close stock exchanges, depending on the degree of submissiveness to the "right economic track." The one and only truth is imposed with a fanaticism worthy of the Inquisition, single-party commissars, or Islamic fundamentalists; exactly the same policy is dictated to countries as diverse as Bolivia and Russia, Mongolia and Nigeria, South Korea and Mexico.

At the end of 1997, Michel Camdessus, president of the International Monetary Fund, declared: "The state should not give orders to the banks." Translated, this means: "It's the banks who ought to give orders to the state." Nearly two years earlier, German banker Hans Tietmeyer, president of the Bundesbank, put it this way: "Financial markets more and more play the role of gendarmes. Politicians should understand that from now on they are under the control of financial markets." Brazilian sociologist Hebert de Souza, "Betinho," once suggested sending all the presidents off on a luxury cruise. Governments govern less and less, and the people who voted for them feel less and less represented by them. Polls reveal this lack of faith: fewer than half of all Brazilians and just over half of all Chileans, Mexicans, Paraguayans, and Peruvians believe in democracy. In the 1997 legislative elections, Chile recorded the largest number of blank ballots in the country's history. And never have so many young people not bothered to register to vote.

GLOBALITARIAN POWER

In the twelve years of her government, from 1979 on, Margaret Thatcher ran a dictatorship of finance capital in the British Isles. The iron lady, much praised for her masculine virtues, brought an end to the era of polite behavior, crushed workers on strike, and reestablished a rigid class society with astonishing speed. Thus Great Britain became the model for Europe. Meanwhile, Chile, under the military dictatorship of General Pinochet, had become the model for Latin America. These two models figure today among the most unjust countries in the world. According to World Bank statistics on income distribution and consumption, a deep chasm currently separates those Britons and Chileans who have plenty left over from the Britons and Chileans who survive on leftovers. In those two countries, incredible as it seems, social inequality is greater than in Bangladesh, India, Nepal, or Sri Lanka. Just as incredibly, since Ronald Reagan took the helm in 1980, the United States has achieved even greater inequality than Rwanda.

Grease

German companies are prohibited from paying bribes to Germans. On the other hand, up until a short while ago, when companies bought off politicians, military officers, or officials from other countries, they were rewarded by the tax man. Bribes could be taken as deductions. According to journalist Martin Spiewak, telecommunications giant Siemens and metals conglomerate Klöckner paid $32 million to officers close to Indonesian dictator Suharto.

In 1997, a spokesman for the Social Democratic Party, Ingomar Hauchler, estimated that German companies spend $3 billion a year to grease the wheels of their businesses abroad. Officials justified the practice as protecting jobs and good trade relations, and they also invoked respect for cultural identity: buying favors is, after all, a way to respect the cultures of countries where corruption is customary.

The logic of the market imposes totalitarian dogmas on a global scale. Ignacio Ramonet, editor of *Le Monda Diplomatique,* calls them "globalitarian." This logic has become a religion that obliges us all to follow its commandments: sit up straight, don't raise your voice, do your chores without asking why. What time is it? Whatever you say, sir.

In the pummeled countries of the South, those on the bottom pay the piper but those on top call the tune, and the consequences are plain to see: hospitals without medicine, schools without roofs, food without subsidies. No judge can send a global system to jail for killing by hunger, but a crime is a crime even when it's carried out as the most normal thing in the world. "Bread is life to the destitute, and to deprive them of it is murder," says Ecclesiasticus, and as theologian Leonardo Boff points out, the market celebrates more human sacrifices than the Aztecs did at the Great Temple or the Canaanites before the idol of Moloch.

The globalitarian order steals with its trade hand what it lends with its finance hand. Tell me how much you sell and I'll tell you what you're worth. Latin America's exports aren't even 5 percent of the world's total, and Africa's add up to 2 percent; what the South buys costs more and more, and what it sells is worth less and less. To buy, governments go further and further into debt, and to comply with the usury on the loans, they sell grandma's jewelry and then grandma herself.

The market gives the order and the state is privatized. Shouldn't we rather "deprivatize" the state, seeing as it's controlled by the international banking cartel and by local politicians who do nothing but slander it so they can unload it at bargain-basement prices? Trafficking in favors and handing out jobs in return for votes has distended the parasite-ridden bellies of Latin America's governments. The insufferable "burrocracy" acts as a procurer, in the original sense of the word: two thousand years ago "procurator" referred to those who arranged administrative transactions in exchange for a tip. Thanks to such inefficiency and corruption, privatizations meet with the approval or indifference of public opinion.

Latin America's countries are being denationalized at a dizzying pace, with the exception of Cuba and of Uruguay, where in a plebiscite at the end of 1992, 72 percent of the country voted to halt the sale of public enterprises. Presidents go about the world like traveling salesmen, selling what doesn't belong to them. "My country is a product, I offer a product called Peru," President Alberto Fujimori has proclaimed on more than one occasion.

Profits are privatized, losses are socialized. In 1990, President Carlos Menem ordered Aerolíneas Argentinas to die. That profitable public enterprise was sold or, better put, given away to another public enterprise, Spain's Iberia, which was a model of poor administration. The Argentine airline's national and international routes were ceded for one-fifteenth their value, and two Boeing 707 planes, still perfectly airworthy, were purchased for the modest price of $1.54 apiece.

On January 31, 1998, the Uruguayan daily *El Observador* congratulated the Brazilian government on its decision to sell the national telephone company, Telebras. On page 2, the paper applauded President Fernando Henrique Cardoso "for getting rid of companies and services that had become a burden on the treasury and on consumers." On page 16 that day, the paper reported that Telebras, "the most profitable company in Brazil, last year made liquid profits of $3.9 billion, a record in the country's history."

The Brazilian government mobilized an army of 660 lawyers to defeat a fusillade of lawsuits against the privatization of Telebras, and it justified its program of denationalization by citing the need to show the world "signs that we are an open country." Writer Luis

Fernando Verissimo noted that such signs were "like the pointy caps they put on village idiots in the Middle Ages."

THE POWER OF THE CASINO

They say astrology was invented to give the impression that economics is an exact science. Economists never know tomorrow why the predictions they made yesterday didn't pan out today. It's not their fault. Frankly, they've been left without much to do since the real economy closed up shop and made way for the virtual economy. Today, finance rules, and frenzy and speculation fall more into the bailiwick of psychiatrists than into that of economists.

The Rothschilds learned of Napoleon's defeat at Waterloo by carrier pigeon. Now news travels faster than the speed of light, and flying alongside it on the computer screen is money. A ring worthy of Saturn spins wildly around the earth: the $2,000,000,000,000 that move on world financial markets every day. Of all those many zeros, so many you get dizzy looking at them, only a minuscule portion corresponds to commercial transactions or productive investments. In 1997, of every $100 in currency transactions, only $2.50 had anything to do with the exchange of goods and services. That same year, on the eve of the hurricane that battered stock markets in Asia and the world, the Malaysian government suggested a commonsense measure: outlawing currency trading for noncommercial purposes. The shouting of floor traders makes a lot of noise, and understandably those who benefit from currency speculation were deaf to the idea. In 1995, only three of the ten largest fortunes in Japan were linked to the real economy. The other seven multimillionaires were speculators.

Ten years ago, the financial markets suffered another collapse.

Language/4

The language of the business world, the universal language, gives new meanings to old words, enriching human communication in the tongue of Shakespeare.

"Options" define not the freedom to chose but rather the right to buy. "Futures" have dropped their mystery and become contracts. "Markets" are no longer boisterous plazas but computer screens. A "lobby" is no longer used to wait for friends but to buy politicians. Not only do ships travel "offshore," now money does too, to evade taxes and questions. "Laundries" that once upon a time washed clothes now wash dirty money.

"Lifting" no longer consists of raising weights or spirits: "lifting" is surgery that keeps the authors of all these good deeds from growing old.

Distinguished U.S. economists from the White House, the Congress, and the New York and Chicago stock exchanges tried to explain what had happened. The word "speculation" was not uttered in any of their analyses. After all, popular sports deserve respect: five out of every ten North Americans play the stock market in one way or another. Just as "smart bombs" killed Iraqis in the Gulf war without anyone except the dead finding out, "smart money" earns 40 percent profits without anyone finding out how. Wall Street, which some say was named for a wall built to keep black slaves from escaping, is today the center of the great global electronic gambling den, and all of humanity is enslaved by the decisions made there. The virtual economy moves capital, trashes prices, plucks fools, ruins countries, and churns out millionaires and mendicants in the time it takes to say, "Amen."

The world may be obsessed with personal insecurity, but reality teaches us that the crimes of finance capital are far more fearsome than those we read about in the papers. Mark Mobius, who speculates on behalf of thousands of investors, told the German magazine *Der Spiegel* at the beginning of 1998, "My clients laugh at ethical criteria. They only want us to increase their profits." During the crisis of 1987, another phrase made him famous: "You've got to buy when blood runs in the streets, even if the blood is mine." George Soros, the most successful speculator in the world, who made a fortune successively bidding down the pound, the lira, and the ruble, knows what he's talking about when he says, "The main enemy of the open society, I believe, is no longer the Communist but the capitalist threat."

Capitalism's Dr. Frankenstein has created a monster that walks on its own, and nobody can stop it. It is a superstate over and above all others, an invisible power that governs us all even though it was elected by no one. In this world there is too much misery but there is also too much money, and wealth doesn't know what to do with itself. In other times, finance capital broadened the consumer market by extending credit. It served the real economy, which to exist needed to grow. Today, utterly bloated, finance capital has put the productive system to work for it, while it plays with the real economy like a cat with a mouse.

Every crash on the stock exchange is a catastrophe for small investors who swallowed the line and bet their savings on the financial lottery. And it's a catastrophe for the poorest barrios of the global village, whose residents suffer the consequences without ever knowing what caused them: in a single blow each "market correction" empties their plates and wipes out their jobs. But rarely do crises on the stock exchange fatally wound the suffering millionaires who, day after day, backs bent over their computers, fingertips calloused from the keyboards, redistribute the world's wealth by moving money, setting interest rates, and deciding the value of labor, commodities, and currencies. They are the only workers who could refute the anonymous scribe who wrote on a wall in Montevideo: "He who works has no time to make money."

LESSONS FOR
RESISTING USELESS VICES

Unemployment sends the crime rate soaring and humiliating wages spike it higher still. Never has the old Spanish proverb been so apt: "The hustler lives from the fool, and the fool from his work." In contrast, no one says, "Work hard and you shall prosper," because no one believes it anymore.

Labor rights have come down to the right to work for whatever you can get under whatever conditions you can stand. Work is the most useless of vices. There is no commodity in the world cheaper than labor. While wages fall and hours rise, the labor market vomits up people. Take it or leave it—there's a long line behind you.

EMPLOYMENT AND UNEMPLOYMENT
IN THE TIME OF FEAR

The shadow of fear is nipping at your heels no matter how fast you go. Fear of losing your job, your money, your food, your home. No talisman can protect you from the curse of sudden bad luck. From one moment to the next, even the greatest winner can turn into a loser unworthy of forgiveness or compassion.

Who is safe from the terror of unemployment? Who doesn't fear being shipwrecked by new technologies or by globalization or any other of the many storms whipping today's world? The waves pound furiously: the ruin or flight of local industries, competition with cheap labor from other latitudes, the implacable advance of machines that need no salary or vacation or bonus or pension or severance pay or anything but the electricity that feeds them.

The development of technology leads not to more free time or freedom, only to more unemployment and fear. Panic at the specter of the pink slip is universal: We're sorry to inform you that due to the new budget policy we must make do without your services. Or simply that's the way it is, without any euphemism to ease the blow. Anyone can get shot down anytime, anywhere. At forty, anyone can become old from one day to the next.

In a report on conditions in 1996 and 1997, the International Labor Organization says, "The evolution of employment in the world continues to be discouraging." In industrialized countries, unemployment remains high and contributes to increasing social inequality, and in so-called developing countries, both unemployment and poverty have risen spectacularly. "That's what spreads fear," the report concludes. And fear does spread: you have a job or you have nothing. At the entrance to Auschwitz the sign said: "Work Shall Make You Free." A little more than half a century later, any worker with a job should thank the company for its kindness in allowing him or her to carry on day after backbreaking day, fodder for the tedium of office or factory life. To find a job, or hang on to one, even if it comes without vacation or pension or any benefits at all and even if the pay stinks, is celebrated as if it were a miracle.

Famous Words

On November 28, 1990, the Argentine papers published a pearl of wisdom from a union leader now in political office. This is how Luis Barrionuevo explained his sudden fortune: "You don't make money by working."

When charges of fraud rained down on him, his friends offered him a testimonial dinner. Later on, he was elected president of a first-division soccer club, and throughout it all he remained at the helm of the food service workers' union.

Saint Cajetan, patron saint of the unemployed, is the most popular saint in Argentina. Crowds come to him begging for work. No other saint, male or female, has such a large clientele. Between May and October 1997, when new jobs suddenly appeared paying two hundred dollars a month, many wondered who was responsible, Saint Cajetan or democracy. With legislative elections on the horizon, the Argentine government astonished the saint by handing out half a million jobs right and left. But they didn't last much beyond the campaign. Some time later, President Menem suggested that Argentines take up golf, because it's relaxing and keeps your mind off your troubles.

The number of unemployed keeps on growing. The world has more and more surplus people. What will the owners of the planet do with so much useless humanity? Send them to the moon? At the beginning of 1998, huge demonstrations in France, Germany,

Italy, and other European countries made headlines around the globe. Some of the marchers acted out the drama of labor in today's world and wore black plastic garbage bags. In Europe there may still be insurance to ease the fate of the unemployed, but the fact remains that even there one young person in every four cannot find a steady job. Work under the table and outside the law has tripled in Europe over the past quarter century. In Great Britain there are more and more stay-at-home workers, always available, who don't earn a thing until that telephone rings. Then they work for a while for an employment agency and go back home to wait for the phone to ring again.

Globalization is a magic galleon that spirits factories away to poor countries. Technology, so dizzying in its ability to reduce the labor time needed to produce anything, impoverishes and oppresses workers instead of liberating them from need and servitude. And labor is no longer necessary for making money. No need to transform raw materials, no need to lay a finger on them, since money is more fertile when it makes love to itself. Siemens, one of the largest industrial companies in the world, earns more from its financial investments than from its productive activities.

In the United States, there is a lot less unemployment than in Europe, but new jobs are temporary, poorly paid, and without benefits. "I see it in my students," says Noam Chomsky. "They're afraid that if they don't behave themselves they'll never get a job, and that has a disciplinary effect on them." At the five hundred largest U.S. companies, only one worker in ten has the privilege of a permanent, full-time job. In Great Britain, nine of every ten new jobs are temporary; in France, eight of every ten. History is leaping two centuries, but backwards: most workers in today's world have neither job stability nor the right to severance, and job insecurity drives wages down. Six out of every ten North Americans are earning less than they did a quarter century ago, even though the U.S. economy has grown 40 percent over the past twenty-five years.

Despite this, thousands and thousands of Mexican braceros, the "wetbacks," continue crossing the river that marks the border, risking their hides in search of a better life. In a couple of decades the ratio of U.S. to Mexican wages has doubled. The U.S. average used to be four times the Mexican; now it's eight. As is well known by those whose investments migrate south in search of cheap labor, and the cheap labor that tries to migrate north, in Mexico work is the only commodity whose price goes down every month. Over the past twenty years, a good part of the middle class has fallen into poverty, the poor have fallen into misery, and the miserable have fallen off the charts. The law guarantees job stability for those who have jobs, but in reality it depends on the Virgin of Guadalupe.

Along with unemployment, job insecurity is the principal factor underlying the decline in pay, and it's as common as the flu. No

one is safe. Not even skilled workers in the most sophisticated and dynamic sectors of the world economy can breathe easy. There, too, contracting and piecework are rapidly replacing steady jobs. In telecommunications and electronics, "virtual companies" already operate with only a handful of employees. Tasks are carried out from computer to computer. Workers never meet one another or their employers, those fugitive ghosts who owe obedience to the laws of no nation. Highly skilled professionals—the poster children you see in magazines that praise the miracles of technology in an era of universal happiness—are condemned to uncertainty and job instability just like any poor kid, even though they earn much more.

Fear of losing your job and terror at the prospect of never finding one can't be separated from a ridiculous statistic that could only seem normal in a world gone mad: over the past thirty years, formal working hours, which tend to be less than real hours worked, have *gone up* significantly in the United States, Canada, and Japan and diminished only slightly in a few European countries. This trend constitutes a treacherous attack on common sense by the upside-down world: the astonishing increase in productivity wrought by the technological revolution not only fails to raise wages but doesn't even diminish working hours in countries with state-of-the-art machines. In the United States, frequent polls indicate that work, far more than divorce or the fear of death, is the principal source of stress, and in Japan *karoshi,* overwork, kills ten thousand people a year.

When the French government decided in May 1998 to reduce the workweek from thirty-nine to thirty-five hours, offering a basic lesson in common sense, the measure set off cries of protest from businessmen, politicians, and technocrats. In Switzerland, where

Capitalist Realism

Lee Iacocca, once a star executive at Chrysler Corporation, visited Buenos Aires at the end of 1993. At a press conference he spoke with admirable sincerity about unemployment and education: "The problem of unemployment is a tough one. Today we can make twice as many cars with the same number of people. When they talk about improving people's educational levels as a solution to the problem of unemployment, I'm always bothered by the memory of what happened in Germany. Education was put forward as the solution to unemployment, and the result was hundreds of thousands of frustrated professionals who then turned to socialism and rebellion. It's not easy for me to admit, but I wonder if it wouldn't be better for the unemployed to smarten up and go straight to McDonald's to find a job."

unemployment is not a problem, I witnessed an event some time ago that left me dumbfounded. A referendum was held on reducing working hours with no reduction in pay, and the Swiss voted the proposal down. I recall that I could not comprehend the result at the time. I confess I still don't. Work has been a universal obligation ever since God sentenced Adam to earn his daily bread by the sweat of his brow, but we don't have to take God's will so literally. I suspect that this urge to work has something to do with fear of unemployment—though in Switzerland unemployment is an abstract threat—and with fear of free time. To be is to be useful; to be you have to be salable. Time that isn't money, free time lived for the pleasure of living and not dutifully in order to produce, provokes fear. There's nothing new about that. Along with greed, fear has always been the most active engine of the system that used to be called capitalism.

Fear of unemployment allows a mockery to be made of labor rights. The eight-hour day no longer belongs to the realm of law but to literature, where it shines among other works of surrealist poetry. And such things as employer contributions to pensions, medical benefits, workers' compensation, vacation pay, Christmas bonuses, and dependents' allowances are relics that belong in an archeological museum. Legally consecrated universal labor rights came about in other times, born of other fears: the fear of strikes and of the social revolution that seemed so close at hand. The powerful who trembled in fear yesterday are the powerful who strike fear today, and thus the fruits of two centuries of labor struggle get raffled off before you can say good-bye.

Fear, father of a large family, also begets hatred. In the countries of the North, it tends to cause hatred of foreigners who offer their labor at desperate prices. It's the invasion of the invaded. They come from lands where conquering colonial troops and punishing military expeditions have disembarked a thousand and one times. Now this voyage in reverse isn't made by soldiers obliged to kill but by workers obliged to sell themselves in Europe or North America at whatever price they can get. They come from Africa, Asia, and Latin America and, since the burial of bureaucratic power, from Eastern Europe as well.

In the years of the great European and North American economic expansion, growing prosperity required more and more labor, and it didn't matter that those hands were foreign, as long as

Statistics

In the British Isles, one out of every four jobs is part-time. And many are so part-time that it's hard to say why they're called jobs. To massage the numbers, as the English say, the authorities changed the statistical criteria for unemployment thirty-two times between 1979 and 1997 until they hit on the perfect formula: anyone who worked more than one hour a week was not unemployed. Not to boast, but that's how we've measured unemployment in Uruguay for as long as I can remember.

they worked hard and charged little. In years of stagnation or weak growth, they become undesirable interlopers: they smell bad, they make a lot of noise, they take away jobs. Scapegoats of unemployment and every other misfortune, they are condemned to live with several swords hanging over their heads: the always imminent threat of deportation back to the grueling life they've fled and the always possible explosion of racism with its bloody warnings, its punishments: Turks set on fire, Arabs stabbed, Africans shot, Mexicans beaten. Poor immigrants do the hardest, poorest-paid work in the fields and on the streets. After work comes the danger. No magic ink can make them invisible.

Paradoxically, while workers from the South migrate north, or at least risk the attempt against all odds, many factories from the North migrate south. Money and people pass each other in the night. Money from rich countries travels to poor countries, attracted by dollar-a-day wages and twenty-five-hour days, and workers from poor countries travel, or try to travel, to rich countries, attracted by images of happiness served up by advertising or invented by hope. Wherever money travels, it's greeted with kisses and flowers and fanfares. Workers, in contrast, set off on an odyssey that sometimes ends in the depths of the Mediterranean or the Caribbean or on the stony shores of the Rio Grande.

In another epoch, when Rome took over the entire Mediterranean and more, its armies returned home dragging caravans filled with enslaved prisoners of war. The hunt for slaves impoverished free workers. The more slaves there were in Rome, the more wages fell and the more difficult it was to find work. Two thousand years later, Argentine businessman Enrique Pescarmona praised globalization: "Asians work twenty hours a day," he declared, "for eighty dollars a month. If I want to compete, I have to turn to them. It's a globalized world. The Filipino girls in our offices in Hong Kong are always willing. There are no Saturdays or Sundays. If they have to work several days straight without sleeping, they do it, and they don't get overtime and don't ask for a thing."

A few months before Pescarmona voiced this elegy, a doll factory caught fire in Bangkok. The workers, women who earned less than a dollar a day and ate and slept in the factory, were burned alive. The factory was locked from the outside, like the slave quarters of old.

Many industries emigrate to poor countries in search of cheap labor, and there's plenty to be had. Governments welcome them as messiahs of progress bringing jobs on a silver tray. But the conditions of the new industrial proletariat bring to mind the word they used for work during the Renaissance, *tripalium,* which was also an instrument of torture. The price of a Disney T-shirt bearing a picture of Pocahontas is equivalent to a week's wages for the worker in Haiti who sewed it at a rate of 375 T-shirts an hour. Haiti was the first country in the world to abolish slavery. Two centuries after that feat, which cost many lives, the country suffers wage slavery. McDonald's gives its young customers toys made in Vietnamese sweatshops by women who earn eighty cents for a ten-hour shift with no breaks. Vietnam defeated a U.S. military invasion. A quarter of a century after that feat, which cost many lives, the country suffers globalized humiliation.

The hunt for cheap labor no longer requires armies as it did during colonial times. That's all taken care of by the misery that most of the planet suffers. What we have is the end of geogra-

---

Law and Reality

Gérard Filoche, a Paris labor inspector, proved that a thief who steals a car radio gets a longer sentence than a businessman who causes the death of a worker through an avoidable workplace accident.

Filoche knows from experience that many French companies that evade health and safety regulations also lie about wages, hours, and seniority. "Employees have to keep their mouths shut," he says, "because they live with the knife of unemployment at their throats."

For every million violations found by labor inspectors in France, only thirteen thousand end in conviction. In nearly all those cases, the sentence is a tiny fine.

phy: capital crosses borders at the speed of light thanks to new communication and transportation technologies that make time and distance disappear. And when an economy anywhere on the planet catches a cold, economies around the world sneeze. At the end of 1997, a currency devaluation in Malaysia killed thousands of jobs in the shoe industry in southern Brazil.

Poor countries have put their heart, soul, and sombrero into a global good-behavior contest to see who can offer the barest of bare-bones wages and the most freedom to poison the environment. Countries compete furiously to seduce the big multinational companies. What's best for companies is what's worst for wage levels, working conditions, and the well-being of people and of nature. Throughout the world, workers' rights are in a race to the bottom, while the pool of available labor grows as never before, even in the worst of times.

Globalization has winners and losers, warns a United Nations report. "A rising tide of wealth is supposed to lift all boats, but some are more seaworthy than others. The yachts and ocean liners are rising in response to new opportunities, but many rafts and rowboats are taking on water—and some are sinking."

Countries tremble at the thought that money will not come or that it will flee. Shipwreck or the threat of it causes widespread panic. If you don't behave yourselves, say the companies, we're going to the Philippines or Thailand or Indonesia or China or Mars. To behave badly means to defend nature or whatever's left of it, to recognize the right to form unions, to demand respect for international norms and local laws, to raise the minimum wage.

In 1995, the Gap sold shirts "made in El Salvador." For every twenty-dollar shirt the Salvadoran workers got eighteen cents. The workers, most of them women and girls, spent fourteen hours a day breaking their backs in sweatshop hell. They organized a union. The contracting company fired 350 of them; the rest went on strike. There were police beatings, kidnappings, jailings. At the end of that year, the Gap announced that it was moving to Asia.

Thanks to the new global reality, the "informal sector" of the economy in Latin America has mushroomed. The "informal sector," which translated into English means work outside the law, generates eighty-five of every hundred new jobs. Workers outside the law put in more hours, earn less, get no benefits, and are not covered by labor legislation won through long, hard years of union struggle. Not that the situation of legal workers is much better: "deregulation" and "liberalization" are the euphemisms used to describe a situation of every man for himself. The elderly Paraguayan woman who told me about her pension summed it up succinctly: "If this is the reward, imagine the punishment!"

Jorge Bermúdez has three children and three jobs. At dawn he heads out to scour the streets of Quito in an old Chevrolet that passes for a cab. From early in the afternoon he teaches English. He has been a public school teacher for sixteen years and earns $150 a month. When the day ends at the public school, it begins at a private school where he works until midnight. Jorge Bermúdez never gets a day off. For a long time he has suffered from stomach trouble, moodiness, and insomnia. A psychologist told him they were psychosomatic symptoms caused by working too hard and suggested he give up two of his three jobs. The psychologist did not explain how he could pay the bills.

In the upside-down world, education does not pay. Public school teachers in Latin America have been among the hardest-hit

Exemplary Lives/3

The middle of 1998 unleashed a whirlwind of popular indignation against the dictatorship of General Suharto in Indonesia. So the International Monetary Fund thanked him for his services and the general retired.

His working life had begun in 1965 when he took power by killing half a million Communists or alleged Communists. In the end he had no choice but to leave the government, but he hung on to the savings he managed to set aside during his more than thirty years of labor: $16 billion, according to the July 28, 1997, issue of *Forbes* magazine.

A couple of months after Suharto's retirement, his successor, President Habibie, made a televised speech: he called for fasting. The president said that if the Indonesian people refrained from eating two days a week, Mondays and Thursdays, the economic crisis could be overcome.

by the new labor regime. Teachers and professors earn praise: hackneyed speeches exalt the stoic efforts of the apostles of education who lovingly mold the clay of the next generation. And they earn salaries you can't see without a magnifying glass. The World Bank calls education "an investment in human capital," which, from their point of view, is homage. But in a recent report they suggested reducing teachers' pay in countries where "the supply of teachers" would allow for it without lowering the level of instruction.

By the Grace of God

At the end of 1993, I attended the funeral of a beautiful trade school that had existed for three years in Santiago, Chile. The students came from the poorest slums of the city, kids condemned to be delinquents, beggars, or whores. The school taught them trades like ironwork, carpentry, and gardening; above all, it taught them to love themselves and to love what they were doing. For the first time they heard people say that they were worth something and that doing what they were learning to do was worth something. The school depended on foreign financing. When the money ran out the teachers turned to the government. They went to the ministry and got nothing. They went to city hall and the mayor suggested, "Turn it into a business."

Reduce pay? What pay? "Poor but docent," we say in Uruguay, or, "I'm hungrier than a schoolteacher." University professors are in the same boat. In the middle of 1995 I saw a job posting in the papers for the School of Psychology at the university in Montevideo. They were looking for someone to teach ethics and were offering a hundred dollars a month. I could only think that you'd have to be a magician at ethics not to be corrupted by such a fortune.

Advantages

At the end of 1997, Leonardo Moledo published an article defending the low salaries paid in Argentina's universities. This professor argued that meager wages contribute to general culture, encourage diversity and the spread of knowledge, and help prevent the problem of overspecialization. Thanks to his puny salary, a professor who in the morning teaches brain surgery can enrich his own culture and the culture of everyone else by making photocopies in the afternoon and showing off his talent on the circus trapeze at night. A specialist in German literature has the stupendous opportunity to run a pizza oven and also be an usher at the Columbia theater. The dean of criminal law can enjoy the luxury of driving a delivery truck from Monday to Friday and working as a security guard on the weekends. And an adjunct in molecular biology can make use of his training by fixing plumbing and painting cars.

Robbery is no less of a crime simply because it
was committed in the name of laws or emperors.
—SENATOR JAMES ALEXANDER MCDOUGALL
OF CALIFORNIA, 1861

MASTER CLASS ON IMPUNITY

- Case Studies
- Hunters of People
- Exterminators of the Planet
- The Sacred Car

CASE STUDIES

There is no doubt about the educational value of these examples. Here we will examine the illuminating experience of the oil industry, whose love of nature is rivaled only by that of the Impressionist painters. We will recount episodes that illustrate the philanthropic vocation of the military and chemical industries. And we will reveal the keys to success that placed the industry of crime in the vanguard of the world economy.

THE HANGED WRITER

Shell and Chevron have destroyed the Niger River delta. Author Ken Saro-Wiwa, of the Ogoni people of Nigeria, wrote: "What Shell and Chevron have done to Ogoni people, land, streams, creeks and the atmosphere amounts to genocide. The soul of the Ogoni people is dying and I am witness to the fact."

At the beginning of 1995, Shell's general manager in Nigeria, Naemeka Achebe, explained why his company supported the military government: "For a commercial company trying to make investments, you need a stable environment. . . . Dictatorships can give you that." A few months later, the dictatorship hanged Ken

Saro-Wiwa along with eight other Ogonis for resisting the companies that were destroying their villages and turning their country
into a vast wasteland. Many Ogonis had already been murdered
for the same reason.

Saro-Wiwa's prestige gave this crime a certain international res-
onance. The president of the United States announced that his
country would suspend arms sales to Nigeria and the world
applauded. The announcement wasn't intended as a confession,
but that's what it was: the president acknowledged that his country
had been selling weapons to the bloody regime of General Sani
Abacha, responsible for executing a hundred people a year by firing squad or hanging in what had become public spectacles.

An international embargo blocked new arms deals with
Nigeria, but the Abacha dictatorship continued adding to its arsenal thanks to "addenda" that appeared miraculously on previously
signed contracts. After a dip in this convenient fountain of youth,
those old contracts lived on forever.

The United States sells about half the weapons in the world
and buys about half the oil it consumes. Its economy and lifestyle
depend to a large degree on arms and oil. Nigeria, the African

dictatorship with the largest military budget, is an oil country. The Anglo-Dutch consortium Shell takes half that oil, and the U.S. company Chevron takes most of the rest. Chevron operates in twenty-two countries, but more than a quarter of all the oil and gas it pumps comes from Nigeria.

THE PRICE OF POISON

Nnimmo Bassey visited the Americas in 1996, a year after his friend and companion in the Ogoni struggle was murdered. In his travel diary, he recounts some telling stories about the giant oil companies and their contribution to public well-being.

Curaçao is an island in the Caribbean, so named, they say, because its breezes cure the sick. Shell built a huge refinery there in 1918 and has been showering poison on that little island of health ever since. In 1983, local authorities ordered the refinery shut down. Experts calculated the company owed a minimum of $400 million in recompense for damages to the environment, not counting damages to the inhabitants.

Shell didn't pay a cent. It bought impunity for a fairy-tale price: Shell sold the refinery to the government of Curaçao, *for one dollar,* in an agreement that freed the company from all responsibility for damages inflicted on the environment at any time throughout history.

THE BLUE BUTTERFLY

In 1994, Chevron, formerly Standard Oil of California, spent many millions of dollars on an advertising campaign praising its tireless efforts to protect the environment in the United States. The campaign focused on a sanctuary the company built for certain blue butterflies in danger of extinction. The sanctuary costs Chevron five thousand dollars a year. Every minute of the advertising blitz that congratulated the company for its ecological conscience cost eighty times that sum to produce and much more than that to actually flutter its blue wings across the TV screens of North America.

The butterfly spa was set up next to the El Segundo refinery on the sands south of Los Angeles. The refinery remains one of the worst sources of water, air, and land pollution in all of California.

THE BLUE STONE

Goiânia City, Brazil, September 1987: two ragpickers find a metal tube in an empty lot. They break it open and discover a stone of blue light, a magic stone that turns the air blue and makes everything it touches shine. The ragpickers break up that stone of light. They give pieces to their neighbors. Whoever rubs it on his skin shines in the night. The entire barrio is a lamp. The poor, suddenly rich in light, celebrate.

The next day the ragpickers start vomiting. They had eaten mango with coconut—that must be why. But the whole neighborhood is vomiting and swelling up and itching. The blue light burns and devours and kills, and it spreads, carried by wind, rain, flies, and birds.

It was one of the greatest nuclear catastrophes in history. Many people died and many more were maimed for life. In that shantytown on the edge of Goiânia, no one knew what the word "radioactivity" meant, and no one had ever heard of Cesium-137. Chernobyl, just the year before, resounded daily in the ears of the world. Of Goiânia, not a word. In 1992, Cuba took in the sick children of Goiânia and gave them free medical care. This event did not merit the slightest coverage either, even though the global factories of public opinion are always, as we know, very concerned about Cuba.

A month after the tragedy, the chief of the federal police in Goiás summed it up: "The situation is absurd. No one is responsible for the radioactive substances used in medicine."

BUILDINGS WITHOUT FEET

Mexico City, September 1985: the earth trembles. A thousand houses and buildings tumble in less than three minutes.

It isn't known, and never will be, how many people died in that moment of horror in the largest and most fragile city in the world. When they first started digging through the rubble, the Mexican government said five thousand. Later on it said nothing. The first bodies recovered carpeted an entire baseball stadium.

Old buildings withstood the earthquake, but new ones fell as if they had no foundations, *because many of them had none* or they had them only in the blueprints. Years have passed and those responsible remain untouched. The developers who built and sold those modern sand castles, the officials who issued permits for skyscrapers in the most sunken parts of the city, the engineers who lied murderously when calculating the foundations and the load, the inspectors who got rich by looking the other way—all of them remain untouched.

The rubble is gone, new buildings have arisen on the ruins, the city keeps on growing.

GREEN, I WANT YOU GREEN

The earth's most successful companies have offices in hell and in heaven too. The more they sell in one, the better they do in the other. The Devil pays and God forgives.

According to World Bank projections, by the year 2000 the environmental industry will be making more money than the chemical industry, and it already makes a bundle. Saving the environment is turning out to be the most brilliant enterprise of the very companies that are destroying it.

In a recent book, *The Corporate Planet,* Joshua Karliner offers three telling examples, well worth studying:

- ◄ General Electric, which owns four of the companies that most poison the air, is the largest U.S. producer of equipment for air pollution control
- ◄ Du Pont Chemical Company, one of the largest producers of toxic waste in the world, has developed a lucrative line of specialized services for incineration and disposal of toxic waste
- ◄ and another multinational giant, Westinghouse, which earns its keep selling nuclear weapons, also sells millions of dollars' worth of equipment to clean up its own radioactive waste.

SIN AND VIRTUE

There are over a hundred million antipersonnel mines spread throughout the world. These artifacts keep exploding years after wars are over. Some mines, shaped like dolls or butterflies or colorful trinkets, are designed to attract children. Of all the victims, half are children.

Paul Donovan, one of the promoters of the global campaign to ban land mines, points out that a new goose is laying golden eggs in the very same arms factories that made and sold mines. These companies now offer their expertise to clean up the vast terrains that have been mined, and it doesn't take a genius to realize that no one knows the business as well as they do. What a deal: removing the mines turns out to be a hundred times more lucrative than placing them.

Until 1991, a company called CMS made mines for the U.S. Army. After the Gulf war it changed tack and has been making $160 million a year in de-mining ever since. CMS belongs to the German consortium Daimler-Benz, which makes missiles with the same enthusiasm that it makes cars, and it continues making mines through another of its affiliates, a company called Messerschmitt-Bölkow-Blohm.

Also traveling the road to redemption is British Aerospace: one of its companies, Royal Ordnance, signed a $90 million contract to remove mines from Kuwait, placed there, coincidentally, by Royal Ordnance. Competing in this selfless task is a French company, Sofremi, which will earn $110 million de-mining Kuwait, while continuing to export weapons for wars throughout the world.

One of the angels carrying out this humanitarian mission on earth with the greatest fervor is a South African specialist named Vernon Joynt, who has spent his life designing antipersonnel mines and other deadly contraptions. This man is in charge of clearing Mozambique and Angola of the thousands of mines he invented for the racist army of South Africa. His task is sponsored by the United Nations.

CRIME AND REWARD

General Augusto Pinochet raped, tortured, murdered, robbed, and lied.

He violated the constitution he had pledged to respect. He was the strongman of a dictatorship that tortured and murdered thousands of Chileans. He sent tanks into the streets to discourage the curiosity of those who wanted to investigate his crimes. And he lied every time he opened his mouth to talk about these things.

Once the dictatorship was over, Pinochet stayed on as head of the army. And in 1998, when he was to retire, he stepped onto the country's civilian stage. As I write these lines, he has, by his own order, become a senator for life. Protest has erupted in the streets, but the buoyant general, deaf to anything but the military hymn praising his achievements, proceeds to take his seat in the Senate. He has plenty of reason to turn a deaf ear: after all, the day of the 1973 coup d'état that ended Chile's democracy, September 11, was celebrated as a national holiday for a quarter of a century, and September 11 is still the name of one of downtown Santiago's main thoroughfares.

CRIME AND PUNISHMENT

In the middle of 1978, while Argentina's soccer team was hosting and winning the World Cup, the country's military dictatorship

was busy throwing prisoners into the ocean *alive.* The planes bearing them took off from Aeroparque airport, a stone's throw from the stadium where the sports event was under way.

Not many people are born with a conscience, that inconvenient gland that haunts your nights and disturbs your sleep worse than the mosquitoes of summer. But sometimes it happens. When Captain Adolfo Scilingo told his superiors he couldn't sleep without pills or drink, they recommended therapy. At the beginning of 1995, Captain Scilingo decided to make a public confession: he said he had thrown thirty people into the sea. Over the course of two years, he added, the Argentine Navy had thrown between fifteen hundred and two thousand political prisoners to the sharks.

After his confession, Scilingo was imprisoned. Not for having murdered thirty people but for having passed a bad check.

CRIME AND SILENCE

On September 20, 1996, the U.S. Defense Department also made a public confession. The story earned little or no coverage from the major news media. That day, the highest military authorities acknowledged that they had made "a mistake": from 1982 to 1991, they had trained Latin American military officers in the arts of threat, extortion, torture, kidnapping, and murder at the School of the Americas in Fort Benning, Georgia, and at the Southern Command in Panama. The "mistake" lasted a decade, but they didn't say how many Latin American officers received the mistaken training or what the consequences had been.

In reality, the Pentagon's classes for future dictators, torturers, and criminals have been denounced a thousand times in the past half century. Their Latin American students numbered some sixty thousand. Many of these same students became dictators or public executioners and left a permanent bloodstain south of the Rio Grande. To cite just one country, El Salvador, and to offer no more than a few examples from an endless list, nearly all the officers responsible for the assassinations of the archbishop, Monsignor Oscar Arnulfo Romero, and four U.S. nuns were graduates of the School of the Americas. So were those who carried out the murders of six Jesuit priests riddled with bullets in 1989.

The Pentagon has always refused to collect author's royalties on the training manuals it finally acknowledged as its own. The confession ought to have been a big story, but few heard it and many fewer were angered: the greatest power in the world, the model, the democracy that inspires the most envy and imitation, acknowledged that its military nurseries had been growing specialists in the violation of human rights.

In 1996, the Pentagon promised to correct the "mistake" with the same seriousness as it had made it. At the beginning of 1998, twenty-two culprits were indeed found guilty and sentenced to six months in jail plus fines. These twenty-two U.S. citizens had committed the atrocity of sneaking into Fort Benning to hold a funeral procession in memory of the victims of the School of the Americas.

CRIME AND ECHOES

In 1995, two Latin American countries, Guatemala and Chile, attracted the attention of the U.S. press, something not at all common.

It came out that a Guatemalan colonel accused of two crimes had for many years been on the CIA payroll. The colonel was charged with the murder of *a U.S. citizen and the husband of a U.S. citizen*. The press ignored the thousands upon thousands of other crimes committed by the military dictatorships the United States had imposed and removed in Guatemala ever since the day in 1954 when the CIA, with the approval of President Eisenhower, overthrew the democratic government of Jacobo Arbenz. The long cycle of horror reached its peak in the massacres of the 1980s. That's when soldiers who brought back a pair of ears were given a necklace with a golden oak leaf as a reward. But the victims of that over-forty-year process—the greatest number of deaths in the second half of the twentieth century anywhere in the Americas—were Guatemalans, and to top off their unimportance, most of them were Indians.

While the story of the Guatemalan colonel was breaking, the U.S. papers reported that two high officials of the Pinochet dictatorship had been sentenced to prison in Chile. The assassination of Orlando Letelier constituted an exception to the norm of impunity in Latin America, but one particular detail caught the journalists' attention: the dictatorship had assassinated Letelier and his U.S. secretary *in Washington, D.C.* What would have happened if he had been killed in Santiago or any other Latin American city? Of the death of Chilean general Carlos Prats, murdered with his Chilean wife in Buenos Aires in an attack identical to the one that killed Letelier, we've still had no news twenty years after the fact.

HUNTERS OF PEOPLE

N ote to criminals starting out: to murder timidly won't do. Like business, crime pays, but only when it's done on a grand scale. The top brass who gave the orders to kill so many people in Latin America are not in jail for murder, even though their service records would make gangsters blush and criminologists go bug-eyed.

We are all equal under the law. Under what law? Divine law? Under earthly law, equality grows less equal every day and everywhere, because power usually sinks its weight onto only one tray on the scales of justice.

OBLIGATORY AMNESIA

Inequality before the law lies at the root of real history, but official history is written by oblivion, not memory. We know all about this in Latin America, where exterminators of Indians and traffickers in slaves have their statues in city plazas, while streets and avenues tend to bear the names of those who stole the land and looted the public purse.

Like the buildings in Mexico City that came tumbling down in the 1985 earthquake, Latin America's democracies have been robbed of their foundations. Only justice could give them a solid base from which to stand up and start walking; instead, we have obligatory amnesia. As a rule, civilian governments are limited to administering injustice and dashing hopes for change in countries where political democracy keeps crashing into the walls erected by economic and social structures that are democracy's enemy.

In the sixties and seventies, Latin America's military leaders took power by assault. To put an end to political corruption, they stole much more than the politicians, an achievement made possible only because they exercised absolute power and started work each day at reveille. Years of blood and dirt and fear: to put an end to the violence of local guerrillas and international red phantoms, the armed forces tortured, raped, or murdered as many people as they could get their hands on, in a vast manhunt that punished every expression of the human desire for justice, no matter how inoffensive.

The Uruguayan dictatorship tortured a lot and killed little. The Argentine one, in contrast, practiced extermination. Despite their differences, the many Latin American dictatorships of those years worked together and were quite similar, as if cut by the same shears. What shears? In the middle of 1998, Vice Admiral Eladio Moll, once chief of intelligence for the Uruguayan military regime, revealed that U.S. advisers had encouraged the regime to eliminate subversives after extracting whatever information it could from them. The vice admiral was arrested—for the crime of candor.

A few months before that, Captain Alfredo Astiz, one of the Argentine dictatorship's chief slaughterers, was demoted for telling the truth: he declared that the navy had trained him to do what he had done and, in a flight of professional arrogance, added

The Devil Was Hungry

El Familiar is a black dog that breathes fire from his nose and ears. At night his fires roam the cane fields of northern Argentina. El Familiar works for the Devil, giving him rebel flesh to eat, keeping watch on and punishing the peons of sugar. Its victims leave this world without saying good-bye.

In the winter of 1976, under the military dictatorship, the Devil was hungry. On the night of the third Thursday in July, the army entered the Ledesma sugar refinery in Jujuy. The soldiers took away 150 workers. Thirty-three disappeared, never to be seen again.

that he was "technically the best prepared in this country to kill a politician or a journalist." At the time Astiz and other Argentinean officers had been charged or tried in several European countries for the murders of Spanish, Italian, French, and Swedish citizens, but the murders of thousands of Argentines had been pardoned by laws intended to wipe the slate clean.

The laws of impunity also seem cut by the same shears. Latin America's democracies were resuscitated only to be condemned to paying debts and forgetting crimes. It was as if the new civilian governments were thankful for the efforts of the men in uniform: military terror had created a favorable climate for foreign investment and paved the way for selling off countries at the price of bananas. It was under democracy that national sovereignty was fully abandoned, labor rights were betrayed, and public services were dismantled. All this was done, or rather undone, with relative ease. Accustomed to surviving amid lies and fear, the societies that recovered their civil rights in the eighties were drained of their best energies, as sick from discouragement as they were needy of the creative vitality that democracy promised but couldn't or didn't know how to deliver.

For the elected governments, justice meant vengeance and memory meant disorder, so they dribbled holy water on the foreheads of the men who had waged state terrorism. In the name of democratic stability and national reconciliation, they passed laws that deterred justice, interred the past, and preferred amnesia. Several of these went beyond even the most horrific precedents in other parts of the world. In its haste to absolve, Argentina's gov-

The Living Thought of Military Dictatorships

During the leaden years of late, Latin American generals managed to make their ideology heard despite the roar of machine guns, bombs, trumpets, and drums.

Carried away with bellicose exhilaration, Argentine general Ibérico Saint-Jean cried: "We are winning the third world war!"

Carried away with chronological exhilaration, his compatriot General Cristino Nicolaides shouted: "For two thousand years Marxism has threatened Western Christian civilization!"

Carried away with mystical exhilaration, Guatemalan general Efraín Ríos Montt bellowed: "The Holy Spirit runs our intelligence service!"

Carried away with scientific exhilaration, Uruguayan rear admiral Hugo Márquez roared: "We have turned the nation's history around by three hundred and sixty degrees!"

Celebrating that epic feat and carried away with anatomical exhilaration, Uruguayan politician Adauto Puñales thundered: "Communism is an octopus that has its head in Moscow and its testicles everywhere!"

ernment passed a "due obedience" law in 1987 (repealed a decade later when it was no longer needed), exonerating soldiers following orders from any responsibility for what they had done. Since there is no soldier who doesn't follow orders, whether from the sergeant, the captain, the general, or God, criminal responsibility ended up in heaven. The German military code that Hitler perfected in 1940 to serve his deliria was in fact more cautious: in article 47 it established that a subordinate was responsible for his acts, "if he knew that the superior's order referred to an action that was a common or military crime."

The rest of Latin America's laws were not as fervent as "due obedience," but they all agreed that civilians should bow to armed arrogance; mandated by fear, they placed massacres beyond the reach of justice and gave the order to sweep all the rubbish of recent history under the rug. Most Uruguayans supported impunity in the plebiscite of 1989, following a media blitzkrieg that threatened a return to violence: what triumphed was fear, which among other things is a source of law. Sometimes hidden, sometimes visible, fear feeds and justifies power throughout Latin America. And power has deeper roots and more lasting structures than the governments that come and go with each democratic election.

What is power? An Argentine businessman, Alfredo Yabrán, defined it unmistakably: "Power is impunity." He knew what he was talking about. Said to be the visible head of an omnipotent mafia, Yabrán started out selling ice cream on the street and ended up making a fortune for himself—or for who knows whom. Not long after he uttered that sentence, a judge issued a warrant for his arrest for the murder of photographer José Luis Cabezas. That marked the beginning of the end of his impunity, the beginning of the end of his power. Yabrán put a gun in his mouth and pulled the trigger.

Impunity is crime's reward, openly promoting and encouraging more of the same. And when the criminal who has raped, robbed, tortured, and murdered without answering to anyone happens to be the state, a green light is flashed to all of society to rape, rob, torture, and kill. The same society that uses punishment like a scarecrow to frighten criminals at the bottom rewards them at the top with a lifetime get-out-of-jail-free card.

Democracy pays the consequences. It's as if any murderer, smoking gun in hand, could ask: "Why should I be punished for killing one person, when those generals killed half the world and are walking the streets proud as can be? They're heroes in the barracks and on Sunday they take Communion."

Under democracy, Argentine dictator Jorge Rafael Videla took Communion in a church in the province of San Luis that refused entry to women in short sleeves or miniskirts. In the middle of 1998, he choked on the host: this pious fellow actually went to jail, though since he was a senior citizen he was soon granted house

Advertising

The Argentine military dictatorship had a habit of sending many of its victims to the bottom of the ocean. In April 1998, a brand of clothing called Diesel placed an ad in *Gente* magazine intended to prove that its pants would hold up to any number of washings. A photograph showed eight young men chained to cement blocks in the depths of the sea. The caption read: "They aren't your first jeans, but they could be your last. At least you'll make a lovely body."

Outlawed Memory

Bishop Juan Gerardi led a task force that rescued the recent history of terror in Guatemala. Bit by bit, through the testimonies of thousands of voices collected throughout the country, he and his colleagues gathered forty years of isolated memories of pain: 150,000 Guatemalans dead, 50,000 disappeared, 1,000,000 displaced refugees, 200,000 orphans, 40,000 widows. Nine out of every ten victims were unarmed civilians, most of them Indians. And in nine out of every ten cases, the responsibility lay with the army and its paramilitary bands.

The Church released the report on a Thursday in April 1998. Two days later, Bishop Gerardi was dead, his skull beaten in with a chunk of concrete.

arrest. It was enough to make you rub your eyes: the exemplary obstinacy of the mothers, grandmothers, and children of the victims had wrought a miracle, an exception, one of very few. Videla, murderer of thousands, was not punished for genocide, but at least he had to answer for the children born in the concentration camps and kidnapped by officers who took them home as war booty after killing their mothers.

Justice and memory are exotic luxuries in Latin America. The murderers of Uruguayan parliamentarians Zelmar Michelini and Héctor Gutiérrez Ruiz stroll calmly down the streets that bear the names of their victims. Forgetting, the powerful say, is the price of peace, and they impose on us a peace based on accepting injustice

Broken Memory

At the end of the eighteenth century, Napoleon's soldiers discovered that many Egyptian children believed the Pyramids had been built by the French or the English.

At the end of the twentieth century, many Japanese children believed the bombs that fell on Hiroshima and Nagasaki had been dropped by the Russians.

In 1965, the people of Santo Domingo resisted an invasion of forty-two thousand U.S. Marines for 132 nights. People fought house by house, hand to hand, with sticks and knives and carbines and stones and broken bottles. What will Dominican children believe a little while from now? The government celebrates this heroic resistance not as a Day of Dignity but as the Day of Brotherhood, placing an equal sign between those who kissed the hands of the invaders and those who bared their breasts to the tanks.

as an everyday norm. They've gotten us used to a peace in which life is scorned and remembering prohibited. The media and the schools don't do much to help us integrate reality and memory. Every fact appears divorced from the rest, divorced from its own past and the past of every other fact. Consumer culture, a culture of disconnectedness, trains us to believe things just happen. Incapable of recalling its origins, the present paints the future as a repetition of itself; tomorrow is just another name for today. The unequal organization of the world, which beggars the human con-

dition, is part of eternity, and injustice is a fact of life we have no choice but to accept.

Does history repeat itself? Or are its repetitions only penance for those who are incapable of listening to it? No history is mute. No matter how much they burn it, break it, and lie about it, human history refuses to shut its mouth. Despite deafness and ignorance, the time that was continues to tick inside the time that is. The right to remember does not figure among the human rights consecrated by the United Nations, but now more than ever we must insist on it and act on it. Not to repeat the past but to keep it from being repeated. Not to make us ventriloquists for the dead but to allow us to speak with voices that are not condemned to echo perpetually with stupidity and misfortune. When it's truly alive, memory doesn't contemplate history, it invites us to make it. More than in museums, where its poor old soul gets bored, memory is in the air we breathe, and from the air it breathes us.

To forget forgetting: the Spanish writer Don Ramón Gómez de la Serna tells a story of a fellow who had such a bad memory that one day he forgot he had a bad memory and remembered everything. To remember the past, to free us of its curse, not to tie the feet of the present but to help the present walk without falling into the same old traps. Up until a few centuries ago, the Spanish word for "remember" also meant "wake up," and it's still used in that sense in some rural parts of Latin America. A memory that's awake is contradictory, like us. It's never still, and it changes along with us. It was born to be not an anchor but a catapult. A port of departure, not of arrival. It doesn't turn away from nostalgia, but it prefers the dangers of hope. The Greeks believed memory was the sister of time and the sea, and they weren't wrong.

Impunity is the child of bad memory. All the dictatorships that have ever existed in Latin America have known this well. They've burned entire mountain ranges of books, books guilty of revealing an outlawed reality and books simply guilty of being books, and mountains of documents as well. Military officers, presidents, priests: the history of burnings is a long one, dating from 1562 in Maní de Yucatán when Father Diego de Landa threw Mayan books into the flames, hoping to reduce indigenous memory to ashes. To mention only a few bonfires: in 1870, when the armies of Argentina, Brazil, and Uruguay razed Paraguay, the historical archives of the vanquished were torched; twenty years later, the government of Brazil burned all the papers that testified to three and a half centuries of black slavery; in 1983, the Argentine brass set fire to all the records of their dirty war against their countrymen; and in 1995, the Guatemalan military did the same.

EXTERMINATORS OF THE PLANET

C rimes against people, crimes against nature: the impunity enjoyed by the masters of war is shared by their twins, the voracious masters of industry, who eat nature on earth and, in the heavens, swallow the ozone layer. The most successful companies in the world are the ones that do the most to murder it; the countries that decide the planet's fate are the same ones that do their best to annihilate it.

NO-RETURN PLANET

Effluence, affluence: inundating the world and the air it breathes are floods of crud and torrents of words—expert reports, speeches, government declarations, solemn international accords that no one observes, and other expressions of official concern for the environment. The language of power diverts blame from consumer society and from those who impose consumerism in the name of development. The large corporations who, in the name of freedom, make the planet sick and then sell it medicine and consolation can do what they please, while environmental experts, who reproduce like rabbits, wrap all problems in the bubble-wrap of ambiguity. The state of the world's health is disgusting, and official rhetoric extrapolates in order to absolve: "We are all responsible" is the lie technocrats offer and politicians repeat, meaning no one is responsible. Official palaver exhorts "the sacrifice of all," meaning screw those who always get screwed.

All of humanity pays the price for the ruin of the earth, the befouling of the air, the poisoning of the waters, the disruption of the climate, and the degradation of the earthly goods that nature bestows. But hidden underneath the cosmetic words, statistics confess and little numbers betray the truth: one-quarter of humanity commits three-quarters of the crimes against nature. Each inhabitant of the North consumes ten times as much energy, nineteen times as much aluminum, fourteen times as much paper, and thirteen times as much iron and steel as someone in the South. The average North American puts twenty-two times as much carbon into the air as an Indian and thirteen times as much as a Brazilian. It may be called "global suicide," but this daily act of murder is being perpetrated by the most prosperous members of the human species, who live in rich countries or imagine they do, members of countries and social classes who find their identity in ostentation and waste. The widespread adoption of such models of consumption faces a small impediment: *it would take ten planets the size of this one for poor countries to consume as much as rich ones do,* according to the well-documented Bruntland Report, presented to the World Commission on Environment and Development in 1987.

The giants of oil, the sorcerer's apprentices of nuclear energy and biotechnology, the large corporations that make weaponry, steel, aluminum, automobiles, pesticides, plastics, and a thousand other products like to shed crocodile tears over the suffering of nature. These companies, the most devastating on the planet, fig-

The Language of International Experts

In the context of evaluating the contributions made by reframing the projects currently under way, we will focus our analysis on three fundamental questions: the first, the second and the third. As can be deduced from the experience of those developing countries where some of the measures which are the object of our study have been put into practice, the first question has many points of coincidence with the third, and one or another of these appear to be intrinsically linked to the second, such that it could well be argued that the three questions are related to one another.

The first . . .

ure among those that make the most money. They also spend the most money—on advertising that magically turns pollution into philanthropy and on high-minded favors for politicians who decide the fates of countries or the world. Explaining why the United States refused to sign the Convention on Biodiversity at the Rio summit in 1992, President George Bush was unequivocal: "It is important to protect our rights, our business rights."

Whether he signed or not mattered little, because such international accords are worth less than a bounced check. The Rio summit was called to keep the planet from dying. But, with the exception of Germany (and even it acted only halfheartedly), none of the great powers kept the agreements they signed, for fear that their companies would lose their competitive edge and their governing politicians would lose elections. And the great power that complied least was precisely the most powerful of all, whose essential objectives were stated clearly in President Bush's confession.

The colossi of the chemical, oil, and automobile industries, so central to the theme of the Rio summit, paid a large portion of the cost of the conference. You can say anything you like about Al Capone, but he was a gentleman: good old Al always sent flowers to the funerals of his victims.

Five years later, the United Nations called another meeting to evaluate the impact of the Rio summit. In those five short years the planet's skin of vegetation had been stripped of its tropical flora over an area two and a half times the size of Italy, and fertile lands the size of Germany had turned arid. A total of 250,000 species of

Morgan

They don't have peg legs or eye patches, but bio-pirates are roaming the Amazon jungle and other tropical lands. They force their way on board, snatch the seeds, patent them, and turn them into successful commercial products.

Four hundred indigenous villages of the Amazon recently decried the seizure of a sacred plant, ayahuasca, "our equivalent," they said, "of the Christian host." At the U.S. Patent Office, International Plant Medicine Corporation patented ayahuasca for making psychiatric and cardiovascular medicine. From now on, ayahuasca is private property.

animals and plants had become extinct; the atmosphere was more polluted than ever; 1.3 billion people were without proper homes or food, and 25,000 were dying each day from drinking water contaminated by chemical poisons or industrial waste. Not long before, twenty-five hundred scientists from a broad array of countries, also called together by the United Nations, concluded that in the near future the planet will face the greatest climate changes in the last ten thousand years.

Those who suffer most from this punishment are, as usual, the poor—poor people and poor countries condemned to expiate the sins of others. Economist Lawrence Summers, with a doctorate from Harvard and a post high in the World Bank hierarchy, bore witness to this fact at the end of 1991. In an internal document leaked by mistake, Summers proposed that the World Bank encourage the migration of dirty industries and toxic waste "toward less developed countries," for reasons of economic logic that had to do with "the comparative advantages" those countries enjoy. Those advantages turned out to be three: pitiful wages, vast expanses where there's still lots of room for polluting, and the low incidence of cancer among the poor, who have a habit of dying young from other causes.

The publication of that document caused quite a furor: such things are to be done but not said. Summers imprudently set to paper what the world has been doing in practice for a long time. The South functions as the garbage can of the North. The factories that most pollute the environment migrate south, and the South is the dump where most of the industrial and nuclear shit the North generates ends up.

Sixteen centuries ago, Saint Ambrose, priest and doctor of the Church, prohibited usury among Christians and authorized it against barbarians. The same thing happens nowadays with the most lethal pollution. What's bad in the North is good in the South; what's outlawed in the North is welcome in the South. In the South lies the vast kingdom of impunity; there are no controls or legal limits and, when there are, it's never hard to discover their price. The complicity of local governments rarely comes free, and then there's the cost of waging advertising campaigns against the defenders of nature and human dignity, dismissing them as advocates of backwardness who only want to scare off foreign investment and sabotage economic development.

At the end of 1984, in the city of Bhopal, India, forty tons of deadly gas leaked from a pesticide factory run by the chemical company Union Carbide. The gas spread through the shantytowns, killing 6,600 people and harming another 70,000, many of whom died shortly thereafter or were maimed for life. Union Carbide in India did not abide by any of the security regulations it must adhere to in the United States.

In Latin America, Union Carbide and Dow Chemical, like the other giants of the world's chemical industry, sell many products that are outlawed in their own country. In Guatemala, for example, crop dusters spray the cotton plantations with pesticides that can't be sold in the United States or Europe. These poisons filter through the food chain into everything from honey to fish and finally reach the mouths of babes. As early as 1974, a study by the Central American Nutrition Institute found that the milk of many Guatemalan mothers contained up to two hundred times the pesticide limit considered dangerous.

Bayer, the world's second-largest producer of pesticides, has been untouchable since the days when it was part of the I. G. Farben consortium and used unpaid labor from Auschwitz. At the

Maps

In the United States, the environmental map is also a racial map. The most polluting factories and the most dangerous dumps are located in the pockets of poverty where blacks, Indians, and Latinos live.

The black community of Kennedy Heights in Houston, Texas, exists on land ruined by Gulf Oil's wastes. The residents of Convent, the Louisiana town where four of the dirtiest factories in the country operate, are nearly all black. Most of those who went to the emergency room in 1993, after General Chemical rained acid on the northern part of Richmond on San Francisco Bay, were black. A 1987 study by the United Church of Christ confirmed that the majority of the population living near hazardous waste dumps was black or Latino.

Indian reservations take in nuclear waste in exchange for money and the promise of jobs.

beginning of 1994, a Uruguayan environmental activist became a Bayer stockholder for a day. Thanks to the solidarity of German friends, Jorge Barreiro was able to raise his voice at an annual stockholders meeting graced with beer, sausage, mustard, and aspirins. Barreiro asked why the company sold toxic agricultural chemicals in Uruguay that were banned in Germany, three of which the World Health Organization considered "extremely dangerous" and another five "highly dangerous." The usual transpired. Every time someone raises the issue of selling in the South poisons prohibited in the North, the executives of Bayer and the other global chemical companies have the same answer: they aren't breaking any laws in the countries where they operate, which could be technically true, and besides, their products are not dangerous. They never explain the enigma of why these balms of nature can't be enjoyed by their own countrymen.

Maximum production, minimum cost, open markets, high profits—the rest is unimportant. Many U.S. industries had already set up shop on the Mexican side of the border long before the two countries signed a free-trade agreement. They turned the border zone into a vast industrial pigpen. All the treaty did was make it easier to take advantage of Mexico's abysmal wages and the freedom to poison its water, land, and air. To put it in the language of the poets of capitalist realism, *the treaty maximized opportunities to make use of the resources of comparative advantage.* Four years before the treaty, the waters near the Ford plant in Nuevo Laredo and the General Motors plant in Matamoros already contained thousands of times more toxins than the maximum allowed on the other side of the border. And in the vicinity of the Du Pont plant, also in Matamoros, the filth was such that people had to be evacuated.

Progress spreads across the globe. Japanese aluminum is made no longer in Japan but in Australia, Russia, and Brazil, where energy and labor are cheap and the environment suffers in silence. To provide electricity for the aluminum industry, Brazil has flooded gigantic tracts of tropical forest. No statistic can register the ecological cost of that sacrifice. After all, it's normal: Amazonian flora and fauna have suffered many sacrifices, mutilated day after day, year after year, in the service of lumber, cattle, and mining companies. Such organized devastation makes "the

Development

A bridge with no river.

A tall façade with no building.

A sprinkler on a plastic lawn.

An escalator to nowhere.

A highway to the places the highway destroyed.

An image on TV of a TV showing another TV on which there is yet another TV.

lungs of the earth" ever more vulnerable. The gigantic fire in 1998 that razed the forests of the Yanomami Indians in Roraima was not just the devilish work of El Niño.

Impunity is fed by fatality, and fatality obliges us to accept whatever orders are dictated by the international division of labor—like the fellow who jumped from the tenth floor to obey the law of gravity.

Colombia grows tulips for Holland and roses for Germany. Dutch companies send tulip bulbs and German companies send rose seedlings to immense plantations on the savannah of Bogotá. When the flowers are ready, Holland gets the tulips, Germany gets the roses, and Colombia gets low wages, damaged land, and poisoned water. Thanks to these floral arrangements of the industrial era, the savannah is drying out and sinking, while the workers, nearly all of them women and children, are bombarded by pesticides and chemical fertilizers.

The rich countries grouped in the Organization for Economic Cooperation and Development cooperate in economically developing the South by sending it radioactive garbage and other toxic expressions of kindness. The very countries that outlaw the importation of polluting substances shower them generously on poor countries. Just as with pesticides and herbicides banned at home, they export hazardous waste to the South under other names. The Basil Convention banned such shipments in 1992, yet there are more today than ever before. They come disguised as "humanitarian aid" or "contributions to development projects," as Greenpeace discovered on several occasions, or they come as contraband hidden inside mountains of legal industrial waste. Argentine law bans the entry of hazardous waste, but to solve that little problem all you need is a certificate of innocuousness issued in the country that wants to get rid of the waste. At the end of

Education

Near Stanford University I visited a smaller university that offers courses in obedience. The students, dogs of all races, colors, and sizes, learn to stop being dogs. When they bark, the professor punishes them by squeezing their snouts with her hand and yanking painfully on collars made of sharp steel points. When they remain quiet, the professor rewards their silence with treats. That is how she teaches them to forget how to bark.

1996, Brazilian ecologists managed to put an end to the importation of used car batteries from the United States that for years had come into the country as "recyclable material." The United States exported used batteries and Brazil *paid* to receive them.

Driven out by the ruin of their lands and the poisoning of their rivers and lakes, twenty-five million people are wandering about, looking for their place in the world. According to the most credible forecasts, in the coming years environmental degradation will be the principal factor causing an exodus of people from the countries of the South. And the countries that smile so nicely for the pictures, those happy protagonists of one economic miracle or another, think they have paid the toll, have passed the pole, and are on a roll, but they are already paying the price of their great leap to modernization: in Taiwan a third of the rice crop is inedible because it's poisoned with mercury, arsenic, or cadmium; in South Korea the water from only a third of the rivers is drinkable. There are no longer edible fish in half the rivers of China. In a letter he

View of Dusk at the End of the Century

Poisoned is the earth that inters or deters us.
There is no air, only despair; no breeze, only sleaze.
No rain, except acid rain.
No parks, just parking lots.
No partners, only partnerships.
Companies instead of nations.
Consumers instead of citizens.
Agglomerations instead of cities.
No people, only audiences.
No relations, except public relations.
No visions, just televisions.
To praise a flower, say: "It looks plastic."

was writing, a Chilean child drew a picture of his country: "Ships depart filled with trees, and ships arrive filled with cars." Chile today is a long highway bordered by shopping malls, arid lands, and industrial forests where no bird sings; the trees, like soldiers at attention, march off to the world market.

The twentieth century, a weary artist, ended its days painting still lifes. The extermination of the planet spares no one, not even the triumphal North that contributes the most to the catastrophe and, at the hour of truth, whistles and looks the other way. At the rate we're going, it won't be long before we'll have to put up new signs in maternity wards in the United States: *Attention, Babies:*

You are hereby warned that your chance of getting cancer is twice that of your grandparents. The Japanese company Daido Hokusan already sells air in cans, two minutes of oxygen for ten dollars. The label assures us: *This is the electric generator that recharges human beings.*

Wild Blue

This sky never grows cloudy; here it never rains. On this sea no one ever drowns; this beach is free of theft. There are no stinging jellyfish, no spiny urchins, no bothersome mosquitoes. The air and the water, climatized at a temperature that never varies, keep colds and flus at bay. The dirty depths of the port are envious of these transparent waters; this immaculate air mocks the poison that people in the city must breathe.

The ticket doesn't cost much, thirty dollars a person, although you pay extra for chairs and umbrellas. On the Internet, it says: "Your children will hate you if you don't take them . . ." Wild Blue, the Yokohama beach encased in glass, is a masterpiece of Japanese industry. The waves are as high as the motors make them. The electronic sun rises and falls when the company wishes, and the clientele is offered astonishing tropical sunrises and rosy sunsets behind swaying palms.

"It's artificial," says one visitor. "That's why we like it."

News

In 1994 in Laguna Beach, southern California, a deer came out
of the forest. Galloping down the street, the deer was struck by
a car. It leapt over a fence, crashed through a kitchen window,
broke another window, threw itself off a second-floor balcony,
burst into a hotel, and, like a bullet stained red with blood,
raced past the astonished patrons of beachfront restaurants
before plunging into the sea. The police trapped it in the water
and hauled it onto the beach, where, bleeding profusely, it died.

"He was crazy," the police explained.

A year later in San Diego, also in southern California, a vet-
eran stole a tank from an arsenal. Driving the tank he crushed
forty cars, damaged several bridges, and, with police cruisers in
hot pursuit, ran down whatever crossed his path. When he got
stuck on a steep rise, the police climbed on the tank, forced
open the hatch, and plugged this ex-soldier full of bullets. TV
viewers saw the entire spectacle live and direct.

"He was crazy," the police explained.

THE SACRED CAR

Human rights pale beside the rights of machines. In more and more cities, especially in the giant metropolises of the South, people have been banned. Automobiles usurp human space, poison the air, and frequently murder the interlopers who invade their conquered territory—and no one lifts a finger to stop them. Is there a difference between violence that kills by car and that which kills by knife or bullet?

THE VATICAN AND ITS LITURGIES

Our age abhors public transportation. In the middle of the twentieth century, Europeans used trains, buses, subways, and streetcars for three-quarters of their comings and goings. Today the figure is a quarter. That's still high compared with the average for the United States, where public transportation, virtually eliminated in most cities, accounts for only 5 percent of all transportation.

Henry Ford and Harvey Firestone were good friends back in the twenties, and they both got on well with the Rockefellers. Their affection for one another reinforced a mutuality of interests that went a long way toward dismantling the railroads and creating a vast network of roads, then highways that spanned the United States. With the passing years, the power of car, tire, and oil magnates has grown ever more ruinous. Of the sixty largest companies in the world, half either belong to this holy alliance or work for it.

Today's high heaven, the United States, has the greatest concentration of cars and the greatest quantity of weapons. Six, six, six: of every six dollars spent by the average North American, one is for the car; of every six hours of life, one is spent traveling in the car or working to pay for it; and of every six jobs, one is directly or indirectly related to the car, and another to violence and its industries. Each murder by cars and guns, of people and of nature, adds to the gross national product.

Talismans against loneliness or invitations to crime? Car sales parallel sales of weapons, and cars could well be considered a form of weapon: they are the principal killers of young people, with guns a close second. Every year cars kill and wound more people in the United States than all the U.S. soldiers killed and wounded throughout the long war in Vietnam, and in many states a driver's license is all you need to buy a machine gun and riddle the entire neighborhood with bullets. A driver's license is also required to pay by check or to cash a check, to sign for documents or notarize a contract. A driver's license is the most common ID: cars give people their identity.

North Americans enjoy some of the cheapest gasoline in the world thanks to sheiks in dark glasses—kings straight out of light opera—and other allies of democracy whose business it is to sell oil at a bargain, violate human rights, and buy U.S. weapons. According to the calculations of the Worldwatch Institute, if ecological damages and other "hidden costs" were taken into account the price of gasoline would at least double. In the United States gasoline is three times as cheap as in Italy, the second-most-

Paradise

If we behave ourselves, it will come to pass. We will all see the same images and hear the same sounds and wear the same clothes and eat the same hamburgers and enjoy the same solitude in our houses all alike in neighborhoods all alike in cities all alike where we will all breathe the same garbage and serve our cars with the same devotion and carry out the orders of the same machines in a world that will be marvelous for all who have no legs or wings or roots.

motorized country in the world, and each American burns on average four times as much gas as the average Italian, which is to say, a lot.

U.S. society, afflicted with autoitis, generates a quarter of the worst gases that poison the atmosphere. Although cars and their unquenchable thirst for gasoline are mostly to blame, it's politicians who give cars the right to roll and rule in exchange for money and votes. Every time some fool suggests raising gas taxes, the Detroit Big Three (General Motors, Ford, and Chrysler) scream to the skies and with broad popular support mount million-dollar campaigns decrying this vile threat to public freedom. And when a wayward politician feels wracked by doubts, the companies prescribe an infallible remedy: as *Newsweek* once put it, "The relationship between money and politics is so organic that seeking reform is tantamount to asking a doctor to perform open-heart surgery on himself."

Rarely is any politician, Democratic or Republican, willing to commit sacrilege against a national way of life that venerates machines, squanders the planet's natural resources, and equates human development with economic growth. Advertising extols the miracles that way of life performs, miracles the entire world would like to deserve. In the United States everyone can achieve the dream of owning a car, and many can trade their vehicles in regularly for new ones. Can't afford the latest model? This identity crisis can be overcome with aerosol sprays that make your autosaurus purchased three or four years ago smell as good as new.

Like death, old age is a sign of failure. The car is the one eternally youthful body you can buy. It eats gasoline and oil in its own restaurants, has its own pharmacies with its own medicine, and its own hospitals for diagnosis and treatment. It even has its own bedrooms and cemeteries.

Cars promise people freedom—highways aren't called "freeways" for nothing—yet they act like traveling cages. Despite technological progress, the human workday continues to lengthen year after year and so does the time required to get to work and back in traffic that moves at a crawl and shreds your nerves. You live in your car and it won't let you go. "Drive-by shooting": without leaving your speeding car you can pull the trigger and shoot blindly, as some people occasionally do in the Los Angeles night. "Drive-thru teller," "drive-in restaurant": without getting out of your car you can get money from the bank and eat hamburgers for supper. And without leaving your car you can also get married— "drive-in marriage." In Reno, Nevada, the car rolls under arches of plastic flowers, a witness appears at one window, the pastor at the other and, Bible in hand, he declares you man and wife. On your way out a woman dressed in wings and a halo gives you your marriage certificate and receives your "love donation."

The automobile, that buyable body, moves while the human body sits still and fattens. The mechanical body has more rights than the one of flesh and bone. As we all know, the United States has launched a holy war against the devil tobacco. I saw a cigarette ad in a magazine with the required public health warning: "Tobacco smoke contains carbon monoxide." But the same magazine had several car ads and not one of them warned that car exhaust, nearly always invisible, contains much more carbon monoxide. People can't smoke. Cars can.

Flight/3

In the sewers, under the asphalt, the abandoned children of the Argentine city of Córdoba make their home. Once in a while they surface to grab pocketbooks and wallets. If the police don't catch them and beat them to a pulp, they use their booty to buy pizza and beer to share. And they buy tubes of glue to inhale.

Journalist Marta Platía asked them what they felt like when they got high.

One of the kids said he whirled his finger and created wind: he pointed at a tree and the tree swayed in the wind he sent forth.

Another recounted that the world filled up with stars and he flew through the sky; there was sky above and sky below and sky to the four corners of the earth.

And another said he was sitting beside the sleekest and most expensive motorcycle in the city. Just by his looking at it, it was his; a harder look and he was riding it full speed while it grew and changed colors.

Rights and Duties

Although most Latin Americans do not have the right to buy a car, it's everyone's duty to pay for that right. For every thousand Haitians, barely five are motorized, but Haiti spends a third of its foreign exchange to import vehicles, spare parts, and gasoline. So does El Salvador, where public transportation is so disastrous and dangerous that people call buses "caskets on wheels." According to Ricardo Navarro, a specialist in these matters, the money that Colombia spends *every year* to subsidize the price of gasoline would pay for handing out 2.5 million bicycles.

Cars are like gods. Born to serve people as good-luck charms against fear and solitude, they end up making people serve them. The church of the sacred car with its U.S.-based Vatican has the entire world on its knees. The spread of car gospel has proven catastrophic, each new version deliriously multiplying the defects of the original.

A tiny proportion of the world's cars circulate on Latin America's streets, but Latin America boasts some of the most polluted cities on the globe. The structures of hereditary injustice, laced with fierce social contradictions, have given rise to cities that are outsized monsters beyond any possible control. The imported faith in the four-wheeled god and the confusion of democracy with consumption have been more devastating than any bombing campaign.

Never have so many suffered so much for so few. Disastrous

public transportation and the absence of bicycle lanes make the use of private cars practically obligatory, but how many people can enjoy the luxury? Latin Americans who don't own a car and can never hope to buy one live engulfed in traffic and suffocated by smog. Sidewalks shrink or disappear altogether; distances increase; more and more cars cross paths while fewer and fewer people meet. Not only are buses scarce, in most Latin American cities public transportation consists of just a few rust-heaps that spew out deadly plumes of exhaust, adding to pollution instead of alleviating it.

In the name of freedom—free enterprise, freeways, and the freedom to buy—the world's air is becoming unbreathable. Cars aren't the only guilty party in this daily act of murder, but they're the worst culprits. In cities the world over, they produce most of the noxious cocktail that destroys our lungs and eyes and everything else. They cause most of the noise and tension that makes our ears hurt and our hair stand on end. In the North, cars are generally obliged to use fuels and technologies that at least limit the poisons they give off—a big improvement, if only cars didn't reproduce like flies. But in the South, it's much worse. Only rarely are unleaded gas and catalytic converters required, and even then the law is respected but not obeyed, as tradition dating from colonial times would have it. Ferocious volleys of lead penetrate the blood with utter disdain, attacking the lungs, liver, bones, and soul.

The inhabitants of Latin America's largest cities spend their days praying for rain to cleanse the air or wind to carry the poison elsewhere. Mexico City, the largest city in the world, lives in a state of perpetual environmental emergency. Five centuries ago, an Aztec song asked:

Who could lay siege to Tenochtitlán?
Who could move the foundations of the heavens?

Today the city once called Tenochtitlán is under siege from pollution. Babies are born with lead in their blood and one person in three suffers frequent headaches. The government's guidelines for dealing with the motorized plague read like a defense against an invasion from Mars. In 1995, the Metropolitan Commission for the Prevention and Control of Environmental Pollution advised residents of Mexico's capital that on so-called days of environmental contingency, they should go out of doors as little as possible, keep doors, windows, and vents closed, not exercise between 10 a.m. and 4 p.m.

On those days, which occur ever more frequently, more than half a million people require some sort of medical attention from breathing what was known not so long ago as "the most transparent of air." At the end of 1996, fifteen poor peasants from the state of Guerrero marched in Mexico City to protest injustices; all of them ended up in the public hospital.

On another day that year, it rained oceans on the city of São

Paulo, creating the largest traffic jam in the country's history. Mayor Paulo Maluf celebrated: "Traffic jams are a sign of progress."

A thousand new cars take to the streets of São Paulo every day. The city breathes on Sunday and chokes the rest of the week. Only on Sunday can you see the skyline from the outskirts. The mayor of Rio de Janeiro, Luiz Paulo Conde, also likes traffic jams. Thanks to that blessing of urban civilization, he once said, motorists can talk on their cell phones, watch their portable TVs, and enjoy music on their cassettes or compact discs. "In the future," the mayor announced, "a city without traffic jams will be considered boring."

His prediction coincided with an ecological catastrophe in Santiago de Chile. Schools were closed and crowds of children packed the emergency rooms. In Santiago, environmentalists say, each child breathes the equivalent of seven cigarettes a day and one child out of four suffers some form of bronchitis. The city is separated from the heavens by an umbrella of pollution that has doubled in density over the past fifteen years, a period when the number of cars has also doubled.

The "airs" of the city called Buenos Aires grow more poisonous year by year, keeping pace with the vehicles, which increase by half a million every twelve months. In 1996, sixteen neighborhoods already suffered "very dangerous" noise levels, a perpetual racket that the World Health Organization says "can produce irreversible damage to human health." Charlie Chaplin liked to say

It's a Joke/1

On a large avenue in a large Latin American city, a man is waiting to cross. He stands at the curb, trapped by the incessant flow of cars. The pedestrian waits ten minutes, twenty minutes, an hour. Then he turns his head and spies a man leaning against a wall, smoking. And he asks, "Tell me, how do I cross to the other side?"

"I don't know," the man responds. "I was born over here."

that silence is the gold of the poor. Years have passed and silence is ever more the privilege of the few who can afford it.

Consumer society imposes its own symbolism of power and its own mythology of social progress. Advertising sends out invitations to join the ruling class; all it takes is a magic little ignition key. "Have it your way!" thunders the voice that gives the orders in the market. "You are in charge!" "Strut your stuff!" And if you put a tiger in your tank, according to the billboards I recall from my childhood, you'll be quicker and stronger than anyone else, crushing whoever blocks your path to success. Language creates a reality that advertising depends on, but real reality isn't at all like the spells of commercial witchcraft.

For every two children born into the world a car is born, and the automotive birthrate is gaining on the human one. Every child wants to own a car, two cars, a thousand cars. How many adults will be able to realize their childhood fantasies? The numbers show cars to be a privilege, not a right. One-fifth of humanity owns

It's No Joke/1

Managua, Las Colinas neighborhood, 1996. It's a night for celebrating: Cardinal Obando, the U.S. ambassador, several government ministers, and the cream of local society attend the
inauguration. They raise their glasses to toast Nicaragua's prosperity. Music and speeches resound.

"This is how you create jobs," declares the ambassador.
"This is how you build progress."

"It's just like being in Miami," gushes Cardinal Obando.
Smiling for the TV cameras, His Eminence cuts the red ribbon
on the new Texaco station. The company announces that it will
build more service stations in the near future.

four-fifths of the cars, even though all five-fifths of humanity have
to breathe the poisoned air that results. Like so many other symbols of consumer society, cars belong to a minority whose habits
are parlayed into universal truths, obliging the rest of us to see cars
as the only possible extension of the human body.

The number of cars in Latin America's Babylons keeps swelling
but it's nothing compared with that in the centers of world prosperity. In 1995, the United States and Canada had more motor
vehicles than the rest of the world combined, Europe aside.
Germany that year had as many cars, trucks, pickups, mobile
homes, and motorcycles as all of Latin America and Africa. Yet it's
in the cities of the South where three out of every four deaths by
car occur. And of the three who die, two are pedestrians. Brazil has

a third as many cars as Germany but three times as many victims. Every year Colombia suffers six thousand homicides politely called "traffic accidents."

Advertisements like to promote new cars as if they were weapons. At least that's one way ads aren't lying. Accelerating is like firing a gun; it offers the same pleasure and the same power. Every year cars kill as many people as were killed at Hiroshima and Nagasaki. In 1990, they caused many more deaths or disabilities than wars or AIDS. According to World Health Organization projections, in the year 2020 cars will be the third-largest cause of death or disability. Wars will be eighth, AIDS tenth.

Hunting down pedestrians is part of daily routine in big Latin American cities, where four-wheeled corsairs encourage the traditional arrogance of those who rule and those who act as if they did. A driver's license is equivalent to a gun permit, and it gives you license to kill. Ever more demons are ready to run down anyone who crosses their path. On top of the traditional thuggery, hysteria about robberies and kidnappings has made it more and more dangerous, and less and less common, to stop at red lights. In some cities stoplights mean, Speed up. Privileged minorities, condemned to perpetual fear, step on the accelerator to flee reality, that dangerous thing lurking on the other side of the car's tightly closed windows.

In 1992, a referendum was held in Amsterdam. People voted to reduce by half the already restricted area where cars can circulate in that kingdom of cyclists and pedestrians. Three years later, Florence rebelled against auto-cracy, the dictatorship of cars, and banned private vehicles from its downtown core. The mayor announced that the prohibition would be extended gradually to the entire city as streetcar, subway, and bus lines and pedestrian walkways expanded. And bike paths, too: according to plans it will

be possible to pedal anywhere in the city safely, on a means of transportation that is cheap, runs on nothing, and was invented five centuries ago by a Florentine, Leonardo da Vinci.

Modernization, motorization: the roar of traffic drowns out the chorus of voices denouncing civilization's sleight of hand that steals our freedom, then sells it back to us, that cuts off our legs to make us buy running machines. Imposed on the world as the only possible way of life is a nightmare of cities governed by cars. Latin America's cities dream of becoming like Los Angeles, with its eight million cars ordering people about. Trained for five centuries to copy instead of create, we Latin Americans aspire to become a grotesque imitation. If we are doomed to be copycats, couldn't we at least be a little more careful about what we choose to copy?

At night, I turn on the light to keep from seeing.
—HEARD BY MERCEDES RAMÍREZ

A PEDAGOGY OF SOLITUDE

- Lessons from Consumer Society
- Crash Course on Incommunications

LESSONS FROM CONSUMER SOCIETY

The punishment of Tantalus is the fate that torments the poor. Condemned to hunger and thirst, they are condemned as well to contemplate the delights dangled before them by advertising. As they crane their necks and reach out, those marvels are snatched away. And if they manage to catch one and hold on tight, they end up in jail or in the cemetery.

Plastic delights, plastic dreams. In the paradise promised to all and reserved for a few, things are more and more important and people less and less so. The ends have been kidnapped by the means: things buy you, cars drive you, computers program you, television watches you.

GLOBALIZATION, GLOBALONEY

Until a few years ago, a man who had no debts was considered virtuous, honest, and hardworking. Today, he's an extraterrestrial. Whoever does not owe, does not exist. I owe, therefore I am. Whoever is not credit-worthy deserves neither name nor face. The credit card is proof of the right to exist; debt, something even those who have nothing have. Every single person or country that belongs to this world has at least one foot caught in this trap.

The productive system, which has become the financial system, multiplies debtors to multiply consumers. Karl Marx, who saw this coming over a century ago, warned that the tendency of the profit rate to decline and the tendency of production to overproduce would oblige the system to seek limitless growth and to extend an insane degree of power to the parasites of the "modern bankocracy," which he defined as a "gang" that "knows nothing about production and has nothing to do with it."

Today's explosion of consumption makes more noise than all the wars that ever were and causes a greater uproar than every Mardi Gras in the world happening at once. As the old Turkish proverb has it, he who drinks on credit gets twice as drunk. This fiesta, this great global binge, makes our heads spin and clouds our vision; it seems to have no limits in time or space. But consumer culture is like a drum: it resonates so loudly because it's empty. At the moment of truth, when the clamor ceases and the party's over, the drunk wakes up and finds himself alone, accompanied only by his shadow and the broken dishes for which he must pay. The system that drives demand and obliges it to expand also builds walls for it to crash into. While the system needs markets that are ever broader and more open, the way lungs need air, at the same time it requires raw materials and human labor that are cheaper and cheaper. This system speaks in the name of all, to all it directs its imperious orders to consume, among all it sows the buying fever. But it won't do: for nearly everyone, this adventure starts and ends on the TV screen. Most people who go into debt in order to have things soon have nothing more than debts taken on to pay debts that lead to more debts, and they end up consuming fantasies that only come true by stealing.

Poverties

Truly poor people have no time to waste time.

Truly poor people have no silence and can't buy it.

Truly poor people have legs that don't remember how to walk any more than chicken wings remember how to fly.

Truly poor people eat garbage as if it were food and pay for it.

Truly poor people have the right to breathe shit as if it were air and not pay for it.

Truly poor people have the freedom to choose—between one TV channel and another.

Truly poor people live passionate dramas with their machines.

Truly poor people are always cheek by jowl and always alone.

Truly poor people don't know they are poor.

With the massive growth of credit, warns sociologist Tomás Moulian, Chile's everyday culture has come to revolve around symbols of consumption: appearance as the essence of personality, artifice as a way of life, "utopia on the installment plan." Consumerism has been imposed bit by bit, year by year, ever since Hawker Hunter jets bombed Salvador Allende's presidential palace in 1973 and General Augusto Pinochet inaugurated the era of the miracle. A quarter of a century later, the *New York Times* explained that it was the "coup that began Chile's transformation from a backwater banana republic to the economic star of Latin America."

On how many Chileans does that star shine? One-fourth of the population lives in absolute poverty and, as Christian Democratic senator Jorge Lavandero has pointed out, the hundred richest Chileans earn more in a year than the entire state budget for social services. U.S. journalist Marc Cooper found quite a few impostors in the paradise of consumption: Chileans who roast in their cars rather than roll down the windows and reveal that they have no air-conditioning, or who talk on toy cellular phones, or who use credit cards to buy potatoes or a pair of pants in twelve monthly installments. Cooper also found several angry workers at the Jumbo supermarket chain. On Saturday mornings, there are people who fill their shopping carts to the brim with the costliest items, then stroll the aisles for a long while, showing off, before abandoning their carts and sneaking out a side door without buying so much as a stick of gum.

The right to waste, privilege of a few, masquerades as freedom for all. Tell me how much you consume and I'll tell you what you're worth. This civilization won't let flowers or chickens or people sleep. In greenhouses, flowers are subjected to twenty-four-hour lighting so they'll grow faster. In egg factories, night is denied to the hens. And people, too, are condemned to insomnia, kept up by the anxiety of buying and the anguish of paying.

A Martyr

In the fall of 1998, in the center of Buenos Aires, a distracted pedestrian got flattened by a city bus. The victim was crossing the street while talking on a cell phone. While talking? While pretending to talk: the phone was a toy.

Magic

In the barrio of Cerro Norte, a poor suburb of the city of Montevideo, a magician gave a street performance. With a touch of his wand, he made a dollar bill sprout from his fist, then from his hat.

When the show was over, the magic wand disappeared. The next day, neighbors saw a barefoot child walking the streets, magic wand in hand. He tapped the wand on everything he came across and stood waiting.

Like many other children in the neighborhood, that nine-year-old boy liked to sink his nose into a plastic bag filled with glue. Once he explained why: "It takes me to another country."

This way of life may not be very healthy, but it's great for the pharmaceutical industry. People in the United States consume half the sleeping pills, tranquilizers, and other legal drugs sold in the world, as well as half the illegal drugs, which ain't chicken feed considering that the United States makes up only 5 percent of the world's population.

"Unhappy people, who live comparing themselves with others," laments a woman in Montevideo's barrio of Buceo. The pain of no longer being, of which the tango once sang, has made way for the shame of not having. A poor man is an object of pity. "When you háve nothing, you think you're worth nothing," says a young man in the barrio of Villa Fiorito in Buenos Aires. And another, in the Dominican town of San Francisco de Macorís, adds, "My

It's a Joke/2

A car crashes on the outskirts of Moscow. The driver crawls
out of the wreckage and moans: "My Mercedes . . . My
Mercedes . . ."

Somebody says to him: "Buddy, who cares about the car!
Don't you see your arm is missing?"

One look at his bleeding stump, and the man cries: "My
Rolex! My Rolex!"

brothers work for brand names. They live to buy labels, and they
work from dawn to dusk to keep up with the payments."

The invisible violence of the market: diversity is the enemy of
profitability, and uniformity rules. Mass production on a gigantic
scale imposes its obligatory patterns of consumption everywhere.
More devastating than any single-party dictatorship is the tyranny
of forced uniformity. It imposes on the entire world a way of life
that reproduces human beings as if they were photocopies of the
consummate consumer.

The consummate consumer is a man who sits still. This civilization, which confuses quantity with quality, also confuses obesity
with good nutrition. According to the British scientific journal the
Lancet, over the past decade "severe obesity" has increased by
nearly 30 percent among young people in the most-developed
countries. Among U.S. children, obesity has increased 40 percent
in the past sixteen years, according to a recent study by the Health

It's No Joke/2

In the spring of 1998 in Vienna, a newborn perfume is baptized. TV cameras record the ceremony, held in the vault of the Bank of Austria. The infant answers to the name "Cash" and she exudes the exciting fragrance of money. More baptismal parties are planned in Germany at the main offices of Deutsche Bank and in Switzerland at the Union des Banques Suisses.

"Cash" can be bought only on the Internet or in the most exclusive boutiques. "We'd like it to be the Ferrari of perfumes," say the creators.

Sciences Center of the University of Colorado. The country that invented "lite," "diet," and "fat-free" foods has the most fat people in the world. The consummate consumer gets out of his car only to work and to watch television. He spends four hours a day sitting in front of the small screen, devouring plastic.

Garbage disguised as food is colonizing palates everywhere and annihilating local cooking traditions in the process. Fine dining, the joy of eating, cultivated and diversified over thousands of years in some countries, constitutes a collective patrimony that finds its way to everyone's hearth, not only to the tables of the rich. Such traditions, such signs of cultural identity, such celebrations of life are being steamrollered by the globalization of hamburgers, the dictatorship of fast food. The worldwide Coca-Colonization of food, successfully imposed by McDonald's, Burger King, and

similar factories, violates cooking's right to self-determination—
a sacred right, since the mouth, as we know, is one of the doorways
to the soul.

The 1998 soccer World Cup confirmed, among other things,
that MasterCard tones muscles, Coca-Cola offers eternal youth,
and a good athlete can't get by without a shot of McDonald's fries.
The golden arches were carried as a standard during the recent
conquest of Eastern Europe. When the first McDonald's opened
with pomp and ceremony in Moscow in 1990, the line outside
symbolized the victory of the West as eloquently as the crumbling
of the Berlin Wall.

It is a sign of the times that this company, which embodies the
virtues of the free world, denies its employees the freedom to join a
union. McDonald's thus violates a legally sanctioned right in many
countries in which it operates. In 1997, a handful of workers,
members of what the company calls the McFamily, tried to form a
union in Montreal; the restaurant closed its doors. A year later, a
group of employees in a small city near Vancouver actually suc-
ceeded, a feat worthy of the *Guinness Book of World Records.*

In 1996, two British environmental activists, Helen Steel and David Morris, sued McDonald's for mistreating its workers, destroying nature, and manipulating the emotions of children. The company's employees are poorly paid, their working conditions are awful, and they can't unionize. Tropical forests are razed and indigenous peoples are run off their lands to produce meat for its hamburgers. What's more, its multimillion-dollar advertising campaigns threaten public health by enticing children to desire food of questionable nutritional value. The lawsuit, which at first seemed like a mosquito bite on an elephant's back, had unexpected repercussions, helped inform public opinion, and is turning into a long and costly headache for a company accustomed to unchallenged power. After all, power is what all this is about. In the United States, McDonald's employs more people than the steel industry, and in 1997 its sales were greater than the total exports of Argentina and Hungary combined. Its star product, the Big Mac, is so very important that in several countries its price is used as a unit of value for international financial transactions: virtual food orienting the virtual economy. According to McDonald's advertising in Brazil, the Big Mac is like love. Two bodies, aroused by cheese and pickle, embrace and kiss, oozing special sauce, while their hearts of onion thrill to the green hope of lettuce.

Cheap prices, quick service: the human machinery gasses up and goes right back to work. The German writer Günter Wallraff worked in one of those gas stations in 1983, a McDonald's in the city of Hamburg, which is certainly innocent of the things being done in its name. He found himself toiling at a feverish pace without a break, spattered with boiling oil: once thawed, the hamburgers have ten minutes to live. After that, they stink. You've got to get them on the stove right away. The fries, the vegetables, the meat, the fish, the chicken, it all has the same taste, an artificial fla-

Faces and Masks/1

Only the poor are condemned to be ugly and old. The rest can buy the hair, noses, eyelids, lips, cheekbones, tits, bellies, asses, thighs, or calves they need to correct the errors of nature and slow the passage of time. The operating rooms of plastic surgeons are shopping malls where you can find the face, body, and age you seek. "Surgery is a necessity of the soul," explains Argentina's answer to Rodin, Roberto Zelicovich. In Lima, billboards offer perfect noses and white skin for every pocketbook that can afford them. Peruvian television interviews a young man who replaced his aquiline Indian nose with a little meatball that he proudly displays, full-face and in profile. He says now he scores with the girls.

In cities like Los Angeles, São Paulo, and Buenos Aires, those with money can indulge in the luxury of going to the operating room the way the rest of us go to the dentist. After a few years and several operations, they all look alike. The men have faces like mummies without wrinkles, the women look like Dracula's girlfriend, and they're all bound to have trouble expressing themselves. When they wink, their belly buttons jump.

vor dictated by the chemical industry, which also supplies the colorants that hide the meat's 25 percent fat content. This garbage is our most successful millennial meal. Its chefs study at Hamburger University in Elk Grove, Illinois. But the owners of the business, according to well-informed sources, prefer elegant restaurants

---

Faces and Masks/2

Latin American cities also get face-lifts to wipe away their age
and erase their identities. Without their wrinkles or long noses,
cities lose their memory. They seem less and less like themselves
and more and more like one another.

The same tall prisms, cubes, and cylinders form the urban
skyline, all crowned by the names of international brands in
gigantic letters. In this era of obligatory cloning, advertisers are
the real urban planners.

---

serving the finest dishes of what has come to be called
"ethnic food": Japanese, Thai, Persian, Javanese, Indian,
Mexican . . . Democracy is nothing to laugh at.

The consuming masses take orders in a language that is universal; advertising has achieved what Esperanto could not. Every person everywhere understands what television broadcasts. Over the past quarter of a century, global spending on advertising has doubled. Thanks to that small fact, poor children drink more Coca-Cola and even less milk, and leisure time is eaten up by obligatory consumption. Free time, time imprisoned: the homes of the very poor have no beds, but they have TVs and the TV has the floor. Bought on credit, this little beast is proof of the democratic nature of progress. It listens to no one but speaks for all. Poor and rich alike thus learn the virtues of the latest car, and poor and rich alike discover the favorable interest rates offered by one bank or another.

"A poor person is someone who has no one," an old woman who talks to herself in the streets of São Paulo says repeatedly. People are ever more numerous and ever more alone. These crowded, lonely souls are then packed into big cities. "Would you please mind taking your elbow out of my eye?" they ask.

Experts know how to turn merchandise into magic charms against loneliness. Things have human attributes: they caress, accompany, understand, help. Perfume kisses you; your car never lets you down. Consumer culture has found in solitude the most lucrative of markets. Holes in your heart can be stuffed with things—or with dreams of things, anyway. And things can be more than embraces, they can be symbols of social mobility, passports to get you by the border guards of class society, keys that open doors usually locked tight. The more exclusive, the better; things lift you out of the crowd and save you from being nobody. Rarely does advertising tell you about the product being sold. That's the least of it. Advertising's primary function is to compensate for frustrations and feed fantasies. Whom do you wish to become by buying this aftershave?

Criminologist Anthony Platt observed that street crime is more than the fruit of extreme poverty. It is also the result of the ethics

of individualism. The obsession with success, says Platt, plays a decisive role in the illegal appropriation of things. I've always heard that money can't buy happiness, but every poor TV viewer has ample grounds for believing money can buy something so close to happiness that the difference can be left to specialists.

According to historian Eric Hobsbawm, the twentieth century put an end to the seven thousand years of human life based on agriculture that started at the end of the Paleolithic age with the first farming communities. The world's population is becoming urban, peasants are becoming citizens. In Latin America we have empty fields and enormous urban ant-hills. Driven off the land by modern export agriculture and the erosion of their plots, peasants invade the shantytowns. They believe God is everywhere, but by experience they know he keeps office hours in the city. Cities promise jobs, prosperity, a future for the children. In the countryside, the hopeful watch life pass by and die yawning; in the cities, life happens and beckons. Packed into slums, the newly arrived soon discover that there aren't enough jobs for the many hands, that nothing is free, and that the most expensive luxuries are air and silence.

At the dawn of the fourteenth century, Father Giordano da Rivalto of Florence offered an elegy to cities. He said that they grow "because people take pleasure in being together." Being together, meeting. Now who meets whom? Does hope meet up with reality? Do desires meet up with deeds? And people, do they meet other people? If human relations have been reduced to the relations among things, how many people meet up with things?

The world is becoming a huge TV screen: look and listen but don't touch. Merchandise on display invades and privatizes public spaces. Bus and train stations, until not long ago meeting places for people, are being turned into commercial bazaars.

The shopping mall, a store window to top all store windows, lords it over us with its imposing presence. Multitudes make the pilgrimage to this, the grandest of all temples, for celebrating the mass of consumption. Most of the devotees contemplate in ecstasy the things they can't afford, while the buying minority submits to the withering bombardment of relentless sales pitches. Going up

---

The Days

We don't know if Christmas celebrates the birth of Jesus or of Mercury, god of commerce, but surely it's Mercury who thought up mandatory shopping days: Father's Day, Mother's Day, Children's Day, Grandparent's Day, Valentine's Day, Friendship Day, Secretary's Day, Policeman's Day, Nurse's Day. Every year there are more Somebody Days on the commercial calendar.

At this rate, soon we'll have days to honor the Unknown Scoundrel, the Anonymous Corrupt Official, and the Last Surviving Worker.

The Great Day

They live off garbage amid garbage, eating garbage in garbage houses. But once a year, the garbage collectors of Managua star in the show that draws the country's largest crowds. "The Ben-Hur Races" were the inspiration of a businessman who came back from Miami to do his part for "the Americanization of Nicaragua."

Riding their garbage carts, fists in the air, Managua's garbage collectors salute the president of the country, the ambassador of the United States, and the other dignitaries who grace the dais of honor. Over their everyday rags, the competitors wear broad colorful capes, and on their heads sit the plumed helmets of Roman warriors. Their dilapidated carts are freshly painted, the better to display the names of their sponsors. The skinny horses, covered with open sores like their owners and punished like their owners, are corsairs that fly to the finish line for the sake of glory, or at least a case of soda.

Trumpets blare. The starting flag drops, and they're off. Whips beat down on the bony haunches of the sorry nags, while the delirious crowd cheers: "Co-ca-Co-la! Co-ca-Co-la!"

and down the escalators the crowds travel the world; they watch mannequins dress in fashions from Paris or Milan and listen to stereos that sound as they would in Chicago, and to see and hear all this you pay no fare. Tourists from the hinterlands or from cities still free of this blessing of modern happiness pose for pictures

beside the best-known international brands the way they used to pose in the plaza beneath the statue of a national hero. For poor residents of the outskirts, notes Argentine sociologist Beatriz Sarlo, the traditional weekend trip downtown has been replaced by an excursion to one of these urban oases. Spruced up and dressed in their Sunday best, the guests arrive at the party well aware they can only be wallflowers. Entire families board the space capsule to tour the universe of consumption and contemplate the hallucinatory display of models, brands, and labels served up by the aesthetics of the market.

Consumer culture, ephemeral culture, condemns everything to immediate obsolescence. Everything changes at the dizzying pace of fashion, at the service of the need to sell. Things grow old in the blink of an eye, only to be replaced by other things no less short-lived. When only insecurity is permanent, merchandise made to wear out is as volatile as the capital that finances it and the labor that produces it. Money flies at the speed of light—yesterday it was over there, today it's here, tomorrow who can say—and every worker is a potential recruit for the vast army of the unemployed.

The Global Field

In its current form, soccer was born over a century ago. It was born speaking English, and it still speaks English everywhere it's played. But now you hear it singing the praises of a good "sponsor" and lauding the virtues of "marketing" with as much fervor as it used to commend a good "forward" and the art of "dribbling."

Tournaments are named for those who pay, not those who play. The Argentine championship is called Pepsi-Cola. Coca-Cola is the name of the world youth soccer tournament. The intercontinental club tournament is called the Toyota Cup.

For the fan of the most popular sport in the world, for the fanatic of the most universally fanatical passion, a team's shirt is a sacred mantle, a second skin, his other breast. But the shirt has also become a walking billboard. In 1998, players for Rapid of Vienna wore four advertisements at once. On their shirts were ads for a bank, a company, and a brand of cars, and on their shorts they advertised a credit card. When River Plate and Boca Juniors play each other in Buenos Aires's soccer classic, it's Quilmes against Quilmes: both teams wear the name of the same brand of beer. In this era of globalization, River also plays for Adidas and Boca for Nike. In fact, you could say Adidas beat Nike when France defeated Brazil in the final of the 1998 World Cup.

Paradoxically, it's shopping malls, the kingdoms of fleeting fashion, that offer the most successful illusion of security. They seem to exist beyond time, ageless and rootless, without night or day or memory, and outside of space, apart from the turbulence of dangerous reality. In these sanctuaries of well-being, you can do everything without ever stepping into the dirty, threatening outdoors. In some, you can even sleep. The newest ones, in places like Los Angeles and Las Vegas, include hotels and health clubs. Oblivious to cold or heat, malls are safe from pollution and violence. Michael A. Petti publishes scientific advice in a syndicated column called "Live Longer." In cities "with poor air quality," Dr. Petti suggests that those who wish to live longer should "walk inside shopping centers." Atomic clouds of pollution hang over Mexico City, São Paulo, and Santiago, and on the corners muggers lie in wait, but in this carefree world outside the world—with its filtered air and guarded walkways—you can breathe and walk safely.

Malls are all more or less alike, in Los Angeles or Bangkok, in Buenos Aires or Glasgow. Uniformity, however, doesn't keep them from competing for clients by inventing new come-ons. At the end of 1991, for example, *Veja* magazine praised a novelty from Praia de Belas mall in Pôrto Alegre, Brazil: "For baby's comfort, they provide strollers to help these small consumers move about." But security is the most important item offered by all shopping centers. A luxury on the outside, it can be had by anyone who penetrates these bunkers. In its infinite generosity, consumer culture issues safe-conduct passes so we can flee the hell of the streets. Surrounded by parking lots like vast moats, these island kingdoms provide closed and protected spaces where people cross paths drawn by the urge to have, the way people used to meet, drawn by the desire for companionship, in the cafés or plazas, parks or mar-

The Injection

More than half a century ago, a writer named Felisberto
Hernández published a prophetic tale. A man dressed in white
and carrying a syringe boards streetcars in Montevideo and ami-
ably injects the arms of all the passengers. Immediately they
hear advertising jingles from the Canary furniture factory. To get
the ads out of their veins, they have to go to the drugstore for
Canary pills that suppress the effect of the shot.

kets of old. The public police and the private police, the visible
police and the invisible police make sure anyone suspicious gets
tossed into the street or thrown into jail. Poor people who don't
manage to disguise their congenital malevolence, especially dark-
skinned ones, are guilty until proven innocent. And if they happen
to be children, so much the worse. Malevolence is inversely proportional to age. Way back in 1979, Colombia's police reported to
the South American Police Congress that their juvenile division
had no choice but to give up social work so that they could
"undercut the evil deeds" of dangerous minors and "avoid the nui-
sance of their presence in shopping centers."

These gigantic supermarkets turned into miniature cities are
also guarded by electronic control systems, eyes that see without
being seen, hidden cameras that follow the steps of the crowd
wandering amid the merchandise. Electronics are useful not only
for watching and punishing undesirables who might succumb to
the temptation of forbidden fruits but for making consumers con-

sume more. In the cybernetic age, when the right to citizenship is based on the duty of buying, large companies take X rays of every citizen's habits, calling up data from credit card, bank machine, and e-mail use to discern a potential customer's earnings and yearnings—and then pummel him with advertising. This happens more and more in highly developed countries, where commercial manipulation of the on-line world freely violates private life and places it at the service of the market. It has become increasingly difficult, for example, for a U.S. citizen to keep secret such things as the purchases he makes, the diseases he suffers, the money he has, and the money he owes. From such data it's not hard to figure out what new services he might pay for, what new debts he might take on, or what sort of new things he might purchase.

No matter how much we buy, it's always little compared with what has to be sold. Over the past few years, for example, the automobile industry has been churning out more cars than the market can absorb. Latin America's huge cities keep on buying and buying, but they're caught between the orders the world market takes and the orders the world market gives, the contradiction between obsessive consumption, which requires higher wages, and the obligation to compete, which demands lower ones.

Take the case of the car, which advertising portrays as a blessing within everyone's reach. A universal right? An achievement of democracy? If that were true and every human being could become the happy owner of one of these four-wheeled good-luck charms, the planet would face sudden death by asphyxiation. Even before that, it would run out of fuel and grind to a halt. The world has already burned up, in a brief span, most of the oil formed in the earth over millions of years. Cars built one after another, at the rate of a beating heart, devour half the oil the world produces every year.

Its owners treat the planet as if it could be discarded, a commodity to be used up, the way images flitting across a TV screen or the fashions and idols launched by advertising fade away shortly after they are born. But what other world are we going to move to? Are we all obliged to swallow the line that God sold the planet to a few companies because in a foul mood he decided to privatize the universe? Consumer society is a booby trap. Those at the controls feign ignorance, but anybody with eyes in his head can see that the great majority of people *necessarily* must consume not much, very little, or nothing at all in order to save the bit of nature we have left. Social injustice is not an error to be corrected, nor is it a defect to be overcome; it is an essential requirement of the system. No natural world is capable of supporting a mall the size of the planet.

The leaders who promise to take the countries of the South into the First World by an act of magic that will turn us all into prosperous subjects of the kingdom of waste ought to be tried for fraud and as accessories to a crime. For fraud because they promise the impossible; if we all consumed like those who are squeezing the earth dry, we'd have no world left. And as accessories to a crime because the lifestyle they promote—the huge orgasm of delirious consumption they call happiness—sickens our bodies, poisons our souls, and leaves us without the home the world wished to become long before it existed.

CRASH COURSE ON INCOMMUNICATIONS

War is the continuation of television by other means. So General Karl von Clausewitz might say if he were to come back to life after a century and a half and start channel surfing. Real reality imitates virtual reality, which imitates real reality in a world that sweats violence from every pore. Violence begets violence, as we all know, but it also begets profits for the industry that turns violence into merchandise, then sells it as spectacle.

The ends no longer need to justify the means. Today the means, the means of mass communication, justify the ends of a system of power that imposes its values on the entire planet. A handful of giant corporations are in charge of the world's Ministry of Education. Never have so many been held incommunicado by so few.

IS THE RIGHT OF FREE EXPRESSION THE RIGHT TO LISTEN?

In the sixteenth century, several theologians of the Catholic Church justified the Conquest of America in the name of commu-

Tell Me Your Secrets/1

Malaysia recently revamped its communications network. A
Japanese company was to do the work, but at the last minute the
U.S. giant AT&T suddenly undercut its offer and snatched the
deal away. AT&T won the contract thanks to the good offices of
the NSA, the National Security Agency, which tracked down
and deciphered the Japanese bid.

The NSA, a U.S. spy agency with a budget four times that of
the CIA, has the technology to record every word transmitted
by telephone, fax, or e-mail in any part of the world. It can inter-
cept up to two million conversations per minute. The NSA's real
mission is to maintain U.S. economic and political control over
the planet, but national security and the struggle against terrorism are its formal covers. Its eavesdropping systems allow it to
track every message that has anything to do with criminal organizations as dangerous as, for example, Greenpeace or Amnesty
International.

All these facts came out in March 1998 when the European
Parliament published an official report entitled, "Evaluation of
the Technologies of Political Control."

nication. *Jus communicationis:* the conquistadors spoke, the
Indians listened. War turned out to be both inevitable and just,
since the Indians pretended to be deaf. Their right to communicate was the right to obey. At the end of the twentieth century, that
rape of America is still called an "encounter," and we still use the
term "communication" for the monologues of the powerful.

Tell Me Your Secrets/2

How does a modern company communicate with its real customers? By means of virtual customers, programmed by computer.

The British supermarket chain Sainsbury has worked up a mathematical model to simulate the movements and sentiments of its shoppers. The computer screen shows the virtual customer walking down the aisles amid shopping carts, revealing his or her tastes and fears, family commitments and personal needs, social position and ambitions. It can also measure the impact of advertising and discounts, the influence of store hours on the flow of customers, and the importance of the location of merchandise.

That's how they study buying behavior and that's how they design sales strategies: virtual media to multiply real profits.

Around the world spins a ring of satellites filled with millions and millions of words and images that come from the earth and are returned to it. Marvelous gadgets the size of your fingernail receive, process, and transmit at the speed of light messages that half a century ago would have required thirty tons of machinery. Miracles of technoscience in these technotimes: the most fortunate members of our media-mad society can now enjoy their vacations at the beach picking up the cell phone, receiving e-mail, checking the beeper, reading faxes, responding to messages on the answering machine by leaving messages on other answering machines, shopping by computer, and spending their free time playing video games or watching tiny portable TVs. In its awesome rise and dizzying flight, communications technology displays almighty powers. At midnight the computer kisses the forehead of Bill Gates, and at dawn he wakes up as the richest man in the world. Now on the market is a computer with a built-in microphone so you can talk to it. In cyberspace's Celestial City, the computer marries the telephone and the television, and all of humanity is invited to the baptism of their astonishing children.

The emerging cybercommunity takes refuge in virtual reality, while real communities are transformed into an immense desert filled with people, each of whom lights a candle to his own saint, each of whom is encased in his own bubble. Forty years ago, according to polls, six out of ten North Americans trusted most people. But the trust index is down: today it's only four out of ten. This sort of progress just promotes separation. The more relations between people get demonized—they'll give you AIDS, or take away your job, or ransack your house—the more relations with machines get sacralized. The communications industry, that most dynamic sector of the world economy, sells abracadabras that open the doors to a new era in human history. But this so-well-communicated world looks too much like a kingdom of loners and the mute.

The dominant means of communication lie in a few hands that are always becoming fewer, and usually serve a system that reduces human relations to mutual use and mutual fear. The Internet galaxy has opened unexpected and valuable opportunities for alternative expression, allowing many voices that are not the echoes of power to broadcast their messages. But access to the information superhighway is still the privilege of developed countries, where 95 percent of users reside, and commercial advertising is doing its all to turn the Internet into the Businessnet. This new medium for freedom of communication is also a new medium for freedom of commerce. On the virtual planet there's no risk of meeting up with customs officers or governments crazed with delusions of independence. In the middle of 1997, when advertising already occupied far more space on the Internet than educational material, the president of the United States ventured that every country in the world should keep the sale of goods and services by Internet duty-free, and from that point on, this issue has been high on the U.S. agenda in international organizations.

Control of cyberspace depends on telephone lines, and it's no accident that the privatizing wave of recent years has yanked the phones out of the public's hands around the world and given them over to the great communications conglomerates. Foreign phone companies have received far more U.S. investment than any other sector, while the concentration of capital has forged ahead at a gallop. Up to the middle of 1998, eight megacompanies dominated the phone trade in the United States; in just a week, these were reduced to five.

Television, the movie industry, the mass-circulation press, the

great publishing houses and record companies, and the biggest radio stations, too, are all marching double-time toward monopoly. The global mass media have set the price of freedom of expression in the clouds; the opinioned, who have the right to listen, are ever more numerous, while the opinionators, who have the right to make themselves heard, are ever fewer. In the years following World War II, independent media still provided broad coverage of news, opinion, and the creative adventures that reveal and nourish cultural diversity. By 1980, the devouring of medium-sized and small companies had put most of the planetary market under the control of fifty corporations. Since then, independence and diversity have become rarer than a green dog.

According to producer Jerry Isenberg, the erosion of independent television in the United States over the past twenty years has been overwhelming. Independent companies used to supply between 30 and 50 percent of what was seen on the small screen; today the figure is barely 10 percent. Also revealing are the world's advertising statistics: currently, half of all the money the world spends on advertising goes down the throat of only ten conglomerates that produce and distribute everything you can imagine involving images, words, and music.

Over the past five years the biggest U.S. communications companies doubled their international sales: General Electric, Disney/ABC, Time Warner/CNN, Viacom, Tele-Communications Inc. (TCI), and Microsoft, Bill Gates's baby, which rules the software market and has successfully broken into cable TV and TV production. These giants exercise oligopolistic power, which they share globally with the Murdoch empire, Sony of Japan, Bertelsmann of Germany, and one or two more. Among them they've woven a global spider's web, their interests linked like so many knotted threads. Although these mastodons of communica-

The Globalized Hero

Secret Agent 007 no longer works for the British crown. Today James Bond is a sandwich-board man for many companies from many countries. Every scene in his 1997 film, *Tomorrow Never Dies*, is an advertisement. The infallible Bond checks his Omega watch, talks on an Ericsson cell phone, leaps from a rooftop onto the roof of a Heineken beer truck, flees in a BMW rented from Avis, pays with a Visa card, drinks Dom Pérignon champagne, undresses women previously dressed by Armani and Gucci and coiffed by L'Oréal, and fights an opponent in Kenzo attire.

tion pretend to compete, and sometimes even come to blows or exchange insults to satisfy the spectators, at the moment of truth the spectacle ends and they calmly carve up the planet.

By grace of cybernetic providence, Bill Gates amassed a sudden fortune equivalent to the entire annual budget of Argentina. In the middle of 1998, the United States government charged Microsoft with using monopolistic methods to crush its competitors. Some time previously, the federal government had put together a similar suit against IBM; after thirteen years of back-and-forth, the matter was left in murky waters. Judicial law can't do much when faced with economic law, and capitalism brings on the concentration of power as inevitably as winter brings on the cold. The antitrust laws that once threatened the kings of oil and steel are unlikely ever to imperil the planetary machinery that sets the stage for the most dangerous of despotisms, that which acts on the heart and conscience of all humanity.

Technological diversity is said to be democratic diversity. Technology places images, words, and music within the reach of all, as never before. But this marvel becomes a dirty trick if private monopoly ends up imposing a one-image, one-word, one-tune dictatorship. Even taking into account the exceptions—and fortunately there are exceptions and they aren't so few—this diversity tends to offer us thousands of ways of choosing between the same and the same. As Argentine journalist Ezequiel Fernández-Moores said of the news: "We're told about everything, but we don't find out a thing."

Although the structures of power have become more international and it's difficult to distinguish any borders, to say that the United States sits at the center of the nervous system of contemporary communications wouldn't be a sin of primitive anti-

Exemplary Lives/4

Admirers and enemies concur: his main virtue is his lack of scruples. They also appreciate his capacity for extermination, essential for success in today's world. Busting unions and devouring competitors, Rupert Murdoch arose from nowhere to become a magnate of world communications. His meteoric career began when he inherited a newspaper in far-off Australia. Today he is the owner of 130 dailies in several countries, including the venerable *Times* of London and the English tabloids that in their glory days reported on who slept last night with Princess Diana. This modeler of minds and consoler of souls made the world's biggest investment in satellite communications technology and controls one of the largest television networks on the planet. He also owns the Fox movie studios and HarperCollins publishing house, where he published several masterworks of world literature, including those of his friends Margaret Thatcher and Newt Gingrich.

imperialism. U.S. companies rule in film and TV, in information and computers. The world, an immense Wild West, begs to be won. For the United States, the global reach of its mass messages is a matter of state. The governments of the South tend to think of culture as playing a decorative function, but the tenants of the White House, at least on this matter, aren't the least bit stupid. Every president knows that the political importance of the culture industry is at least as great as its economic value, great as that is.

For years, to give an example, the government has used diplomatic pressure to promote Hollywood's products, which never err on the side of diplomacy, in countries that attempt to protect their own national film industries.

Over half of Hollywood's earnings already comes from foreign markets, sales that grow spectacularly year by year, while the Oscars attract a universal viewership comparable only to that drawn by soccer's World Cup or the Olympics. The powers that be are no dummies; they know that imperial power largely rests on the unfettered spread of emotion, on illusions of success, symbols of strength, orders to consume, and elegies to violence. In the film *Close to Eden* by Nikita Mikhalkov, the peasants of Mongolia dance to rock music, smoke Marlboros, wear Donald Duck hats, and surround themselves with images of Sylvester Stallone as Rambo. That other great master of the art of pulverizing your neighbor, the Terminator, is the character most admired by the children of the world: a 1997 UNESCO poll taken simultaneously in Europe, Africa, Asia, and Latin America found that nine out of ten children identified with that musclebound purveyor of violence played by Arnold Schwarzenegger.

In the global village of the mediated universe, all continents flow together and all centuries occur at once. "We are from here and from everywhere at the same time, which is to say, from nowhere," says Alain Touraine about television. "Images, always attractive to the public, juxtapose gas station jockeys and camels, Coca-Cola and Andean villages, blue jeans and an imposing castle." Believing themselves condemned to choose between copying and casting themselves adrift, many local cultures, off-balance, torn loose, fading away, take refuge in the past. With desperate frequency, cultures seek shelter in religious fundamentalism or other absolute truths; they propose a return to times gone by, the more

The Spectacle

A criminal trial was the most successful product sold by U.S. television in 1995. The trial of former athlete O. J. Simpson, charged with two murders, filled the networks' programming hours with innumerable episodes that won the fervent allegiance of the television audience.

Crime as spectacle: every one of the trial's many actors played a role, and acting, good or bad, was more important than the guilt or innocence of the defendant, the validity of the charges, the propriety of the investigation, or the truth of the testimony. In his free time, the judge instructed other judges in the secret arts of playing a convincing judge on camera.

---

puritanical the better, as if there were no other response to overpowering modernity than intolerance and nostalgia.

The Cold War has been left behind. Without it, the so-called free world has lost its magical justification for a holy crusade against the totalitarianism that until a short while ago ruled the countries of the East. Yet it grows more evident every day that communications manipulated by a handful of giants can be just as totalitarian as communications monopolized by the state. We are all obliged to accept freedom of expression as freedom of business. Culture is reduced to entertainment, and entertainment is a brilliant global enterprise. Life is reduced to spectacle, and spectacle is a source of economic and political power. News is reduced to advertising, and advertising rules.

Two out of three human beings live in the so-called Third World, but two out of three correspondents of the biggest news agencies work in Europe and the United States. What happened to the free flow of information and the respect for diversity enshrined in international treaties and praised in the speeches of political leaders? Most of the news the world receives comes from and is directed at a minority of humanity—understandably so from the point of view of the commercial operations that sell news and collect the lion's share of their revenue in Europe and the United States. It's a monologue by the North. Other regions and countries get little or no attention, except in the case of war or catastrophe, and then the journalists covering the story often don't speak the language or have the least idea of local history or culture. News tends to be dubious and sometimes plainly, simply wrong. The South is condemned to look at itself through the eyes of those who scorn it.

In the early eighties, UNESCO proposed an initiative based on the truth that news is not a simple commodity but a social right and that the communications media should bear responsibilities commensurate with the educational purpose they serve. UNESCO set out to create an independent international news agency working from the countries that suffer the indifference of the factories of information and opinion. Even though the proposal was framed in ambiguous and cautious terms, the U.S. government thundered furiously against such an attack on freedom of information. What business did UNESCO have sticking its nose into matters pertaining to the living forces of the market? The United States walked out of UNESCO, slamming the door, as did Great Britain, which tends to act as if it were a colony of the country that was once its colony. At that point the idea of promoting international news unhampered by political or commercial interests was shelved. Any

attempt to gain independence, timid as it may be, threatens the international division of labor by which a handful of people actively produce news and opinion and the rest of us passively consume it.

Little is said about the South, and never or almost never from the South's point of view. In general, mass media news of the South reflects the prejudices of an outsider looking on from above and beyond. Between ads, television tends to stick to images of hunger and war. These horrors, these "fatalities," occur in a hellish underworld and serve only to emphasize the paradise of consumer society, which offers cars to suppress distance, facial creams to suppress wrinkles, dyes to suppress gray hair, and pills to suppress pain, among its many suppressive marvels. Frequently, those images of the "other" world come from Africa. African hunger is portrayed as a natural catastrophe, and African wars are strictly "a black thing," bloody rituals of "tribes" who have a savage habit of cutting one another to pieces. Images of hunger never allude, not even in passing, to colonial pillage. Never do they mention the responsibility of Western powers that yesterday bled Africa

The Information Age

Just before Christmas 1989, we all viewed horrendous evidence of the killings ordered by Nicolae Ceauşescu in Romania.

The crazed despot who liked to be called the "Blue Danube of Socialism" killed four thousand dissidents in the city of Timişoara. We saw many of the bodies, thanks to the global reach of television and the good work of the international agencies that feed images to newspapers and magazines. Long rows of dead bodies, deformed by torture, shocked the world.

Later some papers published a correction, though not many read it. Killings had indeed occurred at Timişoara, but the victims numbered about a hundred and included some of the dictatorship's henchmen. What's more, those hair-raising images had been staged. The bodies had nothing to do with the story and were disfigured not by torture but by the passage of time. The news factories unearthed them from a cemetery and had them pose for the camera.

through the slave trade and single-crop plantations and that today perpetuate the hemorrhage through hunger wages and ruinous prices. The same is true of news about wars; there is always the same silence about the colonial legacy, always the same impunity for the white boss who mortgaged Africa's independence, leaving in his wake corrupt bureaucracies, despotic military officers, artificial borders, and mutual hatred. And always the same omission of any reference to the northern industry of death that sells the weapons that so encourage the South to go on killing itself.

At first view, as the writer Wole Soyinka once said, the map of
Africa looks like the creation of a demented weaver who paid no
attention to the texture, color, or design of the cloth he was making. Many of the borders that splintered black Africa into over
forty pieces can only be explained by a desire for military or commercial control; they have nothing at all to do with historical roots
or nature. The colonial powers who drew up the borders were also
good at manipulating ethnic contradictions. *Divide et impera:* one
fine day the king of Belgium decided that Tutsis were those who
had more than eight cows and Hutus were those who had fewer in
the territory today occupied by Rwanda and Burundi. Although
the Tutsis, shepherds, and the Hutus, farmers, had different origins, they shared several centuries of common history in the same
physical space, spoke the same language, and lived together in
peace. They did not know they were enemies but ended up

Let's Play War/1

Yenuri Chihuala died in 1995 during the border war between Peru and Ecuador. He was fourteen. Like many other boys from the poor barrios of Lima, he had been recruited by force. They took him away and left no footprints.

Television, radio, and the print media all praised the child martyr as a role model who gave his life for Peru. During those days of war, the daily *El Comercio* devoted its front page to glorifying the very young people it normally curses on its crime and sports pages. The *cholos trinchudos*—literally "carved-up half-breeds"—grandchildren of Indians, poor kids with spiky hair and dark skin, are heroes of the fatherland when they wear a military uniform on the battlefield, but these same noble savages are dangerous beasts, violent by nature, when they wear civilian clothes on city streets and in soccer stadiums.

believing it with such fervor that in 1994 massacres between Hutus and Tutsis cost close to a million lives. In the news coverage of this butchery, we never once heard, even by chance—and only rarely did we read—any acknowledgment of Germany's or Belgium's colonial assaults on the tradition of peaceful coexistence between two sister peoples or of France's later contribution of weapons and military aid to facilitate mutual extermination.

What happens to poor countries is what happens to the poor of every country: the mass media only deign to glance at them when they suffer some spectacular misfortune that will be a hit in the viewers market. How many people must be slain by war or

Let's Play War/2

Video games have a huge and growing public of all ages. Their proponents say that the violence in video games is innocent because it imitates the news and that such entertainment is good for keeping children off the streets and away from the lure of cigarettes.

Video games speak a language made up of the rat-a-tat-tat of machine guns, horror-movie music, agonized screams, and barked commands: "Finish him!," "Beat 'em up!," "Shoot 'em!," The war of the future, the future as war: the most popular video games take place on battlefields where the player has to shoot without a moment's hesitation, destroying anything that moves. No pause or truce is possible against an enemy stampede of despised extraterrestrials, ferocious robots, humanoid hordes, ghostly cyberdemons, mutant monsters, and skulls that stick out their tongues. The more adversaries the player kills, the closer he comes to winning. In the already-classic *Mortal Kombat,* you get extra points for blows that decapitate the enemy and send his head flying, that knock his bloody heart right out of his breast, or blast his head into a thousand pieces.

There are also a few video games that are not about war. Car races, for example. In one of them, a good way to score points is to run over pedestrians.

earthquake or drowned in floods for their countries to become news and show up on the map of the world? How many ghosts must someone dying of hunger accumulate before the cameras focus on him for once in his life? The world is like a stage for a gigantic reality show. The poor, the ones who always get overlooked, only appear on TV as some hidden camera's object of ridicule or as actors in their own cruelties. Those unknown need to be known, the invisible to become visible, the uprooted to have roots. If something doesn't exist on television, does it exist in reality? Pariahs dream of glory on the small screen, where any sow's ear can turn into a silk purse. To get to the Olympus where the telegods reside, one poor soul on a variety show even shot himself on camera.

Lately, talk shows have become even more popular than soap operas in some Latin American countries. When the girl who was raped is interviewed, she sobs as if the man were raping her all over again . . . This monster is the new Elephant Man. Look, ladies and gentlemen, don't miss this incredible sight . . . The bearded lady wants a boyfriend . . . A fat man says he's pregnant. Thirty or so years ago in Brazil, freak shows brought scores of candidates out of the woodwork and garnered huge TV audiences. Who is the shortest dwarf in the country? Who has a schnoz so long his feet stay dry in the shower? Who is the wretchedest wretch of all? A parade of miracles passed through the studios: a girl with ears eaten by rats; an idiot chained to a bedpost for thirty years; a woman who was the daughter, sister-in-law, mother-in-law, and wife of the drunk who made her a cripple. And every wretch had fans who screamed from the balconies in a chorus: "The winner! The winner!"

The poor nearly always get top billing in crime stories. Any suspect who's poor can be freely filmed, photographed, and put on display when the police arrest him. That way he's sentenced by TV and the press before the trial begins. The media declare the pernicious poor guilty from the word go, the same way they condemn pernicious countries, and there is no appeal.

At the end of the eighties, Saddam Hussein was demonized by the same mass media that had previously idolized him. When he became the Satan of Baghdad, Hussein shone as a star of evil in the

For History Class

During the year 1998 the globalized media dedicated the most space and their best energies to the romance between the president of the planet and a plump, voracious, talkative woman named Monica Lewinsky.

In every country we were all Lewinskyized. We had her for breakfast, reading the papers; we had her for lunch, listening to the radio; and we had her for dinner, watching TV.

I think something else happened in 1998, but I can't remember what.

galaxy of world politics, and the media's lie machine took care of convincing the world that Iraq was a threat to humanity. At the beginning of 1991, the United States launched Operation Desert Storm with the backing of twenty-eight countries and broad public support. The United States, having just invaded Panama, invaded Iraq because Iraq had invaded Kuwait. With a million extras and at a cost of $1 billion a day, the big show, which writer Tom Engelhardt called the greatest megaproduction in the history of television, was a winner in the stadium of international TV, earning high ratings in every country—and on the New York Stock Exchange, which reached record heights.

The art of war, cannibalism as gastronomy: the Gulf war was an interminable, obscene spectacle that paid homage to high-tech weapons and disparaged human life. In that war of machines led by satellites, radars, and computers, TV screens showcased beautiful missiles and marvelous rockets, extraordinary airplanes and smart bombs that with admirable precision turned people into dust. The venture killed a total of 115 North Americans. Nobody bothered to count the Iraqis, though estimates put the figure as high as a hundred thousand. They never appeared on camera; the only victim shown on TV was an oil-slicked duck. Later on, it came out that the image was a fake; the duck was from another war. Retired U.S. Navy Admiral Gene LaRocque commented to Studs Terkel: "We now kill people without ever seeing them. Now you push a button thousands of miles away. . . . Since it's all done by remote control, there's no feeling of remorse. . . . Then we come home in triumph."

A few years later, at the beginning of 1998, the United States tried to repeat this feat. The immense communications apparatus geared up once again to serve the immense military apparatus by convincing the world that Iraq was, again, a threat to humanity.

This time, the excuse was chemical and bacteriological weapons. Years before, Hussein had used U.S.-made poison gas against Iran and then had used the same gas to crush the Kurds, and nobody's hair got the least bit mussed. But panic descended suddenly with the news that Iraq possessed an arsenal of bacteriological weapons: anthrax, bubonic plague, botulism, cancer cells, and other lethal pathogenic agents that any lab in the United States can purchase over the phone or by mail from a company called American Type Culture Collection (ATCC), located just outside Washington. United Nations inspectors, however, found nothing in the palaces of a thousand and one nights, and war was postponed until the next pretext.

The Electronic Friend

The players, absorbed, in a trance, don't speak to one another.

On the way home from work or to work from home, thirty million Japanese find themselves playing Pachinko and to Pachinko they offer their souls. Players spend hours sitting in front of the machine, shooting little steel balls at needles to win prizes. Every machine is run by a computer that makes sure the players nearly always lose and also that they win once in a while to keep the flame of faith burning. Since gambling for money is illegal in Japan, you play with cards bought with money, and the prizes are paid in gadgets that can be exchanged for money around the corner.

In 1998, the Japanese made offerings of $500 million a day in the temples of Pachinko.

Manipulation of world news by the military isn't the least bit surprising if you consider the modern history of communications technology. The Pentagon has always been the principal funder of and the principal client for all new developments. The first electronic computer was created to fill a Pentagon purchase order. Communications satellites grew out of military projects, and it was the Pentagon that first set up the Internet to coordinate its operations across the globe. The multimillion-dollar investments made by the armed forces simplified and accelerated the development of communications technology and made it possible to promote their criminal acts worldwide as if they were contributions to world peace.

Fortunately, history is also nourished by paradox. The Pentagon never suspected that the Internet, born to program the world as a great battlefield, would be used to spread the words of pacifist movements usually condemned to near silence. That said, the primary effect of the spectacular development of communications technology and information systems has been to radiate violence as a way of life and as the dominant culture. The communications media, reaching ever more people in more places, accustom us to the inevitability of violence and train us for it from childhood.

On screens—movie, TV, computer—things blow up and bleed ceaselessly. A research project at two universities in Buenos Aires measured the frequency of violence on children's TV in 1994: one scene every three minutes. The researchers concluded that, by the age of ten, Argentine children have seen eighty-eight thousand acts of violence, not counting the many violent incidents suggested but not portrayed. The dose increases, they found, on weekends. A year before, a poll taken on the outskirts of Lima revealed that nearly every parent condoned that sort of programming: "Those are the programs the kids like." "That way they're entertained." "If they like them, it must be okay." "It's better. That way they learn what life is like." And also, "It doesn't affect them, it's nothing." At the same time, research carried out by the Rio de Janeiro state government concluded that half of all the violent scenes broadcast on the Globo television network were on children's programs; Brazilian children get brutality shot at them every two minutes and forty-six seconds.

Hours spent in front of the television easily surpass those spent in the classroom, when hours are spent in the classroom at all. It is a universal truth that, with or without school, TV programs are children's primary source of formation, information, and deformation, as well as their principal source of topics for conversation. The predominance of TV pedagogy is particularly alarming in Latin America in light of the recent decline of public education. In their speeches politicians are prepared to die for education, and in their acts they proceed to kill it, thus liberating children to take more classes in consumption and violence from the small screen. In their speeches politicians denounce the plague of crime and demand an iron hand, and in their acts they encourage the mental colonization of the next generation. From early on, children are trained to find their identities in merchandise that symbolizes power and to get hold of it with a gun.

Do the media reflect reality or shape it? Who begets whom? Is it the chicken or the egg? Wouldn't a better zoological metaphor be a snake biting its own tail? We give the people what they want, say the media to absolve themselves. But the supply they offer in response to demand creates more demand for more of the same supply; it becomes a habit, creates a need for itself, and turns into an addiction. In the streets there is as much violence as on television, say the media. But violence in the media, which expresses the violence of the world, also promotes more violence.

Europe has had some healthy experiences with the media. In several countries television and radio achieve a high level of quality as public services, run not by the state but directly by organizations that represent diverse sectors of civil society. These experiences, threatened today by a stampede of competition from commercial outlets, offer examples of communication that is truly communicative and democratic, able to speak to people's human dignity and their right to information and knowledge. But that is not the approach that has been promoted internationally. The world has been slipped a lethal cocktail of blood, Valium, and advertising by private U.S. television networks. They've imposed a model based on the proven notion that good is what makes the most profit at the least cost and bad is what pays no dividends.

In Greece at the time of Pericles, there was a tribunal for judging things. It punished the knife, for example, that had been the weapon in a crime, sentencing it to be broken into pieces or thrown into the depths of the sea. Today would it be fair to condemn the television set as the Taliban does? Those who consider TV to have an evil heart slander it by calling it the idiot box. Yes, commercial television reduces communication to business, but obvious though it seems when you say it, TV sets are innocent of the use they are put to and the abuse committed with them. That fact shouldn't stop us from raising an alarm about what all the evi-

Language/5

Several anthropologists traveled about the countryside on Colombia's Pacific coast in search of life stories. An old man told them: "Don't record me, I speak so ugly. Better to get my grandchildren."

Not far from there, anthropologists traveled about the countryside of Grand Canary Island. Another old man welcomed them, served them coffee, and regaled them with hallucinatory tales delightfully recounted. And then he, too, said: "We speak ugly. They're the ones who can talk, the kids."

The grandchildren, the kids, the ones who speak pretty, speak like the TV.

dence makes evident: this, the most worshiped totem of our times, is the medium that has been employed most successfully to impose on the four cardinal points of the earth the idols, myths, and dreams designed by the engineers of emotions and mass-produced by the factories of the soul.

Peter Menzel and other photographers compiled a book of families from all over the planet. Their portraits of family intimacy in England and Kuwait, Italy and Japan, Mexico, Vietnam, Russia, Albania, Thailand, and South Africa are quite different. But all these families have something in common and that something is television. There are 1.2 billion TV sets in the world. Recent surveys in the Americas, from north to south, reveal the omnipresence and omnipotence of the small screen:

- in four out of ten homes in Canada, parents are unable to recall a single family meal eaten without the TV on
- tied to the electronic leash, children in the United States spend forty times as many hours watching TV as talking to their parents
- in most homes in Mexico, the furniture is arranged around the television
- in Brazil, one-fourth of the population admits they would not know what to do with their lives if television did not exist.

Working, sleeping, and watching television are the three activities that eat up most of people's time in today's world—something politicians are well aware of. This electronic network, which brings the pulpit into millions and millions of homes, delivers an audience bigger than any ever dreamed of by the many preachers the world has produced. The power of persuasion depends not on content—the greater or lesser truth of the message—but rather on imagery and the efficacy of the ad blitz to sell the product. Detergents are pushed at shoppers the same way presidents are pushed at the public. Ronald Reagan was the first telepresident in history, a mediocre actor who, in his long years in Hollywood, learned how to lie with sincerity before the camera's eye and whose velvet voice won him a job as spokesperson for General Electric.

In the era of television, Reagan needed nothing else to have a political career. His ideas, not very numerous, came from *Reader's Digest.* (Writer Gore Vidal observes that the complete set of *Reader's Digest* was as important to Reagan as the collected works of Montesquieu were for Jefferson.) With the help of the small screen, President Reagan was able to convince the U.S. public that Nicaragua was a threat. Standing in front of a map of North America with a red stain slowly spreading up from the south, Reagan demonstrated that Nicaragua was planning to invade the United States through Texas.

After Reagan, other telepoliticians started winning. Fernando Collor, once a model for Christian Dior, became the president of Brazil in 1990 thanks to television. The same TV that produced him and blocked a victory of the left overthrew him a couple of years later. The rise of Silvio Berlusconi to the summit of political power in Italy in 1994 would be inexplicable without television. Berlusconi exercised influence over a vast TV audience after he obtained, in the name of democratic diversity, a monopoly on private television. It was that monopoly, along with his success as the owner of the Milan soccer club, that provided an effective catapult for his political ambitions.

In every country, politicians fear being punished or shut out by television. On the news and on the soap operas, there are heroes and villains, victims and executioners. No politician likes to play the bad guy, but bad guys at least get covered. It's far worse to be ignored. Politicians are terrified that television will fail to notice them, condemning them to civic death. Whoever does not appear on TV does not exist in reality; whoever disappears from TV leaves the world. To have a presence on the political stage, you have to appear with a certain regularity on the small screen, and that regularity, not easily achieved, does not tend to come free. The

owners of television offer politicians a platform, and the politicians return the favor by offering the owners impunity; without fear of retribution, they can continue placing a public service at the service of their private pocketbooks.

Politicians are not unaware, can't afford the luxury of being unaware, of the low standing of their profession and the magical, seductive power that television, and to a much lesser degree radio and the press, exercise over the multitudes. A poll taken in several Latin American countries in 1996 confirmed what you hear in the streets: nine out of ten Guatemalans and Ecuadorians have a poor opinion or worse of their parliamentarians, and nine out of ten Peruvians and Bolivians do not trust political parties. In contrast, two out of three Latin Americans believe what they see and hear in the media. José Ignacio López Vigil, an activist in alternative media, summed it up well: "In Latin America, if you want a political career, your best option is to become a TV anchor, a radio host, or a singer."

To win and consolidate popular legitimacy, some politicians take direct control of television. The most powerful and conservative of Brazilian politicians, for example, Antonio Carlos Magalhães, graciously received a concession for private TV in the state of Bahía, and in his fiefdom he runs a virtual monopoly in association with Rede Globo, the Brazilian television giant. Lídice da Mata, the mayor of Bahía, was elected by the voters of the Workers Party, a powerful force that is a party of the left and, what's worse, is proud of it. In 1994, the mayor complained that she was never able to get on Magalhães's stations, not even with paid ads or when there were floods, mud slides, strikes, or other emergency situations that required urgent communication with the public. Bahía's television, a magic mirror, reflected only the face of its owner.

There are channels that claim to be public in many Latin American countries, but that's just one of the things states do to run down the reputation of the state. With a few heroic exceptions, state programming goes over like a lead balloon; thanks to Paleolithic equipment and ridiculous salaries, the picture is often fuzzy. Only private television has the means to capture a mass audience. Throughout Latin America, this prodigious source of

Praise for Imagination

A few years ago, the BBC asked British children if they preferred television or radio. Nearly all favored TV, a finding on the order of saying that cats meow or that dead bodies don't breathe. But among the few children who chose radio, there was one who explained, "I like radio better, because I see prettier pictures."

money and votes lies in a few hands. In Uruguay, three families own all private TV. This family oligolopoly swallows money and spits out advertisements, buys canned programming from other countries for a pittance, and rarely gives work to local artists or runs the risk of producing a quality program of its own; when that miracle occurs, theologians claim it as proof of the existence of God. Two big multimedia conglomerates control the lion's share of Argentina's television. In Colombia two groups hold television and most other important media in their hands. Televisa of Mexico and Rede Globo of Brazil are absolute monarchies barely disguised by the existence of other minor kingdoms.

Latin America is a very lucrative market for the U.S. image industry. It consumes a lot of television and produces little other than a few news shows and successful soap operas. Soap operas, which the Brazilians do wonderfully, are Latin America's only TV export. Once in a while they take up topics from this world, like political corruption, drug trafficking, street children, or landless peasants, but the president of Mexico's Televisa put his finger on what makes soap operas so big when he explained at the beginning of 1998: "We sell dreams. We have no intention of reflecting reality. We sell dreams like Cinderella's."

A hit soap opera is generally the only place in the world where Cinderella marries the prince, evil is punished and good rewarded, the blind recover their sight, and the poorest of the poor receive an inheritance that turns them into the richest of the rich. These "big snakes," as they are called because of their many episodes, create an illusory space where social contradictions dissolve in tears or honey. Religious faith promises you a ticket to paradise in the after-life, but even atheists can get into the soap at the end of a workday. This other reality, that of the characters, takes the place of ordinary reality for as long as each episode lasts, and during that magical time television is a portable temple that offers escape, redemption, and salvation to souls without shelter. Someone, I don't know who, once said, "The poor adore luxury. Only intellectuals like to see poverty." All poor people, no matter how poor, are invited into the sumptuous settings of the soaps, becoming intimates of the rich in their moments of pleasure as well as their bouts of misfor-

tune and tears: one of the most popular Latin American soap operas of all time was called *The Rich Cry Too.*

The intrigues of millionaires constitute the usual plots. For weeks, months, years, or centuries, the people in the telebalconies bite their nails, waiting for the mistreated young servant girl to learn that she is really the daughter of the company president and to beat out the nasty rich girl for the hand of the handsome young man of the house. The poor girl's endless suffering, her unrequited love, her lonely tears in her servant's room are interspersed with entanglements on the tennis court, at pool parties, on the stock exchange, and in the company boardroom, where other characters also suffer, and sometimes kill, to gain a controlling share. It's Cinderella in the time of neoliberal passion.

God is dead. Marx is dead.
And I don't feel so well myself.

—WOODY ALLEN

THE COUNTERSCHOOL

- The End of the Millennium as Promise and Betrayal
- The Right to Rave

The End of the Millennium as Promise and Betrayal

I n 1902, the Rationalist Press Association of London published a *New Catechism* in which the twentieth century was baptized with the names Peace, Freedom, and Progress. Its godparents predicted that the newborn would liberate the world from superstition, materialism, misery, and war.

Years have passed, the century has turned. What world has it left us? A desolate, de-souled world that practices the superstitious worship of machines and the idolatry of arms, an upside-down world with its left on its right, its belly button on its backside, and its head where its feet should be.

QUESTIONS AND ANSWERS THAT POSE MORE QUESTIONS

Faith in the powers of science and technology fed expectations of progress throughout the twentieth century. When the century was halfway through its journey, several international organizations were promoting the development of the underdeveloped by handing out powdered milk for babies and spraying fields with DDT.

Later we learned that when powdered milk replaces breast milk it helps babies die young and that DDT causes cancer. At the turn of the century, it's the same story: in the name of science, technicians write prescriptions for curing underdevelopment that tend to be worse than the disease, and in the process they humiliate people and annihilate nature.

Perhaps the best symbol of the epoch is the neutron bomb, the one that burns people to a crisp and leaves objects untouched. A sad fate for the human condition, this time of empty plates and emptier words. Science and technology, placed at the service of war and the market, put us at their service: we have become the instruments of our instruments. Sorcerer's apprentices have unleashed forces they can neither comprehend nor contain. The world, that centerless labyrinth, is breaking apart, and even the sky is cracking. Over the course of the century, means have been divorced from ends by the same system of power that divorces the human hand from the fruit of its labor, that enforces the perpetual separation of words and deeds, that drains reality of memory, and that turns everyone into the opponent of everyone else.

Stripped of roots and links, reality becomes a kingdom of count and discount, where price determines the value of things, of people, and of countries. The ones who count arouse desire and envy among those of us the market discounts, in a world where respect is measured by the number of credit cards you carry. The ideologues of fog, the pontificators of the obscurantism now in fashion, tell us reality can't be deciphered, which really means reality can't be changed. Globalization reduces international relations to a series of humiliations, while model citizens live reality as fatality: if that's how it is, it's because that's how it was; if that's how it was, it's because that's how it will be. The twentieth century was born under a sign of hope for change and soon was shaken by the hurricanes of social revolution. Discouragement and resignation marked its final days.

Injustice, engine of all the rebellions that ever were, is not only undiminished but has reached extremes that would seem incredible if we weren't so accustomed to accepting them as normal and deferring to them as destiny. The powerful are not unaware that injustice is becoming more and more unjust, and danger more and more dangerous. When the Berlin Wall fell and the so-called Communist regimes collapsed or changed beyond recognition, capitalism lost its pretext. During the Cold War, each half of the world could find in the other an alibi for its crimes and a justification for its horrors. Each claimed to be better because the other was worse. Orphaned of its enemy, capitalism can celebrate its unhampered hegemony to use and abuse, but certain signs betray a rising fear of what it has wrought. As if wishing to exorcise the demons of people's anger, capitalism, calling itself "the market

---

For a Course on the History of Ideas

"Manolo, how you've changed your thinking!"

"No, Pepe, not at all."

"Yes, you have, Manny. You used to be a monarchist. Then you supported the Falange. Then you backed Franco. After that, you were a democrat. Not long ago you were with the socialists and now you're on the right. And you say you haven't changed your thinking?"

"Not at all, Pepe. My thinking has always been the same: to be mayor of this town."

The Stadium and the Boxes

In the eighties, the Nicaraguan people were sentenced to war for believing that national dignity and social justice were luxuries to which a poor little country could aspire.

In 1996, Félix Zurita interviewed General Humberto Ortega, who had been a revolutionary. How quickly times have changed. Humiliation? Injustice? That's human nature, said the general. No one is ever satisfied with what he gets.

"There's a hierarchy," he said. And he explained that society is like a soccer stadium: "A hundred thousand people can squeeze into the stadium, but only five hundred can sit in the boxes. No matter how much you love the people, you can't fit them all in the boxes."

economy," now suddenly discovers its "social" dimension and travels to poor countries on a passport that features its new full name, "the social market economy."

A McDonald's ad shows a boy eating a hamburger. "I don't share," he says. This dummy hasn't learned that now we're supposed to give away our leftovers instead of tossing them in the garbage. Solidarity is still considered a useless waste of energy and critical consciousness is but a passing phase of stupidity in human life, but the powers that be have decided to alternate the carrot with the stick. Now they preach social assistance, which is the only form of social justice allowed. Argentine philosopher Tato Bores, who worked as a comedian, knew all about this doctrine years

The Field

Do people watch the game or do they play it?

When a democracy is real, shouldn't people be on the field? Is democracy exercised only every four, five, or six years, when you cast your vote? Or is it exercised every day of every year?

A Latin American experiment in daily democracy is under way in the Brazilian city of Pôrto Alegre. There residents debate and decide what to do with the municipal funds available for each neighborhood, and they approve, amend, or quash proposals from the local government. Staff and politicians propose, but it's the people who dispose.

before ideologues started promoting it, technocrats started implementing it, and governments started adopting it in what some call the Third World. "You ought to give crumbs to the elderly," Don Tato counseled, "instead of to the pigeons."

The most mourned saint of the end of the century, Princess Diana, having been abandoned by her mother, tormented by her mother-in-law, cheated on by her husband, and betrayed by her lovers, found her vocation in charity. When she died, Diana was the head of eighty-one public charities. If she were still alive, she would make a great minister of the economy in any government of the South. After all, charity consoles but does not question. "When I give food to the poor, they call me a saint," said Brazilian bishop Helder Cámara. "And when I ask why they have no food, they call me a Communist."

Unlike solidarity, which is horizontal and takes place between equals, charity is top-down, humiliating those who receive it and never challenging the implicit power relations. In the best of cases, there will be justice someday, high in heaven. Here on earth, charity doesn't worry injustice, it just tries to hide it.

The twentieth century was born under the sign of revolution, but the adventurous attempts to build societies based on solidarity were shipwrecked, leaving us to suffer a universal crisis of faith in the human capacity to change history. Stop the world, I want to get off. In these days of collapse, the number of penitents—repenters of political passion or of all passion—multiplies. More than a few fighting cocks have become hens a-laying, while dogmatists, who thought they were safe from doubt and discouragement, either take refuge in nostalgia for nostalgia that evokes more nostalgia or simply lie frozen in a stupor. "When we had all the answers, they changed the questions," wrote an anonymous hand on a wall in the city of Quito.

With a speed and efficiency that would arouse Michael Jackson's envy, many revolutionary activists and parties of the red or pink left are undergoing an ideological color change. I once heard it said that the stomach shames the face, but contemporary chameleons prefer to explain it another way: democracy must be consolidated, we have to modernize the economy, there is no alternative but to adapt to reality.

Reality, however, says that peace without justice, the peace we enjoy today in Latin America, is a field sown with violence. In Colombia, the country that suffers the most violence, 85 percent of the dead are victims of "common violence," and only 15 percent die from "political violence." Could it be that common violence somehow expresses the political impotence of societies that have been unable to establish a peace worthy of the name?

History is unambiguous: the U.S. veto has blocked or closed off to the point of strangulation most of the political experiments that have sought to get at the roots of violence. Justice and solidarity have been condemned as foreign aggression against the foundations of Western civilization, leaving it plain as can be that democracy has limits and you'd better not test them. The story is a long one, but it's worth recalling at least the recent examples of Chile, Nicaragua, and Cuba.

At the beginning of the seventies, when Chile tried to take democracy seriously, Henry Kissinger dotted the *i*'s and crossed the *t*'s of the White House decree against that unpardonable foray. "I don't see why," he said, "we need to stand by and watch a country go Communist because of the irresponsibility of its own people."

The process that led up to General Pinochet's coup d'état left hanging a few questions practically no one asks anymore about relations between countries in the Americas and the imbalance in the rights they enjoy. Would it have been normal for President Allende to say that President Nixon was not acceptable to Chile,

just as President Nixon said with a straight face that President Allende was not acceptable to the United States? Would it have been normal for Chile to organize an international credit and investment blockade against the United States? Would it have been normal for Chile to pay off U.S. politicians, journalists, and military officers and then encourage them to drown democracy in blood? And suppose Allende had mounted a coup d'état to block Nixon's inauguration and another to overthrow him? The great powers that govern the world practice terrorism without compunction, since their crimes lead them not to the electric chair but to the thrones of power. And the crime of power is the mother of all crimes.

Nicaragua was sentenced to ten years of war in the 1980s when it committed the insolence of being Nicaragua. An army recruited, trained, armed, and led by the United States tormented the country, while a campaign to poison world opinion portrayed the Sandinista revolution as a conspiracy hatched in the basement of the Kremlin. Nicaragua wasn't attacked because it was a satellite of a great power but to force it back into being one. Nicaragua wasn't attacked because it lacked democracy but so that democracy would be lacking. While fighting the war, the Sandinistas also taught half a million people how to read and write, cut infant mortality by a third, and inspired a sense of solidarity and a yearning for justice in many, many people. That was their challenge and that was their damnation. In the end, exhaustion from the long, devastating war cost the Sandinistas an election. And later, as tends to happen, several of their leaders sinned against hope by disowning their own words and deeds in an astonishing about-face.

During the years of war, peace reigned in the streets of Nicaraguan towns. Since peace was declared, the streets have become scenes of war, the battlegrounds of common criminals and

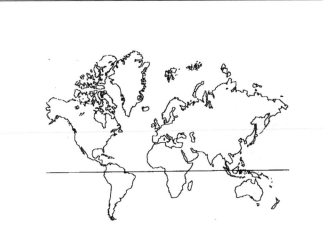

The World Map

The equator did not cross the middle of the world map that we studied in school. More than half a century ago, German researcher Arno Peters understood what everyone had looked at but no one had seen: the emperor of geography had no clothes.

The map they taught us gives two-thirds of the world to the North and one-third to the South. Europe is shown as larger than Latin America, even though Latin America is actually twice the size of Europe. India appears smaller than Scandinavia, even though it's three times as big. The United States and Canada fill more space on the map than Africa, when in reality they cover barely two-thirds as much territory.

The map lies. Traditional geography steals space just as the imperial economy steals wealth, official history steals memory, and formal culture steals the word.

youth gangs. A young U.S. anthropologist, Dennis Rodgers, joined a group of toughs in one of the worst barrios of Managua. He found that such gangs are indeed the violent response of young people to a society that excludes them, and they flourish not only because of grinding poverty and the absence of any hope for work or study but also out of a desperate search for some sort of identity. In the seventies and eighties, years of revolution and war, young people saw themselves in their country, in the colony that wanted to become a country, but the youth of the nineties were left without a mirror. Now they are patriots of the barrio, or of a block in the barrio, and they fight to the death against gangs from enemy neighborhoods or enemy blocks. By defending their territory and organizing themselves to fight and steal, they feel a little less alone and a little less poor in their atomized and impoverished world. They share what they steal and spend the loot from their muggings on glue, marijuana, drink, bullets, knives, Nike shoes, and baseball caps.

In Cuba street violence has also grown, and prostitution has flourished, ever since the country's Eastern European allies collapsed and the dollar became the island's currency. For forty years Cuba was treated as a leper for the crime of having built in this hemisphere a society based more on solidarity and less on injustice. In recent years, that society has lost most of its material base of support: the economy is out of whack, the tourist invasion has warped people's daily lives, work has lost its value, and the dolorous traitors of yesterday have become the dollar-are-us traders of today. Despite these recent sorrows, even the revolution's bitterest enemies admit that some of its achievements still stand, above all in education and health. The mortality rate for Cuban children, for example, is half that for the young of Washington, D.C. Fidel Castro is still the political leader who speaks forbidden truths to

Scrawled on City Walls

I like night so much, I'd throw a blanket over day.
True, crickets don't work. But ants can't sing.
My grandmother said no to drugs. And she died.
Life is a disease that goes away on its own.
This factory smokes birds.
My dad lies like a politician.
No more action! We want promises!
Hope is the last thing we lost.
We weren't asked about coming into the world. But
we demand to be asked about living in it.
There's a different country somewhere.

the world's rulers and the one who most insists that the ruled must unite. As a friend just back from Cuba told me, "There are shortages of everything—except dignity. That they have in such quantities they could give out transfusions." But the crisis in Cuba and the island's tragic isolation have stripped bare the limitations of a top-down system that hasn't shaken the bad habit of believing things do not exist unless they're mentioned in the official press.

The nine U.S. presidents who have screamed successive condemnations of Cuba for its lack of democracy have done nothing more than denounce the consequences of their own acts. It was the ceaseless aggression and the long, implacable blockade that drove the Cuban revolution to become more and more militarized, far removed from the model that was originally envisioned. The omnipotence of the state, which began as a response to the omnipotence of the market, ended up succumbing to the impotence of the bureaucracy. The revolution sought to grow by transforming itself, and it spawned a bureaucracy that reproduces by repeating itself. At this point, the internal blockade, the authoritarian blockade, is turning out to be just as much of an enemy as the external imperial blockade, stifling the creative energy of the revolution. Many Cubans have lost their opinions for lack of use. But others are not afraid to speak and are eager to act. Thanks to their encouragement, Cuba is alive and kicking, offering proof that contradictions are the heartbeat of history, no matter how badly that sits with those who view them as heresies or as wrenches that life throws into the best of plans.

For much of the twentieth century, the existence of the Eastern bloc, so-called real socialism, encouraged the independent forays of countries that wished to escape the trap of the international division of labor. But the socialist states of Eastern Europe had a lot of state and little or nothing of socialist. When they fell, we were all invited to the funeral of socialism, but the undertakers were mistaken about who had died.

In the name of justice, so-called socialism had sacrificed freedom. The symmetry is revealing: in the name of freedom, capitalism sacrifices justice day in, day out. Are we obliged to kneel before one of these two altars? Those of us who believe that injustice is not our immutable fate have no reason to identify with the despotism of a minority that denied freedom, was accountable to no one, treated people as children, and saw unity as unanimity and diversity as treason. Such petrified power was divorced from the people it ruled. Perhaps that explains the ease with which it fell, without pity or glory, and the rapidity with which a new power emerged featuring the same personalities. Bureaucrats turned a

The Other Globalization

The Multilateral Agreement on Investment, a new set of rules to liberate the circulation of money, was a sure thing at the beginning of 1998. The most-developed countries had negotiated the accord in secret and were ready to impose it on all the others and on the bit of sovereignty those countries still retained.

But civil society broke the news. Using the Internet, alternative organizations managed to ring alarm bells throughout the world and pressure governments to good effect. The accord died unhatched.

quick somersault and in a flash reappeared as successful businessmen and mafia capos. Moscow now has twice as many casinos as Las Vegas, while wages have fallen by half and in the streets crime grows like a mushroom after a rain.

We are in the midst of a tragic but perhaps healthy crisis of convictions—a crisis for those who believed in states that claimed to belong to everyone but were really of the few and ended up being no one's; a crisis for those who believed in the magic formulas of the armed struggle; and a crisis for those who believed in political parties that went from withering denunciations to bland platitudes, that began by swearing to bring down the system and ended up administering it. Many party activists now beg forgiveness for having believed that heaven could be built. They work feverishly to erase their own footprints and climb down from hope as if hope were a tired horse.

End of the century, end of the millennium, end of the world? How much unpoisoned air do we have left? How much unscorched earth? How much water not yet befouled? How many souls not yet sick? The Hebrew word for "sick" originally meant "with no prospect," and that condition is indeed the gravest illness among today's many plagues. But someone—who knows who it was?—stopped beside a wall in the city of Bogotá to write, "Let's save pessimism for better times."

In the language of Castile, when we want to say we have hope, we say we shelter hope. A lovely expression, a challenge: to shelter her so she won't die of the cold in the bitter climate of these times. According to a recent poll conducted in seventeen Latin American countries, three out of every four people say their situation is unchanged or getting worse. Must we accept misfortune the way we accept winter or death? It's high time we in Latin America asked ourselves if we are to be nothing more than a caricature of the North. Are we to be only a warped mirror that magnifies the deformities of the original image: "Get out if you can" downgraded to "Die if you can't"? Crowds of losers in a race where most people get pushed off the track? Crime turned into slaughter, urban hysteria elevated to utter insanity? Don't we have something else to say and to live?

At least now we hardly ever hear the old refrain about history being infallible. After all we've seen, we know for sure that history makes mistakes: she gets distracted, she falls asleep, she gets lost. We make her and she looks like us. But she's also, like us, unpredictable. Human history is like soccer: her finest trait is her capacity for surprise. Against all predictions, against all evidence, the little guys can sometimes knock the invincible giants for a loop.

On the woof and warp of reality, tangled though it be, new cloth is being woven from threads of many radically different col-

Latin Americans

They say we missed our date with history, and it's true we're usually late to appointments. Neither have we been able to take power, and the fact is we do sometimes lose our way or take a wrong turn, and later we make a long speech about it.

We Latin Americans have a nasty reputation for being charlatans, vagabonds, troublemakers, hotheads, and revelers, and it's not for nothing. We've been taught by the law of the market that price equals value, and we know we don't rate much. What's worse, our good nose for business leads us to pay for everything we sell and buy every mirror that distorts our faces.

We've spent five hundred years learning how to hate ourselves and one another and work heart and soul for our own ruin. That's what we're up to. But we still haven't managed to correct our habit of wandering about daydreaming and bumping into things or our inexplicable tendency to rise from the ashes.

ors. Alternative social movements don't just express themselves through parties and unions. They do that, but not only that. The process is anything but spectacular and it mostly happens at the local level, where across the world a thousand and one new forces are emerging. They emerge from the bottom up and the inside out. Without making a fuss, they shoulder the task of reconceiving democracy, nourishing it with popular participation and reviving the battered traditions of tolerance, mutual assistance, and communion with nature. One of their spokesmen, ecologist Manfred

The Landless

Sebastião Salgado photographed them, Chico Buarque sang to them, José Saramago wrote about them: five million families of landless peasants wander the deserted vastness of Brazil "between dreams and desperation."

Many of them have joined the Movement of the Landless. From encampments improvised by the sides of roads, rivers of people flow through the night in silence into the immense, empty farms. They break the padlocks, open the gates, enter. Sometimes they're greeted by bullets from hired guns or soldiers, the only ones working on those unworked lands.

The Movement of the Landless is guilty. Not only does it show no respect for the property rights of sponging landlords; even worse, it fails to fulfill its duty to the nation. The landless grow food on the lands they occupy when the World Bank commands the countries of the South not to grow their own food but rather to be submissive beggars on the world market.

Max-Neef, describes these movements as mosquitoes on the attack, stinging a system that repels the hug and compels the shrug: "More powerful than a rhinoceros," he says, "is a cloud of mosquitoes. It grows and grows, buzzes and buzzes."

In Latin America, they are a species at risk of expansion: organizations of the landless, the homeless, the jobless, the whateverless; groups that work for human rights; mothers and

The Zapatistas

Mist is the ski mask the jungle wears. That's how it hides its persecuted children. From the mist they emerge, to the mist they return. The Indians of Chiapas wear majestic clothing, they float when they walk, and they speak softly or remain silent. These princes condemned to servitude were the first and are the last. They've been run off the land and out of the history books, and they've found refuge in mist, in mystery. From there they've emerged, wearing masks, to unmask the power that humiliates them.

grandmothers who defy the impunity of power; community organizations in poor neighborhoods; citizens' coalitions that fight for fair prices and healthful produce; those that struggle against racial and sexual discrimination, against machismo, and against the exploitation of children; ecologists, pacifists, health promoters, and popular educators; those who unleash collective creativity and those who rescue collective memory; organic agriculture cooperatives, community radio and television stations, and myriad other voices of popular participation that are neither auxiliary wings of political parties nor priests taking orders from any Vatican. These unarmed forces of civil society face frequent harassment from the powerful, at times with bullets. Some activists get shot dead. May the gods and the devils hold them in glory: only trees that bear fruit suffer stonings.

With the odd exception, like the Zapatistas in Chiapas or the landless in Brazil, these movements rarely garner much public attention—not because they don't deserve it. To name just one, Mexico's El Barzón emerged spontaneously in recent years when debtors sought to defend themselves from the usury of the banks. At first it attracted only a few, a contagious few; now they are a multitude. Latin America's presidents would do well to learn from that experience, so that our countries could come together, the way in Mexico people came together to form a united front against a financial despotism that gets its way by negotiating with countries one at a time. But the ears of those presidents are filled with the sonorous clichés exchanged every time they meet and pose with the president of the mother country, the United States, always front and center in the family photos.

It's happening all across the map of Latin America: against the paralyzing nerve gas of fear, people reach out to one another, and together they learn to not bow down. As Old Antonio, Sub-commandante Marcos's alter ego, says, "We are as small as the fear we feel, and as big as the enemy we choose." Such people, unbowed, are having their say. There is no greater authority than one who rules by obeying. Marcos represents the sub, the under—the underdeveloped, the underfed, the underrated, the underheard. The indigenous communities of Chiapas discuss and decide, and he is but the mouth that speaks with their voices. The voice of those who have no voice? People obliged to remain silent do have a voice, a voice that deserves to be heard. They speak by their words but also by their silence.

Official history, mutilated memory, is a long, self-serving ceremony for those who give the orders in this world. Their spotlights illuminate the heights and leave the grass roots in darkness. The always invisible are at best props on the stage of history, like Hollywood extras. But they are the ones—the actors of real history, the denied, lied about, hidden protagonists of past and present—who incarnate the splendid spectrum of another possible reality. Blinded by elitism, racism, sexism, and militarism, the Americas continue to ignore their own plenitude. And that's twice as true for the South: Latin America has the most fabulous human and vegetal diversity on the planet. Therein lies its fecundity and its promise. As anthropologist Rodolfo Stavenhagen puts it, "Cultural diversity is to the human species what biological diversity is to the genetic wealth of the world." If Latin America is to realize the marvels promised by our people and our the land, we'll have to stop confusing identity with archeology and nature with scenery. Identity isn't frozen in museums and ecology can't be reduced to gardening.

Five centuries ago, the people and the land of the Americas were incorporated into the world market as things. A few of the conquistadors, those who were themselves conquered, managed to see America's splendor and to revel in it. But the powers behind the Conquest, a blind and blinding enterprise like every other

Warning

The duly appointed authorities hereby warn the population that a number of lazy and bored young ne'er-do-wells are on the loose, wandering con men who carry the malevolent virus that spreads the plague of disobedience.

Fortunately for public health, these subjects are easy to spot, since they have the scandalous habit of thinking out loud, dreaming in color, and violating the norms of collective resignation that constitute the essence of democratic culture. They refuse to carry the mandatory old-age cards, even though, as everyone knows, these are dispensed free of charge on every street corner and in every village in the countryside thanks to the "Elderly Mind, Healthy Body" campaign, which has been such a great success for many years.

Ratifying the principle of authority and overlooking the provocations of this minority of upstarts, the Higher Government reiterates its irrevocable decision to keep a watchful eye on the development of our youth, who are our country's principal export product and who constitute the foundation of our balance of trade and of payments.

imperial invasion, could see Indians and nature only as objects of exploitation or as obstacles. In the name of the one and only God, the one and only language, and the one and only truth, cultural diversity was written off as ignorance and criminalized as heresy, while nature, that ferocious beast, was tamed and obliged to turn itself into money. The communion of indigenous peoples with the earth was the essential truth of American cultures, a sin of idolatry that merited punishment by lash, gallows, and the pyre.

We no longer speak of "taming" nature; now its executioners like to say it must be "protected." Either way, nature was and still is viewed as *outside* us: civilization, which confuses clocks with time, also confuses postcards with nature. But the vitality of the world, which wriggles out of all classifications and is beyond explanation, never sits still. Nature realizes itself in movement and we, too, children of nature, exist in motion. We are who we are

---

Kin

We are family of everything that buds, grows, matures, tires, dies, and sprouts again.

Every child has many parents, aunts and uncles, brothers and sisters, grandparents. The grandparents are the dead and the hills. Children of the earth and of the sun, watered by she-rains and he-rains, we are all related to the seeds, to the corn plants, to the rivers, and to the foxes that announce how the year will unfold. The stones are related to the snakes and to the lizards. Corn and beans, brothers to each other, grow up together without squabbling. Potatoes are the daughters and mothers of those who plant them, because he who creates is created.

Everything is sacred, and we are too. Sometimes we are gods and the gods, sometimes, are just little people.

That's what is said, what is known, among the Indians of the Andes.

328

The Music

He was a magician with the harp. On the prairies of Colombia, no fiesta could take place without him. Mesé Figueredo had to be there with his dancing fingers that delighted the breeze and made legs go wild.

One night, on his way to a wedding, he was mugged on a lonely path. Mesé was on one mule, the harp on another, when the robbers jumped him and beat him to a pulp.

The next day someone found him lying in the road, a bloody bunch of rags more dead than alive. In what remained of his voice, that scrap of flesh said, "They took the mules."

He said, "They took the harp."

"But," he breathed and laughed, "they didn't take the music."

and at the same time are what we do to change who we are. As Paulo Freire, the educator who died learning, liked to say, "We become by walking."

Truth lies in the voyage, not the port. There is no greater truth than the search for truth. Are we condemned to crime? We all know that we human creatures are busy devouring our neighbors and devastating the planet, but we also know that we would not be here if our distant Paleolithic grandparents hadn't learned to adapt to the natural world to which they belonged and hadn't been capable of sharing what they hunted and gathered. Living wherever, living however, living whenever, each person contains many possible persons. Every day, the ruling system places our worst characteristics at center stage, condemning our best to languish behind the backdrop. The system of power is not in the least eternal. We may be badly made, but we're not finished, and it's the adventure of changing reality and changing ourselves that makes our blip in the history of the universe worthwhile, this fleeting warmth between two glaciers that is us.

THE RIGHT TO RAVE

The new millennium is upon us, though the matter shouldn't be taken too seriously. After all, the year 2001 for Christians is 1379 for Moslems, 5114 for Mayans, and 5762 for Jews. The new millennium starts on January 1 only because one fine day the senate of imperial Rome decided to end the tradition of celebrating the new year at the beginning of spring. The number of years in the Christian Era is a matter of whim as well: another fine day the pope in Rome decided to assign a date to the birth of Jesus, even though nobody knows when he was born.

Time pays no attention to the borders we erect to fool ourselves into believing we control it. Even so, the millennium is a frontier the whole world both celebrates and fears.

AN INVITATION TO FLIGHT

The millennium is a good opportunity for orators of inflated eloquence to spout off on the destiny of humanity and for the agents of God's ire to announce the end of the world and other assorted calamities, while time itself continues its long, tight-lipped march through eternity and mystery.

The truth is, who can resist? On such a date, arbitrary though it is, everyone is tempted to wonder about the time to come. And just how is anyone to know? Only one thing is certain: in the twenty-first century, we'll all be people from the last century and, what's worse, we'll be from the last millennium.

If we can't guess what's coming, at least we have the right to imagine the future we want. In 1948 and again in 1976, the United Nations proclaimed long lists of human rights, but the immense majority of humanity enjoys only the rights to see, hear, and remain silent. Suppose we start by exercising the never-proclaimed right to dream? Suppose we rave a bit? Let's set our sights beyond the abominations of today to divine another possible world:

- the air shall be cleansed of all poisons except those born of human fears and human passions;
- in the streets, cars shall be run over by dogs;
- people shall not be driven by cars, or programmed by computers, or bought by supermarkets, or watched by televisions;
- the TV set shall no longer be the most important member of the family and shall be treated like an iron or a washing machine;
- people shall work for a living instead of living for work;
- written into law shall be the crime of stupidity, committed by those who live to have or to win, instead of living just to live like the bird that sings without knowing it and the child who plays unaware that he or she is playing;
- in no country shall young men who refuse to go to war go to jail, rather only those who want to make war;

- economists shall not measure living standards by consumption levels or the quality of life by the quantity of things;
- cooks shall not believe that lobsters love to be boiled alive;
- historians shall not believe that countries love to be invaded;
- politicians shall not believe that the poor love to eat promises;
- earnestness shall no longer be a virtue, and no one shall be taken seriously who can't make fun of himself;
- death and money shall lose their magical powers, and neither demise nor fortune shall make a virtuous gentleman of a rat;
- no one shall be considered a hero or a fool for doing what he believes is right instead of what serves him best;
- the world shall wage war not on the poor but rather on poverty, and the arms industry shall have no alternative but to declare bankruptcy;
- food shall not be a commodity nor shall communications be a business, because food and communication are human rights;
- no one shall die of hunger, because no one shall die from overeating;
- street children shall not be treated like garbage, because there shall be no street children;
- rich kids shall not be treated like gold, because there shall be no rich kids;
- education shall not be the privilege of those who can pay;
- the police shall not be the curse of those who cannot pay;
- justice and liberty, Siamese twins condemned to live apart, shall meet again and be reunited, back to back;
- a woman, a black woman, shall be president of Brazil, and another black woman shall be president of the United States; an Indian woman shall govern Guatemala and another Peru;

- in Argentina, the crazy women of the Plaza de Mayo shall be held up as examples of mental health because they refused to forget in a time of obligatory amnesia;

- the Church, holy mother, shall correct the typos on the tablets of Moses and the Sixth Commandment shall dictate the celebration of the body;

- the Church shall also proclaim another commandment, the one God forgot: You shall love nature, to which you belong;

- clothed with forests shall be the deserts of the world and of the soul;

- the despairing shall be paired and the lost shall be found, for they are the ones who despaired and lost their way from so much lonely seeking;

- we shall be compatriots and contemporaries of all who have a yearning for justice and beauty, no matter where they were born or when they lived, because the borders of geography and time shall cease to exist;

- perfection shall remain the boring privilege of the gods, while in our bungling, messy world every night shall be lived as if it were the last and every day as if it were the first.

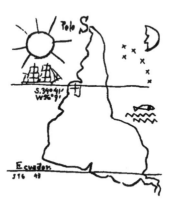

A Question

In the twelfth century, the official geographer of the kingdom of Sicily, al-Idrisi, drew a map of the world, the world that Europe knew about, with south on top and north on the bottom. That was common in mapmaking back then. And that's how the map of South America was drawn eight centuries later, with south on top, by Uruguayan painter Joaquín Torres-García. "Our north is south," he said. "To go north, our ships go down, not up."

If the world is upside down the way it is now, wouldn't we have to turn it over to get it to stand up straight?

This book was completed in August 1998. Check your local newspaper for an update.

Sources Consulted

THE LOOKING-GLASS SCHOOL

THE STUDENTS

Brisset, Claire. *Un monde qui dévore ses enfants* (Paris: Liana Levi, 1997).

ChildHope. *Hacia dónde van las niñas y adolescentes víctimas de la pobreza.* Report on Guatemala, Mexico, Panama, the Dominican Republic, Nicaragua, Costa Rica, El Salvador, and Honduras. April 1990.

Comexani. *IV informe sobre los derechos y la situación de la infancia* (Mexico: Colectivo Mexicano de Apoyo a la Niñez, 1997).

Dimenstein, Gilberto. *A guerra dos meninos: Assassinato de menores no Brasil* (São Paulo: Brasiliense, 1990).

Gibert, Eva, et al. *Políticas y niñez* (Buenos Aires: Losada, 1997).

Iglesias, Susana, with Helena Villagra and Luis Barrios. "Un viaje a través de los espejos de los Congresos Panamericanos del Niño," in UNICEF/UNICRI/ILANUD, *La condición jurídica de la infancia en América Latina* (Buenos Aires: Galerna, 1992).

Monange/Heller. *Brésil: Rapport d'enquête sur les assassinats d'enfants* (Paris: Fédération Internationale des Droits de l'Homme, 1992).

Organización International del Trabajo. *Todavía queda mucho por hacer: El trabajo de los niños en el mundo de hoy* (Geneva: OIT, 1989).

Pilotti, Francisco, and Irene Rizzini. *A arte de governar crianças* (Rio de Janeiro: Amais, 1995).

Tribunale Permanente dei Popoli. *La violazione dei diritti fondamentali dell'infanzia e dei minori* (Rome: Nova Cultura, 1995).

United Nations Children's Fund. *State of the World's Children 1997* (New York: UNICEF, 1997).

———. *State of the World's Children 1998* (New York: UNICEF, 1998).

INJUSTICE 101

Ávila Curiel, Abelardo. *Hambre, desnutrición y sociedad: La investigación epidemiológica de la desnutrición en México* (Guadalajara: Universidad, 1990).

Barnet, Richard Jr., and John Cavanagh. *Global Dreams: Imperial Corporations and the New World Order* (New York: Simon & Schuster, 1994).

Chesnais, François. *La mondialisation du capital* (Paris: Syros, 1997).

Food and Agriculture Organization. *Production Yearbook* (Rome: FAO, 1996).

Goldsmith, Edward, and Jerry Mander. *The Case against the Global Economy* (San Francisco: Sierra Club, 1997).

Hobsbawm, Eric. *Age of Extremes: The Short Twentieth Century, 1914–1991* (New York: Pantheon, 1994).

Instituto del Tercer Mundo. *Guía del Mundo, 1998* (Montevideo: Mosca, 1998).

International Monetary Fund. *International Financial Statistics Yearbook* (Washington: IMF, 1997).

McNamara, Robert. *In Retrospect* (New York: Times Books, 1995).

Ramonet, Ignacio. *Géopolitique du chaos* (Paris: Galilée, 1997).

United Nations Development Program. *Human Development Report 1995* (New York: UNDP, 1995).

———. *Human Development Report 1996* (New York: UNDP, 1996).

————. *Human Development Report 1997* (New York: UNDP, 1997).

World Bank. *World Bank Atlas* (Washington: World Bank, 1997).

————. *World Development Indicators* (Washington: World Bank, 1997).

————. *World Development Report, 1995* (Oxford: Oxford University Press, 1996).

RACISM AND SEXISM 101

Berry, Mary Frances, and John W. Blassingame. *Long Memory: The Black Experience in America* (New York: Oxford University Press, 1982).

Commager, Henry Steele. *The Empire of Reason: How Europe Imagined and America Realized the Enlightenment* (New York: Doubleday, 1978).

Escobar, Ticio. *La belleza de los otros* (Asuncion: CDI, 1993).

de Friedemann, Nina S. "Vida y muerte en el Caribe afrocolombiano: Cielo, tierra, cantos y tambores." *América negra* (Bogotá), no. 8, 1994.

Galton, Francis. *Herencia y eugenesia* (Madrid: Alianza, 1988).

Gould, Stephen Jay. *Ever Since Darwin* (New York: Norton, 1977).

————. *The Mismeasure of Man* (New York: Norton, 1981).

Graham, Richard, et al. *The Idea of Race in Latin America, 1870–1940* (Austin: University of Texas, 1990).

Guinea, Gerardo. "Armas para ganar una nueva batalla" (Government of Guatemala, 1957).

Herrnstein, Richard, and Charles Murray. *The Bell Curve: Intelligence and Class Structure in American Life* (New York: Free Press, 1994).

Iglesias, Susana, with Helena Villagra and Luis Barrios. "Un viaje a través de los espejos de los Congresos Panamericanos del Niño," in UNICEF/UNICRI/ILANUD, *La condición jurídica de la infancia en América Latina* (Buenos Aires: Galerna, 1992).

Ingenieros, José. *Crónicas de viaje* (Buenos Aires: Elmer, 1957).

Ingrao, Pietro. "Chi é l'invasore." *Il Manifesto* (Rome), November 17, 1995.

Kaminer, Wendy. *It's All the Rage: Crime and Culture* (New York: Addison-Wesley, 1995).

Lewontin, R. C., et al. *No está en los genes: Racismo, genética e ideología* (Barcelona: Crítica, 1987).

Lombroso, Cesare. *L'homme criminel* (Paris: Alcan, 1887).

————. *Los anarquistas* (Madrid: Júcar, 1977).

Lozano Domingo, Irene. *Lenguaje femenino, lenguaje masculino* (Madrid: Minerva, 1995).

Martínez, Stella Maris. *Manipulación genética y derecho penal* (Buenos Aires: Universidad, 1994).

Mörner, Magnus. *La mezcla de razas en la historia de América Latina* (Buenos Aires: Paidós, 1969).

Organización de las Naciones Unidas (CEPAL/CELADE). *Población, equidad y transformación productiva* (Santiago, 1995).

Palma, Milagros. *La mujer es puro cuento* (Bogotá: Tercer Mundo, 1986).

Price, Richard. *First Time: The Historical Vision of an Afro-American People* (Baltimore: Johns Hopkins University, 1983).

Rodrigues, Raymundo Nina. *As raças humanas e a responsabilidade penal no Brasil* (Salvador de Bahía: Progresso, 1957).

Rojas-Mix, Miguel. *América imaginaria* (Barcelona: Lumen, 1993).

Rowbotham, Sheila. *La mujer ignorada por la historia* (Madrid: Debate, 1980).

Rubin, William, et al. *"Primitivism" in Twentieth-Century Art* (New York: Museum of Modern Art, 1984).

Shipler, David K. *A Country of Strangers: Blacks and Whites in America* (New York: Knopf, 1997).

Spencer, Herbert. *Man versus the State* (London: Caldwell, 1940).

Tabet, Paola. *La pelle giusta* (Turin: Einaudi, 1997).

Taussig, Michael. *Shamanism, Colonialism, and the Wild Man* (Chicago: University of Chicago Press, 1987).

Trexler, Richard. *Sex and Conquest* (Cambridge: Polity, 1995).

United Nations Children's Fund. *State of the World's Children 1997* (New York: UNICEF, 1997).

———. *State of the World's Children 1998* (New York: UNICEF, 1998).

United Nations Population Fund. *The State of World Population 1997* (New York: UNFPA 1997).

Vidart, Daniel. *Ideología y realidad de América* (Bogotá: Nueva América, 1985).

Weatherford, Jack. *Indian Givers: How the Indians of the Americas Transformed the World* (New York: Fawcett, 1988).

Zaffaroni, Eugenio Raúl. *Criminología: Aproximación desde un margen* (Bogotá: Temis, 1988).

———. Introduction. *La industria del control de delito,* by Nils Christie (Buenos Aires: Del Puerto, 1993).

LECTURES ON FEAR

THE TEACHING OF FEAR

Baratta, Alessandro. *Criminología crítica y crítica del derecho penal* (Mexico: Siglo XXI, 1986).

Batista, Nilo. "Fragmentos de um discurso sedicioso. *Discursos sediciosos,* no. 1 (Rio de Janeiro: Instituto Carioca de Criminología, 1996).

Batista, Vera Malaguti. "Drogas e criminalização da juventude pobre no Rio de Janeiro," PhD thesis, Niterói, Universidade Federal/História Contemporânea, 1997.

Blixen, Samuel. "Para rapiñar a lo grande," *Brecha* (Montevideo), February 13, 1998.

Chevigny, Paul. *Edge of the Knife: Police Violence in the Americas* (New York: New Press, 1995).

Data Bank on Human Rights and Political Violence in Colombia. Reports published in *Noche y niebla* (Bogotá: CINEP/Justicia y Paz, 1997–98).

Girard, René. *Le bouc émissaire* (Paris: Grasset, 1978).

Monsiváis, Carlos. "Por mi madre, bohemios." *La Jornada* (Mexico), September 29, 1997.

Otis, John. "Law and Order." *Latin Trade* (Miami), June 1997.

Pavarini, Massimo. *Control y dominación: Teorías criminológicas burguesas y proyecto hegemónico.* Epilogue by Roberto Bergalli (Mexico: Siglo XXI, 1983).

Platt, Anthony M. *The Child Savers: The Invention of Delinquency* (Chicago: University of Chicago Press, 1977).

———. "Street Crime: A View from the Left." *Crime and Social Justice* (Berkeley), no. 9, 1978.

Ruiz Harrell, Rafael. "La impunidad y la eficiencia policiaca." *La Jornada* (Mexico), January 22, 1997.

Sudbrack, Umberto Guaspari. "Grupos de extermínio: Aspectos jurídicos e de política criminal." *Discursos sediciosos,* no. 2 (Rio de Janeiro: Instituto Carioca de Criminología, 1996).

Van Dijk, Jan J. M. *Responses to Crime across the World: Results of the International Crime Victims Survey* (University of Leyden/Ministry of Justice of Holland, 1996).

Ventura, Zuenir. *Cidade partida* (São Paulo: Companhia das Letras, 1994).

THE INDUSTRY OF FEAR

Bates, Eric. "Private Prisons." *Nation* (New York), January 5, 1998.
Burton-Rose, Daniel, with Dan Pens and Paul Wright. *The Ceiling of America: An Inside Look at the U.S. Prison Industry* (Monroe, Maine: Common Courage, 1998).
Christie, Nils. *La industria del control del delito. ¿La nueva forma del holocausto?* (Buenos Aires: El Puerto, 1993).
Crónica (Guatemala), July 19, 1996.
Foucault, Michel. *Vigilar y castigar. Nacimiento de la prisión* (Mexico: Siglo XXI, 1976).
Human Rights Watch. *Prison Conditions in the United States* (New York: Human Rights Watch, 1992).
La Maga (Buenos Aires), August 13, 1997.
Lyon, David. *El ojo electrónico* (Madrid: Alianza, 1995).
Marron, Kevin. *The Slammer: The Crisis in Canada's Prison System* (Toronto: Doubleday, 1996).
Morrison, Toni. Interview. *Die Zeit.* February 12, 1998.
Neuman, Elías. *Los que viven del delito y los otros: La delincuencia como industria* (Buenos Aires: Siglo XXI, 1997).
New Internationalist (Oxford), August 1996.
Rusche, Georg, and Otto Kirchheimer. *Pena y estructura social* (Bogotá: Temis, 1984).
U.S. News & World Report. May 1995.

SEWING: HOW TO MAKE ENEMIES TO MEASURE

Amnesty International. *Report 1995* (London, 1995).
———. *Report 1996* (London, 1996).
———. *Report 1997* (London, 1997).
Batista, Nilo. "Política criminal com derramamento de sangue." *Revista Brasileira de Ciências Criminais* (São Paulo), no. 20, 1997.
Bergalli, Roberto. "Introducción a la cuestión de la droga en Argentina." *Poder y Control* (Barcelona), no. 2, 1987.
Del Olmo, Rosa. "La cara oculta de la droga." *Poder y Control* (Barcelona), no. 2, 1987.
———. *¿Prohibir o domesticar? Políticas de drogas en América Latina* (Caracas: Nueva Sociedad, 1992).
———, et al. "Drogas: El conflicto de fin de siglo." *Cuadernos de Nueva Sociedad* (Caracas), no. 1, 1997.
Human Rights Watch. "Colombia's Killer Networks: The Military-Paramilitary Partnership and the United States" (New York: Human Rights Watch, 1996).
International Institute for Strategic Studies. *The Military Balance, 1997–98* (Oxford: Oxford University Press, 1997).
Levine, Michael. *The Big White Lie: The CIA and the Cocaine/Crack Epidemic: An Undercover Odyssey* (New York: Thunder's Mouth, 1993).
Miller, Jerome. *Search and Destroy: African-American Males in the Criminal Justice System* (Cambridge: Cambridge University Press, 1996).
National Institute on Drug Abuse. "National Household Survey on Drug Abuse: Population Estimates, 1990" (Washington: GPO, 1991).
Niño, Luis Fernando. "¿De qué hablamos cuando hablamos de drogas?" in Niño et al., *Drogas: Mejor hablar de ciertas cosas* (Buenos Aires: Facultad de Derecho y Ciencias Sociales, Universidad, 1997).
Reuter, Peter. *The Organization of Illegal Markets: An Economic Analysis* (Washington: Department of Justice, 1985).

Schell, Jonathan. "The Gift of Time: The Case for Abolishing Nuclear Weapons." *Nation* (New York), February 2 and February 9, 1998.
Wray, Stefan John. "The Drug War and Information Warfare in Mexico." Unpublished thesis, University of Texas at Austin, August 1997.
Youngers, Coletta. "The Only War We've Got: Drug Enforcement in Latin America." *NACLA Report on the Americas* (New York), September–October 1997.

SEMINAR ON ETHICS

PRACTICUM: HOW TO MAKE FRIENDS AND SUCCEED IN LIFE

Arlt, Roberto. *Aguafuertes porteñas* (Buenos Aires: Losada, 1985).
Boff, Leonardo. *A nova era: A civilização planetaria* (São Paulo: Atica, 1994).
Calabrò, Maria Antonietta. *Le mani della Mafia: Vent'anni di finanza e politica attraverso la storia del Banco Ambrosiano* (Rome: Edizioni Associate, 1991).
Di Giacomo, Maurizio, and Jordi Minguell. *El finançament de l'Església Catòlica* (Barcelona: Index, 1996).
Feinmann, José Pablo. "Dobles vidas, dobles personalidades." *Página 30* (Buenos Aires), September 1997.
Greenberg, Michael. *British Trade and the Opening of China* (New York: Monthly Review Press, 1951).
Hawken, Paul. *The Ecology of Commerce: A Declaration of Sustainability* (New York: Harper Business, 1993).
Henwood, Doug. *Wall Street* (New York: Verso, 1997).
Lietaer, Bernard. "De la economía real a la especulativa." *Revista del Sur/Third World Resurgence* (Montevideo), January–February 1998.
Newsinger, John. "Britain's Opium Wars." *Monthly Review* (New York), October 1997.
Pérez, Encarna, and Miguel Angel Nieto. *Los cómplices de Mario Conde: La verdad sobre Banesto, su presidente y la Corporación Industrial* (Madrid: Temas de Hoy, 1993).
Ramonet, Ignacio. *Géopolitique du chaos* (Paris: Galilée, 1997).
Saad Herrería, Pedro. *La caída de Abdalá* (Quito: El Conejo, 1997).
Silj, Alessandro. *Malpaese* (Milan: Donzelli, 1996).
Soros, George. "The Capitalist Threat." *Atlantic Monthly* (Boston), February 1997.
Spiewak, Martin. "Bastechend einfach." *Das Sonntagsblatt* (Hamburg), February 24, 1995.
Verbitsky, Horacio. *Robo para la Corona: Los frutos prohibidos del árbol de la corrupción* (Buenos Aires: Planeta, 1991).
World Bank. *World Bank Atlas* (Washington: World Bank, 1997).
———. *World Development Indicators* (Washington: World Bank, 1997).
———. *World Development Report, 1995* (Oxford: Oxford University Press, 1996).
Ziegler, Jean. *La Suisse lave plus blanc* (Paris: Seuil, 1990).
———. *La Suisse, l'or et les morts* (Paris: Seuil, 1997).

LESSONS FOR RESISTING USELESS VICES

Cerrutti, Gabriela. Interview with Enrique Pescarmona. *Página 12* (Buenos Aires), February 18, 1997.
Chomsky, Noam. Interview. *La Jornada* (Mexico), February 1, 1998.
"Conferencia de Lee Iacocca en Buenos Aires." *El Cronista.* (Buenos Aires), November 12, 1997.
Economic Policy Institute. *The State of Working America, 1996–1997* (Washington: Sharpe, 1997).

Figueroa, Héctor. "In the Name of Fashion: Exploitation in the Garment Industry." *NACLA* (New York), January–February 1996.

Filoche, Gérard. *Le travail jetable* (Paris: Ramsay, 1997).

Forrester, Viviane. *El horror económico* (Mexico: FCE, 1997).

"The Gap and Sweatshop Labor in El Salvador." *NACLA* (New York), January–February 1996.

Gorz, André. *Misères du present, richesse du possible* (Paris: Galilée, 1997).

International Labor Organization. *World Employment Report 1996–1997* (Geneva: ILO, 1997).

————. *Yearbook of Labor Statistics 1996* (Geneva: ILO, 1996).

————. *Yearbook of Labor Statistics 1997* (Geneva: ILO, 1997).

Méda, Dominique. *Le travail: Une valeur en voie de disparition* (Paris: Aubier, 1995).

Moledo, Leonardo. "En defensa de los bajos sueldos universitarios." *Página 12* (Buenos Aires), December 2, 1997.

Montelh, Bernard, et al. *C'est quoi le travail?* (Paris: Autrement, 1997).

New York Newsday, August 7, 1992.

Rifkin, Jeremy. *The End of Work* (New York: Putnam's, 1995).

Stalker, Peter. *The Work of Strangers: A Survey of International Labour Migration* (Geneva: ILO, 1994).

Van Liemt, Gijsbert. *Industry on the Move* (Geneva: ILO, 1992).

Verity, J. "A Company That's 100% Virtual." *Business Week* (New York), November 21, 1994.

MASTER CLASS ON IMPUNITY

CASE STUDIES

Bañales, Jorge A. "La lenta confirmación." *Brecha* (Montevideo), September 27, 1996.

Bassey, Nnimmo. "Only Business: A Pollution Tour through Latin America." *Link* (Amsterdam), no. 80, September–October 1997.

Beristain, Carlos Martín. *Viaje a la memoria: Por los caminos de la milpa* (Barcelona: Virus, 1997).

Donovan, Paul. "Making a Killing." *New Internationalist* (Oxford), September 1997.

Greenpeace International. *The Greenpeace Book on Greenwash* (Washington: Greenpeace, 1992).

Helou, Suzana, and Sebastião Benicio da Costa Neto. *Césio 137: Conseqüências psicossociais do acidente de Goiânia* (Goiás: Universidade Federal, 1995).

"Informe." *Uno más uno* (Mexico), September 1985.

International Finance Corporation. *Investing in the Environment: Business Opportunities in Developing Countries* (Washington: World Bank, 1992).

Karliner, Joshua. *The Corporate Planet: Ecology and Politics in the Age of Globalization* (San Francisco: Sierra Club, 1997).

Monsiváis, Carlos. *Entrada libre* (Mexico: Era, 1987).

Poniatowska, Elena. *Nada, Nadie: Las voces del temblor* (Mexico: Era, 1988).

Saro-Wiwa, Ken. *Genocide in Nigeria: The Ogoni Tragedy* (London: Saros, 1992).

Schlesinger, Stephen, and Stephen Kinzer. *Bitter Fruit: The Untold Story of the American Coup in Guatemala* (New York: Anchor, 1983).

Strada, Gino. "The Horror of Land Mines." *Scientific American* (Washington), May 1996.

Tótoro, Dauno. *La cofradía blindada* (Santiago de Chile: Planeta, 1998).

Verbitsky, Horacio. *El vuelo* (Buenos Aires: Planeta, 1995).

World Bank. *Priorities and Strategies for Education* (Washington: IBRO, 1995).

HUNTERS OF PEOPLE

Americas Watch. *Human Rights in Central America: A Report on El Salvador, Guatemala, Honduras, and Nicaragua* (New York, 1984).
————. *Into the Quagmire: Human Rights and U.S. Policy in Peru* (New York, 1991).
Amnesty International. *Human Rights Violations in Guatemala* (London, 1987).
Cerrutti, Gabriela. Interview with Alfredo Astiz. *Trespuntos* (Buenos Aires), January 28, 1998.
Comisión de la Verdad para El Salvador. *De la locura a la esperanza* (San Salvador: Arcoiris, 1993).
Comisión Interamericana de Derechos Humanos, Organización de Estados Americanos. *Informe sobre la situación de los derechos humanos en la república de Bolivia* (Washington: OAS, 1981).
Comisión Nacional de Verdad y Reconciliación. *Informe Rettig* (Santiago de Chile: La Nación, 1991).
Comisión Nacional sobre la Desaparición de Personas. *Nunca más* (Buenos Aires: EUDEBA, 1984).
Guena, Marcia. *Arquivo do horror: Documentos da ditadura do Paraguai* (São Paulo: Memorial de América Latina, 1996).
Inter-Church Committee on Chile. *Le cône sud de l'Amérique Latine: Une prison gigantesque. Mission d'observation au Chili, en Argentine et en Uruguay* (Montreal, 1976).
Jonas, Susanne. *The Battle for Guatemala: Rebels, Death Squads, and U.S. Power* (Boulder: Westview, 1991).
Klare, Michael T., and Nancy Stein. *Armas y poder en América Latina* (Mexico: Era, 1978).
Marín, Germán. *Una historia fantástica y calculada* (Mexico: Siglo XXI, 1976).
Ribeiro, Darcy, *Aos trancos e barrancos: Como o Brasil deu no que deu* (Rio de Janeiro: Guanabara, 1985).
Rouquié, Alain. *El estado militar en América Latina* (Mexico: Siglo XXI, 1984).
Servicio Paz y Justicia. *Nunca más: Informe sobre la violación a los derechos humanos en Uruguay, 1972–1985* (Montevideo, 1989).
Verbitsky, Horacio. *El vuelo* (Buenos Aires: Planeta, 1995).

EXTERMINATORS OF THE PLANET

Baird, Vanessa. "Trash." *New Internationalist* (Oxford), October 1997.
Barreiro, Jorge, "Accionista de Bayer por un día." *Tierra Amiga* (Montevideo), June 1994.
Bowden, Charles. *Juárez, the Laboratory of Our Future* (New York: Aperture, 1997).
Bruno, Kenny. "The Corporate Capture of the Earth Summit." *Multinational Monitor* (Washington), July–August 1992.
Carson, Rachel. *Silent Spring* (New York: Houghton Mifflin, 1994).
Colborn, Theo, with Dianne Dumanoski and John Peterson Meyers. *Nuestro Futuro Robado* (Madrid: Ecoespaña, 1997).
Durning, Alan Thein. *How Much Is Enough?* (London: Earthscan, 1992).
Lisboa, Marijane. "Ship of Ills." *New Internationalist* (Oxford), October 1997.
Lutzenberger, José. "Re-Thinking Progress." *New Internationalist* (Oxford), April 1996.
National Toxic Campaign. *Border Trouble: Rivers in Peril* (Boston, May 1991).
Payeras, Mario. *Latitud de la flor y del granizo* (Tuxtla Gutiérrez: Instituto Chiapaneco de Cultura, 1993).
Salazar, María Cristina, et al. *La floricultura en la sabana de Bogotá* (Bogotá: Universidad Nacional/CES, 1996).
Simon, Joel. *Endangered Mexico* (San Francisco: Sierra Club, 1997).
Worldwatch Institute, *State of the World, 1996* (New York: Norton, 1996).

THE SACRED CAR

American Automobile Manufacturers Association. *World Motor Vehicle Data* (Detroit: AAMA, 1995).

Barrett, Richard, and Ismail Serageldin. *Environmentally Sustainable Urban Transport: Defining a Global Policy* (Washington: World Bank, 1993).

Cevallos, Diego. "El reino del auto." *Tierramérica* (Mexico), June 1996.

Faiz, Asif, et al. *Automotive Air Pollution: Issues and Options for Developing Countries* (Washington: World Bank, 1990).

"Global 500: The World's Largest Corporations." *Fortune* (New York), August 7, 1995, and April 29, 1996.

"The Global 1,000." *Business Week* (New York), July 13, 1992.

Greenpeace International. *El impacto del automóvil sobre el medio ambiente* (Santiago de Chile: Greenpeace, 1992).

Guinsberg, Enrique. "El auto nuestro de cada dia." *Transición* (Mexico), February 1996.

International Road Federation. *World Road Statistics* (Geneva: IRF, 1994).

Marshall, Stuart. "Gunship or Racing Car?" *Financial Times* (London), November 10, 1990.

Navarro, Ricardo, with Urs Heirli and Victor Beck. *La bicicleta y los triciclos* (Santiago de Chile: SKAT/CETAL, 1985).

World Health Organization. *City Air Quality Trends* (Nairobi: WHO, 1995).

———. *World Health Report* (Geneva: WHO, 1996).

———, and United Nations Environment Program. *Urban Air Pollution in Megacities of the World* (Cambridge: Blackwell, 1992).

Wolf, Winfried, *Car Mania: A Critical History of Transport* (London: Pluto, 1996).

Worldwatch Institute. *State of the World, 1996* (New York: Norton, 1996).

A PEDAGOGY OF SOLITUDE

LESSONS FROM CONSUMER SOCIETY

"Annual Report on American Industry." *Forbes* (New York), January 12, 1998.

Bellah, R. N., et al. *Habits of the Heart: Individualism and Commitment in American Life* (Berkeley: University of California Press, 1985).

Centre de Recherches Historiques, École Pratique des Hautes Études. Special issue of *Annales* (Paris), July–August 1970.

Cooper, Marc. "Twenty-five Years after Allende." *Nation* (New York), March 23, 1998.

de Jouvenal, Bertrand. *Arcadie, essai sur le mieux-vivre* (Paris: Sedeis, 1968).

Flores Correa, Mónica. "Alguien está mirando." *Página 12* (Buenos Aires), January 4, 1998.

Hernández, Felisberto. "Muebles El Canario." *Narraciones incompletas* (Madrid: Siruela, 1990).

Informe de la Policía de Colombia al Primer Congreso Policial Sudamericano (Montevideo, December 1979).

Majul, Luis. *Las máscaras de la Argentina* (Buenos Aires: Atlántida, 1995).

Marx, Karl. *Capital: A Critique of Political Economy,* vol. 3 (New York: International, 1929).

Moulian, Tomás. *Chile actual: Anatomía de un mito* (Santiago: Arcis/Lom, 1997).

Sarlo, Beatriz. *Instantáneas: Medios, ciudad y costumbres en el fin de siglo* (Buenos Aires: Ariel, 1996).

Steel, Helen. Interview. *New Internationalist* (Oxford), July 1997.

Wachtel, Paul. *The Poverty of Affluence* (New York: Free Press, 1983).

Wallraff, Günter. *Cabeza de turco* (Barcelona: Anagrama, 1986).

Zurita, Félix. *Nica libre.* Video documentary (Managua: Alba Films, 1997).

CRASH COURSE ON INCOMMUNICATIONS

Alfaro Moreno, Rosa María, with Sandro Macassi. *Seducidos por la tele* (Lima: Calandria, 1995).

Asociación Latinoamericana de Educación Radiofónica. *Un nuevo horizonte teórico para la radio popular en América Latina* (Quito: ALER, 1996).

Auletta, Ken. "Life in Broadcasting." *New Yorker,* April 13, 1998.

Chomsky, Noam, and Edward S. Herman. *Manufacturing Consent* (New York: Pantheon, 1988).

Davidson, Basil. *The Black Man's Burden* (New York: Times Books, 1992).

Engelhardt, Tom. *The End of Victory Culture* (New York: Basic Books, 1995).

Gakunzi, David. "Ruanda." *Archipel* (Basel), January 1998.

Gatti, Claudio. "Attention, vous êtes sur écoûtes: Comment les États-Unis surveillent les européens." *Courrier International/Il Mondo* (Paris), April 2–8, 1998.

González-Cueva, Eduardo. "Heroes or Hooligans: Media Portrayals of Peruvian Youth." *NACLA* (New York), July–August 1998.

Herman, Edward S., and Robert N. McChesney. *The New Missionaries of Corporate Capitalism* (London: Cassell, 1997).

Hertz, J. C. *Joystick Nation* (Boston: Little, Brown, 1997).

Herz, Daniel. *A história secreta da Rede Globo* (Pôrto Alegre: Tchê!, 1987).

International Labor Organization. *Symposium on Multimedia Convergence* (Geneva: ILO, 1997).

Leonard, John. *Smoke and Mirrors: Violence, Television, and Other American Cultures* (New York: New Press, 1997).

López Vigil, José Ignacio. *Manual urgente para radialistas apasionados* (Quito: AMARC/ALER, 1997).

Martín-Barbero, Jesús. *De los medios a las mediaciones* (Barcelona: Gili, 1987).

———, et al. *Televisión y melodrama* (Bogotá: Tercer Mundo, 1982).

Mata, Lídice da. "Salvador resiste." *Folha de São Paulo,* April 28, 1994.

Miller, Mark Crispin, et al. "The National Entertainment State." *Nation* (New York), June 3, 1996, and June 8, 1998.

Noble, David. *The Religion of Technology* (New York: Knopf, 1997).

Pasquini Durán, José María, et al. *Comunicación: El Tercer Mundo frente a las nuevas tecnologías* (Buenos Aires: Legasa, 1987).

Postman, Neil. *Amusing Ourselves to Death: Public Discourse in the Age of Show Business* (New York: Penguin, 1986).

———. *Technopoly* (New York: Vintage, 1993).

———, with Steve Powers. *How to Watch TV News* (New York: Penguin, 1992).

Ramonet, Ignacio. *La tiranía de la comunicación* (Madrid: Debate, 1998).

Santos, Rolando. *Investigación sobre la violencia en la programación infantil de la TV argentina* (Buenos Aires: Universidades de Quilmes y de Belgrano, 1994).

Terkel, Studs. *Coming of Age: The Story of Our Century by Those Who've Lived It* (New York: New Press, 1995).

Touraine, Alain. *¿Podremos vivir juntos?* (Mexico: FCE, 1997).

United Nations Educational, Scientific, and Cultural Organization. *Many Voices, One World* (New York: UNESCO, 1980).

Zerbisias, Antonia. "The World at Their Feet." *Toronto Star,* August 27, 1995.

THE COUNTERSCHOOL

THE END OF THE MILLENNIUM AS PROMISE AND BETRAYAL

Blackburn, Robin, et al. *After the Fall: The Failure of Communism and the Future of Socialism* (London: Verso, 1991).

Burbach, Roger. "Socialism Is Dead, Long Live Socialism." *NACLA* (New York), November–December 1997.

Ejército Zapatista de Liberación Nacional. *Documentos y comunicados* (Mexico: Era, 1994–95).

Fals Borda, Orlando, et al. *Investigación participativa y praxis rural* (Santiago: CEAAL, 1988).

———. *Participación popular: Retos del futuro* (Bogotá: ICFES/IEPRI/Colciencias, 1998).

Fernandes, Bernardo Marcano. *MST, Movimento dos Trabalhadores Rurais Sem-Terra: Formação e territorialização en São Paulo* (São Paulo: Hucitec, 1996).

Freire, Paulo. *La educación como práctica de la libertad* (Mexico: Siglo XXI, 1995).

Gallo, Max. *Manifiesto para un oscuro fin de siglo* (Madrid: Siglo XXI, 1991).

Genro, Tarso, and Ubiratam de Souza. *Orçamento participativo. A expêriencia de Pôrto Alegre* (Pôrto Alegre: Fundação Abramo, 1997).

Grammond Barbet, Hubert. "El Barzón: ¿Un movimiento social contra la crisis económica o un movimiento social de nuevo cuño?" Paper given at UNAM/PHSECAM/AMER, Querétaro, March 1998.

Latouche, Serge. *La planète des naufragés* (Paris: La Découverte, 1993).

López Vigil, María. "Sociedad civil en Cuba: Diccionario urgente." *Envío* (Managua), July 1997.

Max-Neef, Manfred. *La economía descalza* (Montevideo: Cepaur/Nordan, 1984).

———. "Economía, humanismo y neoliberalismo," in Fals Borda, *Participación popular.*

Rodgers, Dennis. "Un antropólogo-pandillero en un barrio de Managua." *Envío* (Managua), July 1997.

Rengifo, Grimaldo. "La interculturalidad en los Andes." Paper given at *Con los pies en la tierra,* Asociación para el Desarrollo Campesino/Colombia Multicolor, La Cocha, Colombia, 1998.

Stavenhagen, Rodolfo. "Racismo y xenofobia en tiempos de la globalización." *Estudios sociológicos,* no. 34 (Mexico: Colegio de México, 1994).

United States Senate. *Covert Action in Chile, 1963–1973: Staff Report of the Select Committee to Study Governmental Operations with Respect to Intelligence Activities* (Washington: GPO, 1975).

Zurita, Félix. *Nica libre.* Video documentary (Managua: Alba Films, 1997).

Index

OCT 1 6 2000

361.1   Galeano, Eduardo H.,
G   1940-

Upside down.

10/4 in New

24.00

DATE			

3/01-2

3/01-2

06/03-3
2/07-4 (7/05)
9/08-5
12/12 - 8

2/16-11

∂PLe

BAKER & TAYLOR